P9-CQI-298

THE KOREAN WAR

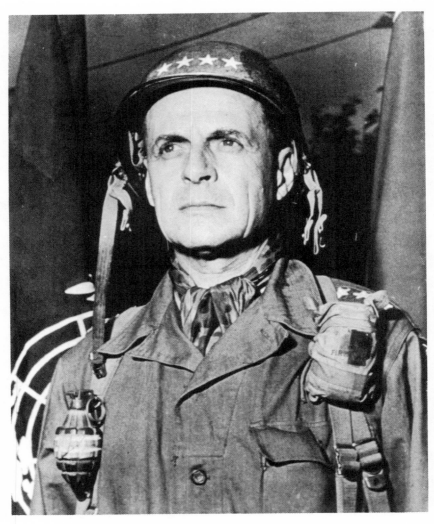

GENERAL MATTHEW B. RIDGWAY. *U.S. Army Photograph.*

MATTHEW B. RIDGWAY
GENERAL, UNITED STATES ARMY, RETIRED

THE KOREAN WAR

How We Met the Challenge

How All-Out Asian War Was Averted

Why MacArthur Was Dismissed

Why Today's War Objectives Must Be Limited

A DA CAPO PAPERBACK

Library of Congress Cataloging in Publication Data

Ridgway, Matthew B. (Matthew Bunker), 1895–
  The Korean War.

  (A Da Capo paperback)
  Reprint. Originally published: Garden City, N.Y.:
Doubleday, 1967.
  Bibliography: p.
  1. Korean War, 1950–1953. I. Title.
DS918.R49   1986   951.9′042   86-2029
ISBN 0-306-80267-8 (pbk.)

This Da Capo Press paperback edition of *The Korean War*
is an unabridged republication of the edition published
in New York in 1967. It is reprinted by arrangement with
Doubleday & Co., Inc.

Copyright © 1967 by Matthew B. Ridgway

Published by Da Capo Press, Inc.
A Subsidiary of Plenum Publishing Corporation
233 Spring Street, New York, N.Y. 10013

All Rights Reserved

Manufactured in the United States of America

DEDICATION

To GEORGE CATLETT MARSHALL

Whose character and achievements in peace
and in war have been surpassed by no wearer of
the uniform of the United States, save only by
our first Commander in Chief, George Washington.

PREFACE

The Korean conflict marked the end, in the United States, of the Fortress America era and the beginning of an age when it would no longer be possible for our nation to ensure peace merely by avoiding foreign entanglements. When war broke out in Korea, we found ourselves for the first time in our history plunged headlong into war without even a week's warning and involved half a world away in a struggle our people neither understood nor felt a part of.

In every previous war, beginning with the one that gave our country birth, there had been time to gird our loins, recruit our spirits, and deliberate over where and how best to apply our force. Even in 1776, when many a patriot stepped right out of his cornfield into battle, there had been that "long train of abuses and usurpations" to fire up the indignation of our citizenry and ready them for taking arms. In other conflicts, our ocean moats and our distance from the battle enabled us to delay long enough to tool our industries for war, to train our armies, build our stockpiles, and take counsel with ourselves over the disposition of our forces.

Korea, however, burst into flame without apparent warning. There was no time allowed in 1950 to arrive at our major decisions through conferences, debate, legislative action, and careful clearances. The outbreak of hostilities found us at peace and awoke us to full-scale war. It took young family men, hardly settled down after dreary months of warfare, and transported them at airplane speed straight to the fighting front. It found a prosperous nation, with a new era of labor-management peace apparently dawning, with taxes diminishing, wartime restrictions vanishing, and a tranquil future unfolding—and it offered it, once more, shortages and strife and sacrifices and doubt.

The war in Korea was perhaps the last one to be fought with conventional weapons solely. It was the last in which we would be free from fear of thermonuclear disaster. And it heralded drastic changes in our relationship with the rest of the world.

In the course of the conflict we met and decided several questions of major import, some of which have been only dimly understood by the masses of our people. Facing the issue of whether to act in concert with other free nations, or go it alone, we decided that our national security lay in collective action. Forced to choose between civilian authority and military, we emphasized once more the constitutional supremacy of the civilian authority. Abruptly faced with the need to decide whether to stand up to aggression or abandon the Republic of Korea to her enemies, we chose the path of honor and met the aggressor head-on. And for the first time in our history, we became acquainted with the concept of "limited" war.

There remained, however, a number of hard questions that troubled our people throughout the war and for a long time afterward: How could it happen that a major conflict like this could explode without warning? Was there ineptitude among our decision makers or were our intelligence forces lacking? Were we the victims of dark schemes by Chiang Kai-shek or Syngman Rhee to achieve on one hand an invasion of mainland China and on the other the reunification of Korea by force? Why did the outbreak of war find us so ill-prepared to fight? And how did we get into such a state that our moral position before the free world was salvaged only by the swift decision of a courageous President— who alone had the decision-making power?

The answer to all these questions perhaps lay in our preoccupation with all-out war. Before Korea, all our military planning envisioned a war that would involve the world, and in which the defense of a distant and indefensible peninsula would be folly. But Korea taught us that all warfare from this time forth must be limited. It could no longer be a question of *whether* to fight a limited war, but of *how* to avoid fighting any other kind. Unlimited war, now that many nations own thermonuclear weapons or the skill to build them, is no longer thinkable, for it would mean mutual annihilation. Our dealings with friends and potential enemies, after Korea, would all be colored by this realization.

Perceptive people then foresaw that this change in our thinking would bring other changes in its train. The realization began to dawn that military force alone could no longer solve problems such as faced us in Vietnam, Laos, and the Congo but that mutually supporting political, economic, and military policies must be evolved that would be acceptable to all peoples concerned, and they would have to be implemented through strong leadership. It became clear too that policy could no longer be formulated by the White House alone, or by the Department of State, or by the Defense Department; that neither civilian statesmen nor military professionals, working in separate compartments, could by themselves lay down the lines that would give direction to our intercourse with other sovereignties. It is clear now, or should be clear, that best results flow from intimate day-to-day collaboration among military and civilian leaders, wherein the civilian leaders propose the *ends* that must be achieved and the military leaders supply their estimate of how much can be attained by military *means* and how those means may be best employed.

Such collaboration is possible only when civil and military authorities seek and earnestly consider each other's point of view. Sound decisions will not be reached through automatic overruling of the preponderant recommendations of the nation's senior military advisers by their civilian superiors. The civilian authority, under our Constitution, of course remains supreme. But a failure to seek, hear, and weigh the counsel of our experienced military advisers is to court disaster.

Many of our citizens, absorbed as they properly are by the struggle to maintain the security and health of their families and to educate their children, have not had the time to grasp the full significance of these changes in our situation and in our thinking. Too often they are still beguiled by the thoughtless old slogans of "all-out war" and "unconditional surrender" and "complete victory," slogans that are frequently employed to serve partisan

vii

political ends. It is no wonder then that widely divergent views on foreign policy, heated debates, confused thinking, and feelings of frustration still persist throughout the country.

Fortunately there seems to be a growing body of citizenry who, while perhaps themselves not fully understanding the depth and force of the changes that have engulfed us since Korea, still perceive that we live in a wholly new world that calls for new ways of thinking and planning.

And in between the unthinking and the more perceptive, there remains the group of people who, confused by the vehement utterances of the opposing schools of thought, find it more and more difficult to decide which group to support.

In this book, I do not mean to indulge in polemics for any point of view. Rather I hope to contribute what I can to a better understanding of a much-misunderstood conflict that marked a major turning point in the nation's history.

Nor does this book pretend to be a definitive treatment of the operations of United Nations air and naval forces in Korea. Those have been well covered in volumes prepared by the services themselves. Insofar as tactical operations are covered at all, they are those of the ground forces of the United Nations Command, and the terminology used is theirs. The measure of the role the ground forces played in Korea may be judged from the fact that, of the total United States battle casualties for the entire conflict, the Army and Marines accounted for 97 percent. And it was the performance of the ground forces that determined the success or failure of the United Nations effort, which in turn determined the course of United States and United Nations policy.

There is little doubt that had our ground forces been compelled to operate without air or naval support, the Communist tide would have rolled on to the Strait of Tsu Shima within the first sixty to ninety days. And again, in the crises of action in late November and early December 1950, had our air and naval forces not supported the ground armies to the limit of their capabilities, losses would have been far greater and our cause might have suffered a disaster. And it certainly may be said that the gallant airmen and sailors who contributed so much to the effort are nowhere more highly honored than in the hearts of the doughboys and Marines who fought the ground battles. Still, if it seems that we deal largely here with the foot soldiers who spent so many days and nights in the zone of fire, one must keep in mind that Fate dealt largely with them too, as their casualty lists will testify.

Beyond that, I have in this book no point to prove nor case to argue and only the purpose I have stated above: to shed some light on what we tried to do in Korea and point up the lessons we learned from the effort.

I am grateful to Brigadier General Hal C. Pattison and Dr. Stetson Conn, Chief, Office of Military History, Department of the Army, and Chief Historian, respectively, and to their staffs, on whose excellent histories I have freely drawn, as I also have done on the excellent *U. S. Marine Operations in Korea 1950–53*, Historical Branch, G-3, Headquarters U. S. Marine Corps, Washington, D.C., 1962.

I gratefully acknowledge the valuable assistance of Curt Anders, former captain, U. S. Army, and an infantry platoon and company commander in the Korean combat zone.

I wish to acknowledge with grateful appreciation the generous and talented contribution of Robert Smith in helping put the manuscript in final form for publication.

General S. L. A. Marshall has been unsparing of time in reading proofs and making suggestions toward correction of facts and emphasis in treatment. I am most grateful.

M. B. Ridgway

Pittsburgh, Pennsylvania
January 1967

CONTENTS

ILLUSTRATIONS

MAPS

ABBREVIATIONS USED IN THIS BOOK

CCF   Chinese Communist Forces
CINCUNC   Commander in Chief, United Nations Command
COMNAVFE   Commander, Naval Forces Far East
GHQ   General Headquarters (situated in Tokyo)
JCS   Joint Chiefs of Staff
KMAG (pronounced *Kay*mag)   Korea Military Advisory Group
LST   Landing Ship, Tank
MLR   Main Line of Resistance
MP   Military Police
NKPA   North Korean Peoples Army
RCT   Regimental combat team
ROK   Republic of Korea (South Korea)
ROKA   Republic of Korea Army
VIP   Very important person

NOTE   Spellings of Korean place names have been used that are slightly simplified versions of the official spellings. The Changjin Reservoir is also named the Chosin Reservoir.

THE KOREAN WAR

CHAPTER ONE

THE LAND OF MORNING CALM –
PRELUDE TO THE STORM

No ONE CAN fully understand the Korean War who does not own at least an elemental knowledge of the geography, the history, the climate, and the economic lot of that country and its people. Korea is not naturally divided in two, except by the spine of mountains, the Taebaek Range, that runs from north to south close to the Sea of Japan. It is geographically, strategically, economically, and ethnically a single entity with each part as necessary to all the rest as a man's arms and legs are to his body. Its division at the 38th parallel was almost accidental, a mere military convenience, of such minor concern to military historians at the time that no one today can say for certain just who first suggested it.

The 38th parallel is not a border in any true sense. It is not militarily defensible, nor does it wear any traditional significance. Koreans who live north of the parallel speak the same language, eat the same foods, favor the same clothing and customs, and nourish the same national pride as do those who live in the south.

Korea, despite a history of invasion and enslavement by powerful neighbors, has always existed as an independent nation in the hearts of its inhabitants; and the desire to run their own affairs has slumbered there for centuries. A geographical misfortune has made it a battleground for nearly as long as men have kept records of their doings. China, Russia, and Japan have all at one time or another and in spite of international commitments to the contrary,

1

tried to annex its territory to their own. And the United States, no matter that our government has several times pledged itself to assist Korea in the event of attack, had never, prior to June 1950, raised a hand to rescue this tiny, hapless kingdom from its foes next door.

The 600-mile-long peninsula of Korea protrudes like a small fat thumb from the land mass of Asia. It is pointed directly at Kyushu, the southernmost of the four major islands of Japan, offering or inviting invasion across the narrow Strait of Tsu Shima. From Korea's principal port of Pusan to Shimonoseki, at the entrance to Japan's Inland Sea, is a voyage of a little more than a hundred miles. The Korean peninsula divides the subarctic Sea of Japan from the subtropical Yellow Sea, and this may account in some degree for the extremes of temperature this country knows. Although Korea lies in the temperate zone, in the same latitude as Kentucky, it suffers wintry cold on the craggy 6000-foot ridges in the north that can reach fifty degrees below zero Fahrenheit; while it experiences, in the rice country of the south, summer heat that can make men gasp. All the afflictions of the foot soldier are here: deep snows, viscous mud, very heavy summer rains, bitter biting dust—but then there is also the green of growing rice fields, so rich and bright it can take your breath away.

There is one feature of Korea that every fighting man will remember—the smell. The use of human excrement—night soil—to fertilize the fields, the husbanding of that commodity in pails and barrels, and in leaky wagons, give to the atmosphere of the country a fragrance so overpowering that the soul at first rebels.

Korea is a poor country. In the lowlands of the south, its natural cover, the grasses and trees, have long ago been cropped for fuel, food, and fodder, and now the chief growth there is a gnarled and scrubby brush that offers almost no concealment, little fuel, and a minimum of shelter and greenery. Villagers in the south scratch the earth with sticks to collect every last bit of burnable substance to feed their fires. Roots, twigs, straw, rags, trash of every sort are patiently scraped up and stored to keep the stoves going. In the villages the gutters are open sewers and contribute their own savor to the universal stench. Pigs, the chief livestock, roam in indescribable filth. Wary and hungry dogs gobble even the most offensive droppings of offal. Little children play outside the cottages, the trousers of the tiniest cut right out in the rear so they may answer the call of nature wherever it comes to them.

The rice fields of the south provide a rich yield and the Koreans raise large crops of cabbage, which often grows overripe on the stalk, and is brought in to be preserved in a great crock, along with fish heads and other delicacies, by the kitchen stove, to serve as a staple called Kim-Chi that most Western people would find it impossible to stomach. Yet it is relished by the Koreans and is undoubtedly a rich source of vitamins.

The cottages are skimpy, scantily furnished, and illuminated by windows that are covered with oiled paper to allow the daylight through. The flat land in the south is all closely cultivated and there are habitations everywhere.

Northern Korea, which holds the industrial section that is largely dependent on the south for its food, shows stands of tall evergreens upon its steep mountains, where sheer granite cliffs sometimes drop off from 6000-foot ridges. And the country as a whole, viewed from the air, or while walking in peace among its hills or on its seashores, seems especially blessed with beauty. When the summer fades, the foothills of the spinal range where hardwood trees grow in some profusion turn gold, and yellow, and all the breathtaking shades of red and brown. The skies are often a bottomless blue and the seas on either side of the peninsula stretch out deep and clean.

The far north, however, offers a more forbidding prospect, particularly in the winter when storms that make up in the distant Manchurian wastes scream down unheralded and lay ten-foot drifts on the mountains. In this section, as the mountain ranges reach toward the Yalu River, the country is truly divided so that it is impossible for an army to maintain a solid front, or even liaison, across the trackless and impassable summit ridges. Throughout the country roads are sinuous and far between. The highlands are traced largely by footpaths where men or ponies must go one after one. The forests here offer excellent cover to an enemy on foot,

3

while the innumerable narrow valleys, the painfully straitened and scanty roads, and the knifelike ridges stall every movement of a heavily mechanized army that dares not take to the trackless hills. Without armor, with little artillery, unencumbered by complex communications, lightly equipped and carrying hand weapons only, the Chinese armies, which were all inured to the extremes of weather and the scantiness of food, superbly disciplined and thoroughly trained, found choice opportunities here for maneuver and concealment.

Our ignorance of the terrain and the extreme faultiness of the maps we tried to make use of gave the enemy an added advantage and made his own familiarity with the landscape a sort of secret weapon. Roads we looked for often did not exist, or turned out to be mere footpaths that no wheeled vehicle could negotiate.

Unlike the terrain, the people of Korea are thoroughly hospitable, a docile gentle folk for the most part, potentially fine soldiers when properly trained, thrifty farmers, and fierce patriots who harbor a century-old hatred for the Japanese, whose brutal police they well remember. Individualistic as the Irish, the Koreans are just as unlikely as the Irish are ever to submit to enforced political unanimity. They had no training in self-government and very little in the uses of modern machinery, so they were severely handicapped in trying to build themselves a modern, self-sufficient nation. Their unfamiliarity with our ways and our inability to breach the language barrier with consistency, combined with the blundering nature of so many of our dealings with their nation, made cooperation extremely difficult, particularly when the pressure of mortal danger allowed no time for planning or protocol.

The United States has known of the existence of Korea (originally spelled Corea in our geography books) for a relatively short time and has dealt with her diplomatically for far less time than that. In 1834, Americans concerned with opening Japan to trade expressed some interest in trade with Korea, but even after Commodore Matthew C. Perry "opened the door" to Japan, Korea was neglected. In 1866 French and American nationals were put to death in Korea and for a time the two offended governments contemplated a joint punitive expedition. This plan, happily, was abandoned; but later efforts to open negotiations with Korea resulted only in an exchange of gunfire between U.S. naval vessels and Korean shore batteries, and the taking of a few Korean prisoners. The efforts persisted, however, with first Japan and then China acting as intermediary. Ultimately, in 1882, our first treaty with Korea was drawn up in Tientsin, establishing commercial relations between the United States and the Kingdom of Korea. An especially interesting feature of this treaty was a clause that pledged "mutual aid in case either country should be unjustly treated by another." Just what constituted "unjust treatment" seems to have been open, throughout the succeeding seventy years, to rather restricted interpretation.

In nearly all subsequent treaties, documents, decisions, and declarations on the subject of Korea the word "independent" recurs again and again. Yet in all the years since the Tientsin treaty, independence has been only a fairy tale. What it meant to us was that we held Korea to her trade agreements but made no effort to interfere as other nations struggled over the right to occupy and exploit this "Land of Morning Calm."

When the Tientsin treaty was signed, we specifically recognized China's sovereignty. Later as Japan and China both endeavored to seize control of Korea, we studiously avoided giving offense to either, even recalling our envoy after the Chinese Resident objected to his attitude toward China's efforts to strengthen her hold. When the China-Japan rivalry over Korea exploded into warfare in 1894, we again took pains to choose neither side and confined our good offices to the expression of a polite hope that Japan would not visit an unjust war upon a defenseless neighbor. So the basis of our diplomatic "writing off" of Korea was laid before Dean Acheson could spell his own name.

During the Sino-Japanese conflict, we rejected a British proposal that we intervene jointly with her and with Germany, Russia, and France. And when Japan won complete control of Korea, we once again recognized Korea's "independence" while acknowledging Japanese rights. In subsequent months, as Russia and Japan began their own struggle to take over the peninsula, our State Department instructed our Minister in Seoul to warn all Americans there against expressing any anti-Japanese opinions.

In the next two decades we were twice invited to honor our original pledge to protect Korea from being eaten alive and twice we rejected the request, specifically and forthrightly. When Japan, in the first month of the Russo-Japanese War, made Korea a protectorate, President Theodore Roosevelt wrote off Korea in these words: "We cannot possibly interfere for the Koreans against the Japanese. They [the Koreans] could not strike a blow in their own defense." This was our "reply" to requests made five and six years earlier that we undertake to secure from the Great Powers an agreement guaranteeing the integrity of Korea. Our hands-off policy was made official by the Taft-Katsura agreement in 1905 in which we consented to a Japanese protectorate in Korea in exchange for a Japanese disclaimer of any aggressive intentions toward our own recent Far East acquisition, the Philippines.

Following the First World War, when subject peoples everywhere thrilled at the Wilsonian declaration of the right of self-determination, there was a violent surge of nationalism in Korea. Men met secretly in Korean cellars to print a declaration of independence with wooden type that had been hewed out by hand. Schoolgirls, with the secret declaration hidden in their flowing sleeves, walked from village to village, without once awakening the suspicions of the sharp-eyed Japanese police or ever being detected by the countless Japanese spies who dwelt among the Korean people, alert for just such efforts as this to rally an open revolt.

In hundreds of villages, north and south, Korean patriots met secretly to plan the day of liberation—tens of thousands of men and women altogether, yet no whisper of their plans ever reached the Japanese. On March 1, 1919, thirty-three Korean leaders, excluding Syngman Rhee, met at the Bright Moon restaurant in Seoul for a last meal together, read the declaration of independence aloud, signed their names with a flourish, and called in the police. At the same moment, all over the land, millions gathered in the streets to hear the declaration read, then marched joyfully through every village, carrying the forbidden flag of Korea. The marchers were unarmed and threatened no violence. But in the next few weeks thousands were put to death by the Japanese. Meanwhile, our State Department was solemnly warning the Consul in Seoul that he should be "extremely careful not to encourage any belief that the United States would assist Korean nationalists in carrying out their plans" or to give the Japanese any basis for believing that the United States government even sympathized with the Korean nationalist movement.

It was therefore entirely consistent with tradition when, in April 1948, with Korea divided into Soviet and United States zones, President Harry S. Truman, at the urging of the Joint Chiefs of Staff, approved this policy statement: "The United States should not become so irrevocably involved in the Korea situation that an action taken by any faction in Korea or by any other power in Korea could be considered a *casus belli* for the United States."

Despite open avowals, at Cairo and at Potsdam, of a desire to establish an independent Korea, the United States had returned to its traditional hands-off policy. At Cairo, the United States, Great Britain, and China agreed that Korea should be independent "in due course" (Soviet Premier Joseph Stalin approved of this declaration when he met with President Franklin D. Roosevelt in Teheran). At Potsdam, just before the Japanese surrender, in 1945, Truman and Stalin approved a statement assuring Korea her independence after a five-year trusteeship under the Soviet Union, Great Britain, and China, with no mention of the United States. (Stalin later insisted the United States be included.)

The United States, finding itself, after the Japanese surrender, unexpectedly in charge of the southern half of the Korean peninsula, moved without forethought, with little planning, and without reckoning of the consequences, to fulfill its obligations under a trusteeship that had never been formally approved. It made a major blunder almost at once that cost it the confidence and the cooperation of the Korean people: It confirmed in office the despised Japanese administrative officials. Alarmed at the prompt outburst of indignation that followed this move, the United States then compounded the mistake by hastily flinging out the Japanese and filling the posts with well-meaning but wholly unqualified

7

American civilians, without knowledge of the tongue or understanding of the problems posed by a need to formulate banking and currency policies for a new-born Republic.

Of course the failure to reach an over-all agreement with the Soviet Union aggravated the crisis and left both Moscow and Washington accusing each other of devious activities directed by one against the other. The Korean people meanwhile seethed with unrest and began to turn violently against both sides, whom they suspected of preparing to renege once again on the oft-ruptured promise of independence.

Despairing at last of winning Russian cooperation in setting up the trusteeship, the United States turned the problem over to the United Nations—which prompted the Soviet Union to charge a betrayal of the original agreement. The United Nations moved to conduct free elections in both zones, but the Soviets refused to permit the UN Temporary Committee to enter the Soviet Zone. They had earlier insisted that only those parties might participate in the election who had given "full support" to the Moscow agreement on trusteeship. This disqualified practically all the parties in the United States zone, where freedom of speech had allowed openly expressed dissatisfaction with any postponement of independence—trusteeship or no.

The ultimate outcome was an election in May 1948 in South Korea that led to the establishment of the Republic of Korea with Syngman Rhee as President, followed by a Soviet countermove—the creation of the "Democratic People's Republic of Korea" with its capital at Pyongyang.

The United States then terminated the military occupation and in September 1948 began the withdrawal of all United States troops, thus exhibiting once more our traditional devotion to the theory of noninvolvement. While the Soviet Union had earlier announced her intention to withdraw all her forces from Korea by the year's end, and in due time was reported to have completed the withdrawal, a hard-eyed examination of the resultant situation might have revealed that we were laying our baby Republic naked on the altar.

The difference between our approach to the Korean problem

and the Soviet approach is that we had no real goal to aim for beyond a rather dimly visualized "independence" that would leave us free to hasten home and pick up the threads of our domestic concerns. The Soviets, by contrast, visualized from the very beginning an "independence" that would leave the Korean peninsula independent of all nations but Russia. She began to work toward this end almost from the moment the United States entered the war and made victory a certainty.

To begin with, she started early in the game to train selected Korean cadres to establish and maintain a Soviet-style Republic in which all anti-Soviet groupings would be voiceless. And she made immediate provision for the training and arming of a North Korean force of impressive size, including infantry, mechanized divisions, and border constabulary. Originally these forces were supplied with arms taken from the Japanese at the time of surrender. Then, as Russian forces were withdrawn, in 1948, their arms were left behind for the newly trained North Koreans. In the first months of 1950, just prior to the irruption across the 38th parallel, Russia supplied the North Korean Peoples Army with large quantities of modern arms, including heavy artillery, T-34 tanks, trucks, automatic weapons and about 180 new aircraft, of which about 40 were YAK fighters and 70 were attack bombers.

Before the NKPA invaded South Korea she could field eight infantry divisions, all at full strength, two divisions at half strength, a motorcycle reconnaissance regiment, an armored brigade equipped with T-34 medium tanks, and five brigades of border constabulary—a total strength of 135,000.

But there was more to this army than mere numbers and modern equipment. It contained a great many Koreans who had fled from the Japanese into Russia and had been trained under fire with the Russian and Chinese Red armies, plus several thousand who had completed a three-year training period in the Soviet Union beginning in 1946. The government too was manned by personnel well-trained for their posts, most of whom had, like the Premier, Kim Il Sung, undergone thorough indoctrination in the Soviet Union since 1943. Divisions and other large units in the NKPA were commanded largely by men who as junior officers had served

9

with credit in the Soviet Army in World War II; and each NKPA division had assigned to it approximately fifteen Soviet Army advisers.

South of the 38th parallel, to cope with this well-trained and thoroughly disciplined modern army, we left a rather sorry force that we did not even dare call an army. (So obsessed was the United States with its aim of disengagement that our people in South Korea were not permitted to use the word "army" in referring to the police force we were endeavoring to build to keep order after our withdrawal.) The Koreans south of the parallel were no less freedom-loving and no less devoted to their homes than those in North Korea. There were many Koreans in our zone who had fled from the Soviet take-over. It was not willingness to fight or courage in battle that was lacking on the ROK side, so much as intensive training and good leadership. These were but two of the major needs which we failed to fill.

It is not enough merely to say that we were inept and that we lacked foresight. And it is a gross and misleading simplification to lay the blame for the outbreak of the Korean War upon Dean Acheson's public "writing off" of Korea as beyond our defense perimeter. He was merely voicing an already accepted United States policy. Korea had always been outside our defense perimeter and we had written her off several times in the history of our dealings with her. The ROK forces lacked equipment and lacked trained leaders largely because we attached almost no strategic importance to Korea and were chiefly concerned that we did not become so involved there as to find ourselves fighting in the wrong place at the wrong time. We therefore would not equip her army properly nor take a strong hand in correcting the deficiencies in ROK army leadership, where military knowledge was at a very low level indeed.

There were real obstacles, of course. The Republic of Korea had no pool of returnees from Manchuria and relatively few of her people had been trained in modern warfare. Only a few Korean officers could speak English and even fewer American advisers could speak Korean. American military terms had almost no counterparts in the Korean tongue. In the ROK army, "Face" was

10

of top importance, and Korean officers found it difficult to accept advice from junior American advisers, and often expressed open resentment at views contrary to their own, so that their own staffs hesitated to disagree with them. Many ROK officers had been appointed for political reasons, as had been so many of the officers in our own peacetime National Guard in pre-World War I days, and so their military competence had never been examined. Many of the troops were scattered here and there on antibanditry missions and other internal security tasks. Training was incomplete, with fewer than half of the sixty-seven battalions having passed the battalion phase of their training by the end of 1949. The ROK had no heavy artillery, no tanks, no antitank weapons, and no air power. It was no wonder that Syngman Rhee and other ROK leaders voiced dismay at the buildup in North Korea and the corresponding weakness south of the parallel.

But this was a true reflection of our policy toward Korea at the time. In 1948, the National Security Council of the United States had given serious thought to helping create a field army in South Korea but the plan was abandoned on MacArthur's recommendation, largely because of the "diminished capabilities of U.S. occupation forces." By 1949, we were completely committed to the theory that the next war involving the United States would be a global war, in which Korea would be of relatively minor importance and, in any event, indefensible. All our planning, all our official statements, all our military decisions derived essentially from this belief. The concept of "limited warfare" never entered our councils. We had faith in the United Nations. And the atomic bomb created for us a kind of psychological Maginot line that helped us rationalize our national urge to get the boys home, the armies demobilized, the swords sheathed, and the soldiers, sailors, and airmen out of uniform. In the light of later events it was easy for all to criticize this wholesale urge to dismantle and disperse the greatest military establishment our nation had ever owned. But would any political candidate in that era have been able to survive had he urged keeping the nation still under arms and large forces still posted 8000 miles from home?

It is true that in our assessment of the Korean situation we gave too much weight to our own interpretation of the enemy's intentions and too little to the facts we knew about his capability. The existence of the powerful striking force in North Korea and the massing of troops near the border were no secret from our intelligence. It was our evaluation that was at fault and in this I think we were largely guided by our conviction that the Communist forces in the world were not ready to risk atomic war by resorting to armed aggression. Limited war, as I noted earlier, was a concept still foreign to us, except in the sense that all wars are limited by the willingness of the participants to pay the price required.

Under these circumstances, one may certainly find fault with the timing of Dean Acheson's speech (January 1950) in which he excluded Korea from our defense perimeter. While the weakness of the ROK forces and the strong popular pressure on the administration to bring *all* United States forces home certainly were well known to the Soviets, this clear indication that we had no intention of defending Korea did nothing to give the enemy even momentary pause. It is true of course that the drawing of a defense perimeter that excluded Korea was not the work of Dean Acheson, or of the Truman administration alone. As early as September 1947, studies by the Joint Chiefs of Staff (Leahy, Eisenhower, Nimitz, and Spaatz), made at the direction of President Truman, resulted in a memorandum to the Secretary of State that included this statement: ". . . from the standpoint of military security, the U.S. has little strategic interest in maintaining the present troops and bases in Korea. . . ." It is certainly not surprising that the considered views of these four great military authorities should have met with presidential approval.

In 1949, in separate interviews, first with British journalist G. Ward Price and later with Walter B. Mathews of the Arizona *Daily Star*, General Douglas MacArthur was reported to have outlined a defense perimeter that clearly excluded Formosa. This caused no particular stir because it had been almost taken for granted among our military authorities that Formosa would soon fall to the Chinese Communists. And the United States Emergency Plans for the Far East did not provide for the defense of either

Korea or Formosa. When the State Department began to brief diplomatic missions as to what they might say to offset any loss of prestige caused by the fall of Formosa, Republicans in Congress were aroused to demand United States defense for the island. But there was no move to alter our policy toward Korea. The traditional "write-off" was apparently still in effect.

How to explain our flagrant misinterpretation of intelligence reports is a more complex question. We knew the approximate strength of the North Korean Peoples Army, which had been doubled in strength with a total mobilization in 1949 and the addition of thousands of draftees. And we knew our own weakness. Indeed General MacArthur had been sounding warnings since 1947 of the dangers that threatened in the Far East and insisting that there was no substitute for troop strength. The administration, however, was under severe pressure to cut the military budget and every arm of the services felt the surgeon's knife. The Navy was tragically short of combat ships, of amphibious craft of every kind, of minesweepers and of equipment for mine warfare. The Air Force initially had no jet fighters and was short of conventional combat and troop-carrier planes. Its reduced potential for photo-reconnaissance and the crucial lack of photo-interpreters placed the ground forces under severe handicaps. At home, where arms and armor stockpiles had been permitted to dwindle to a hatful, production facilities had been dismantled or placed in dead-storage. We had complete confidence in the ability of the United Nations to forestall any serious aggression; we knew that the world was weary of war and the Communists were "not ready" to involve themselves in a nuclear holocaust; and besides we were taking extreme pains not to provoke our potential enemies into a major dispute.

Some of this wishful thinking may have entered into our misinterpretation of the intelligence reports received just prior to the invasion. Only six days before the NKPA crossed the border in force a Central Intelligence field agency reported "extensive troop movements" north of the 38th parallel, together with "evacuation of all residents from the Northern side of the parallel to a depth of two kilometers; suspension of civilian freight service from Wonsan to Chorwon and reservation of this line for transporting military supplies only; movements of armed units to border areas; and movement of large shipments of ordnance and ammunition to border areas." How anyone could have read this report and not anticipated an attack is hard to fathom. Yet this report was not used as a basis for *any* conclusion by G-2 at General Headquarters in Tokyo and it was forwarded to Washington in routine fashion, with no indication of urgency. Later GHQ was to disclaim all responsibility for failure to interpret these almost classic preparations and to insist that it had "forwarded all the facts" to Washington. But this does not explain the fact that, six days before the North Korean army struck, GHQ sent this interpretative report to Washington: "Apparently Soviet advisers believe that now is the opportune time to attempt to subjugate the South Korean government by *political means* [my emphasis], especially since the guerrilla campaign in South Korea recently has met with serious reverses."

No, I think it obvious that GHQ, like so many others of our people, at home and abroad, was influenced by its conviction that all these alarums and excursions were just a normal aspect of the psychological "cold war" in which we were engaged, not only in Korea but in sectors deemed far more crucial to us. Besides, there was a tendency in Tokyo to place minimum credence in Oriental agents and a feeling that South Koreans especially had a tendency to cry "Wolf" when there was no beast in the offing. It was also true that movements following this pattern had been observed in 1947 when the North Korean armies had initiated an annual rotation of completely equipped units between the 38th parallel and rear areas.

What is truly inexcusable, I believe, and what cost us dearly in blood, was a failure to assess properly the high level of combat effectiveness that the North Korean Peoples Army had attained. When the fighting began, GHQ had to increase almost daily its estimate of the force that would be needed to stop the invaders. We simply had never properly reckoned the strength of the foe.

We began to withdraw our last combat troops from Korea in the very face of these obvious intensifications of the strain between the two Koreas. We did so, it was asserted, in deference to a resolution by the General Assembly of the United Nations. But that resolution, calling for a withdrawal of all foreign troops, had been drawn up and introduced by the United States itself, and in spite of warnings by the United Nations Temporary Commission and by Syngman Rhee that Korea was on the verge of a "barbarous civil war." Our national mind was made up to liquidate this embarrassing military commitment and we closed our ears to the clashing of arms that sounded along the border as our last troops were taking ship for home. Our sole concession to the realities of the situation had been a decision in March 1949 to complete the equipment of a 65,000-man constabulary (the Republic of Korea authorities promptly changed this word in the resolution to "army") and a 4000-man coast guard with requisite vessels "for suppressing smuggling, piracy and hostile penetration by sea." The "armor" for this army consisted of a few scout cars and some half-tracks. Four of the army's infantry divisions had only two instead of the normal allotment of three infantry regiments and the entire army had only ninety-one 105-mm. howitzers. (Under the United States Army's Table of Organization there would have been 432 divisional artillery pieces backed up by nondivisional battalions of the same and heavier calibers.)

Our own forces in South Korea, first reduced to a single Regimental Combat Team, consisted finally of a Military Advisory Group—the famous KMAG (pronounced *Kay*mag)—of approximately 500 officers and men under the command of Brigadier General William L. Roberts. This group was charged with the task of providing advisers to the Republic of Korea Army down to battalion level. This was all we had left in Korea while the North Koreans were engaged in the final softening-up process preparatory to the invasion. In June 1949, following a series of minor forays along the 38th parallel, the North Korean forces invaded Republic of Korea territory in the Ongjin Peninsula, almost at the same time that the last of the United States tactical units were being withdrawn. The border was not restored until July. In this same month the city of Kaesong, south of the 38th parallel, was attacked by North Korean infantry and artillery. Again in August

15

the Ongjin Peninsula was invaded, the North Koreans being finally driven back after heavy fighting. In May 1950, Kaesong once more came under heavy artillery fire from the north. Meanwhile our own disengagement moved on apace.

It must not be thought, however, that our military or even our civilian authorities were unanimous in urging withdrawal from Korea or in trying to look on the bright side of affairs in that unhappy country. As early as 1948, General Omar N. Bradley, Army Chief of Staff, with characteristic discernment, challenged the view of the majority of the Joint Chiefs of Staff, that Korea was "of little strategic value" and that "any commitment to the use of U.S. military forces in Korea would be ill-advised." He recognized the strong possibility of a North Korean invasion and recommended that if such an invasion did take place United States nationals should be promptly evacuated and the matter should be presented without delay to the Security Council of the United Nations. And he strongly urged a reappraisal of the Korean situation before our combat troops were withdrawn. His views were rejected.

A senior American officer in KMAG, Colonel John E. Baird, also sounded a lonely warning. He informed our newly appointed ambassador to Korea, John Muccio, that the type and quality of material available to the ROK army was not sufficient to maintain existing borders. He reported that the outnumbered ROKs were thoroughly outgunned by the NKPA, who had 122-mm. guns with a range of roughly seventeen miles as against the American-supplied 105-mms with an effective range of about seven miles. And he urged that the ROKs be given some means of defense against air attack, recommending that we supply them with F-51 aircraft. His urging went unheeded.

Civilian voices, too, including President Truman's, had earlier spoken out against the rapid dismantling of our war machine and the mothballing of our arms industry. But, as Mr. Truman phrased it in his *Memoirs,* these voices were "drowned out by Congress and the press." So when the big guns finally did signal the eruption of full-scale warfare in Korea, the little Republic we had created found herself completely unready to offer more than token resistance—and we found ourselves militarily unprepared to implement our agreement for mutual aid.

CHAPTER TWO

CHALLENGE AND RESPONSE – THE
GALLANT STAND OF TASK FORCE SMITH

CONSIDERING THE RELATIVE strength and combat readiness of the forces that faced each other across the 38th parallel in June 1950, it was a marvel that the North Korean armies were delayed at all in their drive to overrun all of South Korea. They had armor, where the ROKs had none. They had artillery that far outnumbered and outranged what we had provided for the ROK. And most of the ROK artillery had not been fired for years. The NKPA had air cover, and the ROKs lacked even antiaircraft batteries. Nor did the ROKs have any gun capable of slowing a tank. It was as if a few troops of Boy Scouts with hand weapons had undertaken to stop a Panzer unit.

Before artillery can be effective, its fire must be concentrated on a target of military importance. That means that concentrations must be plotted and crews trained and guns test-fired. In most instances, this had not been done by the ROK army at all. On the other hand, the NKPA howitzers had been zeroed in on major targets for months and had already shelled the city of Kaesong on two previous occasions. The NKPA was not only thoroughly prepared for this attack. It had planned it in fine detail, even to assigning certain units to the task of mingling with civilian refugees to infiltrate ROK territory, to disrupt communications, spread terror, and neutralize strong points.

The attack began at dawn on a rainy summer morning, June

25, 1950, with heavy artillery fire in the various attack zones—which were the main valley roads or corridors leading to Seoul and Chunchon. The main thrusts came down these valleys, with T-34 tanks rumbling ahead and infantry spreading out quickly into battle line whenever resistance was met. Coordinated with these drives were the complete overrunning of the Ongjin Peninsula and an amphibious flanking move along the east coast to cut off ROK units who were covering the north-south coastal road as well as the roads extending southwest to Hongchon, Wonju, and Chechon. Anyone who has stood up to hostile armor, with no weapon in sight capable of piercing it, can understand the terror that gripped the outnumbered ROK forces who faced the two-pronged tank-supported attack toward Seoul. Relatively few of these troops —only those who had been engaged in antiguerrilla activity in the past few months—had ever faced hostile fire at all. Many were almost completely untrained, unsure of their own weapons, lacking confidence in their leaders (some of whom abandoned their troops in the opening days), and without any knowledge of how to deal with an enemy who outnumbered and outflanked them. Almost no provision had been made for defense in depth or for a supply system. The ROK forces were essentially equipped and prepared for internal security and many of them found no way of fighting the disciplined hordes that fanned out grimly through the countryside. Indeed by the time United States forces moved into action there were many South Korean troops who had not fought at all—from lack of knowing how and from complete collapse of discipline.

There were valiant exceptions however. If it were not for the fierce courage of those few ROK units that had been properly prepared for the fight, another day or two of priceless time might have been lost and disaster might have been complete. The ROK 6th Division was one unit that had been made combat-ready before the invasion began. Lieutenant Colonel Thomas D. McPhail of KMAG had been assigned to the 6th Division as senior adviser and he quickly won the permission of the Division Commander, General Kim, to initiate an intensive training program. The 6th Division, charged with the defense of the approach to Chunchon had to deal frequently with guerrilla bands who crossed the border on well-established routes between Chunchon and Kangnung. Battles with these invaders, who crossed in bands of varying sizes, were frequent in the weeks just prior to the major incursion, so the ROK 6th got part of its training in hot action.

Artillery and Engineer units were also included in the training program. Limited firing of the long-still howitzers was conducted, concentrations were surveyed and plotted, and positions were improved. Under Colonel McPhail's shrewd direction, intelligence units were recruited and trained and sent on frequent missions across the 38th parallel, whence they returned with information that strongly indicated an imminent attack. Well-camouflaged tanks were observed, new enemy troop units, and antiaircraft batteries, all of which indicated to Colonel McPhail (although not to the superiors to whom he conveyed this information) that time was pressing. McPhail persuaded the Division Commander to cancel all passes for the weekend of June 23 and to keep the defensive positions fully manned. As a result, when the attack did come, the ROK 6th Division was prepared to make a stand. They fought a gallant battle that stalled the NKPA drive on Seoul for three precious days. Had adjoining units been similarly prepared the attack might have been blunted long enough to permit some sort of stand along the Han River, with consequences now past imagining. But, after the ROK 6th had repulsed several attacks, had startled and disrupted the enemy by the accuracy of the artillery concentrations, and had reduced the early penetrations through use of reserve forces, word came that friendly units on either flank had fled, leaving the 6th Division exposed on both sides and open to immediate envelopment. There was no choice then but to withdraw. Defensive positions had already been established south of Chunchon where the 6th was to make a further stand. But KMAG meanwhile had received orders to leave Seoul, and Colonel McPhail was directed to proceed to Taegu to be evacuated by air. When he was able to return to help reorganize the reeling South Korean troops, Seoul was in enemy hands and the retreat had become a rout.

The ROK 1st Division made an equally gallant fight in defense of the capital. One infantry company stood and fought on the hill above Seoul until its last man had been killed. Elsewhere however there was panic. The Ongjin Peninsula was completely overrun by dark of the second day, and the troops from that action were released to join the drive on Seoul. Surviving ROK troops had to be evacuated by LSTs to help in the futile defense of the capital. Kaesong, the ancient capital of the country, fell to the NKPA only four hours after the dawn jump-off on the first day. By dark of the following day the enemy's armor-supported columns had driven down along the narrow corridor to Uijongbu, and had invested the city, thus opening the straight and unobstructed road to Seoul. Civilians, disorganized troops, carts loaded with bedding and supplies, ponies, oxen, all fled in a clamoring, yet strangely patient stream before the approaching rumble of the guns. A piecemeal counterattack hardly slowed the enemy advance on the capital.

But before the NKPA had entered the outskirts of the city, the ROK Chief of Staff had gathered up his entire retinue and fled south across the Han. According to ROK sources, General Chae, "over his protest," had been "placed in a jeep and sent south across the river." Just what form his protest took or what authority placed him in the jeep, our own people in Seoul were unable to discover. According to the United States Army Official History of the action in Korea, the entire headquarters of the ROK army moved to Sihung, halfway between Seoul and Suwon, without notifying KMAG. When the Americans did learn of the move, the senior U.S. officer present, Colonel (later Lieutenant General) William H. S. Wright, gathered his own staff and started south to persuade the Koreans to return. Arguments were vain, however, and the ROK units still engaged north of Seoul were left without communications to their headquarters. The civilian population then began to panic and a wholesale exodus began. (Three days later, on June 30, the ROK government relieved General Chae and replaced him with General Chung Il Kwon, whose service was exemplary. He later became Ambassador to the United States and is now—May 1967—Prime Minister.

Early on the morning of June 28, the NKPA moved into Seoul, where fires were already burning and Communist flags were showing. With the loss of Seoul—the cultural, political, communications, and psychological heart of the new Republic—all effective resistance collapsed and the ROK troops, along with hordes of white-clad refugees including many trained infiltrators from the north) swarmed back across the Han, a river that for a time GHQ in Tokyo had believed might provide a suitable barrier beyond which to make a stand.

On June 29 however the Commander in Chief, General Mac-Arthur, acting as he so often did without thought of personal danger, made a personal reconnaissance that persuaded him the tide could not be stemmed without massive reinforcement. Mac-Arthur and seven high-ranking officers on his staff, including Generals Edward M. Almond and George E. Stratemeyer, flew from Tokyo to Suwon, twenty miles south of Seoul, and were briefed at Advance Command Headquarters by two KMAG officers who had just returned from Seoul. Riding with them in two commandeered jeeps, the Commander in Chief and his staff set out for the Han River, bucking the southward flow of refugees, carts, baggage, troops and trucks. From a hill looking down on the Han Valley, MacArthur viewed the rout. He then reported in a radio message to the JCS: "The South Korean forces are in confusion, have not seriously fought, and lack leadership . . . They are incapable of gaining the initiative . . ."

While MacArthur spent only five hours on the ground in Korea at this time and, with time out for briefing and traveling, probably could spare only an hour for direct observation, his assessment of the ROK resistance was a fair one, apart from those exceptions to these strictures that have already been noted. The ROKs were beaten. And unless we came in quickly, with massive strength on the ground, the peninsula would soon be overrun.

(There is an amusing sidelight to the MacArthur reconnaissance: In his *Reminiscences,* MacArthur calls up a vivid picture of the retreat, "the dreadful backwash of a defeated and dispersed army. The South Korean forces were in complete and disorganized flight." From the hill overlooking the river, he watched "towers of smoke rising from the ruins of Seoul" and "the retreating panting columns of disorganized troops" which were "clog-

ging all the roads in a writhing dust-shrouded mass of humanity."
But the report of General Almond, who watched the same scene
from MacArthur's side, gave a picture not quite so despairing. The
troops he saw were neither panting nor disorganized but "all smil-
ing, all with rifles, all with bandoliers of ammunition, all saluting"
while sporadic mortar fire fell, but not near enough to be a peril.
Nor is it quite clear how the "mass of humanity" could be "dust-
shrouded" when it had been raining intermittently for twelve hours.
But in many of MacArthur's ghostwritten reports the same
tendency to paint the dark side blacker and the bright side shinier
than in life has been detected by eyes more perceptive than my
own.)

The plans of the United States to stave off the looming disaster
were subject now to hour-by-hour reappraisal, with an almost geo-
metric expansion of the estimate of the force that would be needed.
Our intelligence had given us facts enough to go on, but we had
failed to interpret them properly or even to take them with sufficient seriousness. We had never, for instance, imagined that the
NKPA was a force so well-trained, so superbly disciplined, so bat-
tle-ready—and in consequence we had not adjusted our thinking
to the actual dimensions of the fight. Now we had to shake ourselves out of our slumber, count over our tragically diminished
forces, and hasten to salvage what we could from the imminent
catastrophe.

Our immediate concern was the safe evacuation of American
nationals endangered by the invasion. To effect this rescue, we had
prepared plan Cruller, worked out a year before by the staff of
the GHQ in Tokyo in coordination with KMAG and the United
States Embassy. Ambassador Muccio was charged with putting the
plan into effect in the event of a major emergency. The emergency
at hand, the plan was implemented without delay. The Navy, the
Air Force, and the Embassy all worked with consummate smooth-
ness, dispatch, and efficiency, so that not a man, woman, or child
involved was lost—not even one seriously injured. This minor
triumph by our forces in the Far East was so quickly lost sight of
in the swirl of major tragedies that the richly deserved WELL
DONE message from Washington was never sent.

The Commander's immediate concern now was scratching together men and munitions enough to fight a battle five times as big as we were ready for. It was a time for instant decisions and swift action. To the credit of our President, and our military leaders, there was neither hesitation nor doubt in the response. The message announcing the invasion of ROK territory by the forces of North Korea reached Washington from Seoul at about 9:30 P.M. on Saturday, June 24.* Before 10 P.M. a copy of the message had been handed to Secretary of State Acheson, who immediately telephoned President Truman in Independence, Missouri, where the President was beginning a brief vacation. Throughout the early hours of Sunday morning, duty officers in the various government departments worked down their *must call* lists to notify the men who first needed to know that warfare had broken out in Korea.

It was not a foregone conclusion by any means that the United States, after its long history of leaving Korea to its fate, would this time respond any differently. We were not prepared for war, and most of us who first heard this ominous message from the other side of the world told ourselves that World War III had begun. No one would have criticized the President had he stopped to take solemn counsel with all his advisers before he decided what move he should make first. But it was not in President Truman's nature to waver or step backward in the face of a challenge like this. Within hours he had ordered the use of "U.S. air and sea forces to give the ROK government troops cover and support." On June 30 he approved MacArthur's request to use one regimental combat team and shortly thereafter gave MacArthur "full authority to use the ground forces under his command."

The impact of those decisions was not immediately felt in the United States. I believe the majority of our citizens, convinced by press and politician, and by the promptings of their own deepest desires, thought of the Korean outbreak as hardly more than a bonfire that would be extinguished soon enough by the people we had left in charge of such matters. But soldiers everywhere received the news with deep misgiving. They knew too well how the Congressional budget-paring had cut our forces down to mere

* Washington time was fourteen hours earlier than Seoul and Tokyo time.

23

skeletons. They had long been concerned, not with Soviet intent but with Soviet capability. Now most military men feared that the Communists had finally chosen to put the whole issue to the touch.

I well recall how the news came to me and how deep an effect it had upon me. At the time, June 1950, I was Deputy Chief of Staff of the Army on duty at the Pentagon and had just completed a visit to the 28th Infantry Division of the Pennsylvania National Guard. Like a hundred other sleepy men that night I was awakened by the tinkle of the telephone at my bedside and listened with growing uneasiness as the quiet, correct voice in midnight Washington told me of the message from Ambassador Muccio. I awakened my patient wife, to share my fears with her and to tell her to dress and make ready to go right back to the capital. A country stillness wrapped the VIP quarters at Carlisle Barracks as we made our way to our car. Long before the countryside was awake we were out on the dark road, talking very little, but sharing I know the same conviction that the short peace we had known since the Nazi surrender was ended now for a long, long time. I could not help dwelling on the hundreds of thousands of souls who slept, not only along the road we traveled, but all through the nation, without a hint of how suddenly and how brutally their lives might be changed when the sun came up.

Naturally, the first forces we could commit in Korea were the naval and air forces, already concerned with bringing to safety all American civilians there and a few designated foreigners. The Navy, with the Seventh Fleet commanded by Vice-Admiral Arthur D. Struble as its principal element, assigned its major tactical organization, Task Force 77, to the job of blockading the Korean coastline, after destroying whatever minor enemy naval forces existed. The annals of the Korean War concern themselves largely with the bitter fighting on the ground. This is only just, for the ground forces had to slug it out night and day with a resourceful and (for a long time) a numerically superior foe. But the men of the United States Navy afloat and aloft fought with characteristic gallantry and effectiveness, carrying out interdiction missions along the Korean coast, grimly devoting themselves to the thankless and dangerous job of sweeping mines out of the channels, or engaging

in underwater demolition tasks, often in subzero weather. As for
the airmen, without them, the war would have been over in sixty
days, with all Korea in Communist hands. Handicapped in their
task of reconnaissance by a lack of trained photographic inter-
preters, the fliers of the Army, the Navy, and the Marine Corps,
and the ground crews, working around the clock in every kind of
weather, operating from scanty runways, or slippery decks,
managed to eliminate the North Korean Air Force early in the
battle, destroyed much of the NKPA armor, and transported criti-
cally needed men and supplies to spots of greatest danger. With
the Navy controlling the shipping lanes and preventing even small
hostile forces from side-slipping along the coast, while transporting the bulk of supplies and equipment needed for rapid buildup
of the Eighth Army, and the Air Force providing complete mastery
of the skies, our ground forces managed to seize a flimsy toehold
in Korea and hang on to it until help arrived.

With no hope of getting the authorized Regimental Combat
Team (a reinforced infantry regiment) from Hawaii to the battle
zone in time, General MacArthur had ordered a makeshift infantry
battalion to be flown to Korea without delay, with orders to make
contact with the enemy as far forward as possible and, by fighting
a delaying action, to buy time to bring more troops across. Destined for the airport at Suwon, at the time still in friendly hands,
these troops were delayed by foul weather and landed eventually
at Pusan Airport. From there they moved forward, along road and
rail line to meet the steadily advancing enemy.

This was Task Force Smith, named for its Commanding Officer,
Lieutenant Colonel C. B. Smith, and for several bitter days it
was the entire United States fighting force on the ground. It numbered just 500 men—two rifle companies, two platoons of 4.2
mortars (all it had to pass for artillery), a single 75-mm. recoilless rifle crew, and six 2.36″ bazooka teams. Against them were
ranged more than a hundred times as many enemy troops, with
T-34 tanks and artillery. Task Force Smith had no reserves, no
weapon capable of knocking out the thick-skinned tanks, and nothing to match the enemy howitzers. (Task Force Smith did include
Battery A of the 52nd Field Artillery Battalion but this unit was

25

slowed in its forward movement and was absent when action opened on July 5.)

It was tragic to picture this handful of poorly equipped men, trained for occupation rather than for battle, fresh from the idleness and luxury of peacetime Japan, where they lived on delicacies, whiled time away with girl friends, and even found servants to shine their shoes—to picture them plodding forward without question or complaint to meet death on some nameless Korean hillside, where there was neither cover nor concealment, or in some foul-smelling rice paddy where filth rose calf-deep. The action they fought may have seemed futile and without hope. All they could do, at best, was to hold their place on some rise of ground until the hostile troops had almost completely encircled them or ammunition had run out. Then it was fall back through unknown countryside where every man might be an enemy and try feverishly to regroup somewhere for another hopeless stand. There was some panic, and much confusion, when the first battle was joined. At 8 A.M. on July 5, the enemy attacked near Osan with thirty tanks and a strong force of infantry. Task Force Smith soon had to choose between retreat and annihilation. Having held their positions until their ammunition was gone, they withdrew in some disorder, receiving heavy casualties.

This was the pattern of the fighting for the next several weeks, with the enemy attacking in overwhelming numbers, continually probing for the open flanks, and moving his armor against our fire as if we had been using bean-blowers. The men of the 24th Infantry Division, having no reserves, were almost constantly engaged, half-sleeping on their feet sometimes, forgetting when they had last known a hot meal, but hanging on determinedly to gain time and time and time. By the evening of July 5, all of the 1st Battalion, 21st Infantry, had entered the fight, while the balance of the 24th Division began to set up defensive positions in the Taejon area.

General MacArthur's plans were far-ranging and all-inclusive, right from the start: He would make contact as far forward as possible, throw whatever troops he could quickly transport there into the path of the enemy, and take immediate advantage of the natural barrier offered by the wide Han River (one of the very few streams in Korea too deep to be forded on foot). He would rapidly build up to a force of two United States divisions which, when combined with the ROK forces, would be sufficient (in Mac-Arthur's first estimate) to delay the enemy and assure retention of an adequate lodgment area on the peninsula. Then, when sufficient forces were at hand (this, the Commander in Chief reckoned, would take two months), he would pass to the offensive with an amphibious assault by a two-division corps, seize the Inchon-Seoul area, sit astride the enemy lines of communication and supply, and then destroy the hostile army.

But this plan had been completed before GHQ knew the caliber of the enemy. Once the fighting had begun, General MacArthur's estimates skyrocketed. The Han River hardly slowed the enemy down, with the ROK infantry on the south bank disintegrating quickly under heavy artillery fire that could not be returned. The NKPA crossed this obstacle quickly and began to flow south. Forward elements of the 24th Division retired along the general axis of the main highway and double-track railroad running from Seoul to Pusan. Our Air Force knocked out much of the enemy armor, inflicted casualties on his foot soldiers, and kept close check on his movement. But only the remnants of one understrength, badly battered, and outgunned division was there to dispute the ground.

In seventeen days of bitter fighting, these bone-weary soldiers fought five major delaying actions while falling back seventy miles. They made their first stand near Osan, on July 5 and 6; then they stood again near Chonan on the eighth; between Chonui and Chochiwon on the eleventh; and then for three days, July 13 through 15, they held back the enemy along the Kum River. Perhaps their bitterest fight, and the one that cost them the services of their gallant commander, Major General William F. Dean (who was taken prisoner there), took place in and around the city of Taejon. Here they battled through the treacherous streets, with sniper fire, even automatic weapons, from rooftops on every side.

The enemy, after penetrating the defenses with his armor, would envelop both flanks with infantry, surround artillery units, and roll on rearward. Everyone then—cannoneers, MPs, even medics

—would take up carbines or rifles, set up a hasty perimeter defense and make ready to fight their way to the rear.

Supply routes, overrun by guerrillas and trained Communist agitators, who had infiltrated our lines among the countless refugees, were constantly disrupted, and rear areas offered no safety. It was endless fighting, endless falling back, endless danger. Patrols who went seeking men who had been cut off from their units often found them, arms tied behind their backs, lying dead, each with a single bullet wound in the back of the head. It rained in torrents. Or the summer sun steamed the men's clothing, or baked their skin, and ravaged them with thirst.

On July 20, Taejon was abandoned. A very few days after this, the 25th and the 1st Cavalry Divisions, raised to a minimum combat level through cannibalizing the 7th Infantry Division (now our entire remaining combat garrison in Japan), were in action at various points along a hundred-mile front extending from west of the Taejon-Taegu highway and rail line to the Sea of Japan, north of Pohang-dong. The 24th Division, riddled with casualties, sore, weary, and dirty, looked around for respite—and found none. They were promptly shifted west and south to the Naktong River where they were to block enemy attempts to turn our south flank.

Enemy pressure against our reinforced line continued to increase, and it soon became obvious that the front would have to be shrunk further to provide sufficient depth for defense and to prevent breakthroughs. Fortunately at this juncture additional forces came ashore at Pusan to add flesh to our battle line. The Army's 5th Regimental Combat Team arrived from Hawaii on August 1 and the 2nd Infantry Division began debarking at Pusan on the same day. The next day the 1st Provisional Marine Brigade came ashore. Their arrival seemed timed to the second, for the danger was acute.

Observers in the Pentagon had long been aware of the disaster that threatened on the south, for air reconnaissance had kept us informed of the movement of an enemy column down the west coast of the peninsula, heading toward Masan, at the tip. A breakthrough at that point could have meant complete disaster, abandonment of the peninsula, and a bloody slaughter of our pieced-out forces as they tried to fight their way to safety.

But Lieutenant General Walton H. Walker, in command of the Eighth Army, had already announced there would be no Bataan. While the Army's situation was still deteriorating rapidly after the fall of Chinju on July 29, he announced: "There will be no more retreating! . . . We must fight to the end! . . . We are going to hold this line! We are going to win!"

Win they did, through desperate fighting and brilliant maneuver. First, with his skeleton force finally beefed up to near battle strength, Walker hastened to meet the most serious threat—the approaching enemy column on the south that could roll up his whole front. The 25th Division, moving with skill and despatch, was shifted from the north, where the enemy force was still relatively meager, to the south, where the Masan-Chinju front was in danger of collapse. The 1st Provisional Marine Brigade, newly landed, was sent immediately to the same sector. The brigade provided real muscle. Commanded by Brigadier General Edward A. Craig, it included the 5th Marines and Marine Aircraft Group 33. While it arrived understrength, with unit shortages akin to those of the Army (infantry battalions with two instead of three rifle companies and artillery firing batteries with four rather than six guns), it had a strength of 6500 men and could enter the fight with M-26 Pershing tanks which, with their 90-mm. guns, were more than a match for the T-34. This force saved the day in the south and stopped the enemy column in its tracks. (Because of night marches, our aircraft had not been able to slow this advance.)

Now the Eighth Army had set up their final defense line—what became known as the "Pusan Perimeter"—in a great three-sided front that protected the railroad quadrilateral—the Taegu-Masan-Pusan-Kyongju connection that fed the lifeblood to our scattered forces. To keep this line free from enemy interruption and fire, Walker decided to try to hold the general line along the Naktong River, even though the enemy had penetrated well beyond this stream in places.

The front was by no means continuous. There simply was not manpower enough to hold a solid line. Instead it was made up of scattered strong points from which our forces could sally forth to "put out one fire after another," as General Leven C. Allen, Eighth Army Chief of Staff, worded it. There was no rest for the weary troops. There were no reserves. And for six weeks the enemy continued his strong thrusts against both flanks while probing for weak spots in the center. At any time, dawn or midnight, the call might come to round up whatever men could be spared—a battalion from one division, a company from another, fifty or a hundred men from some other unit, to meet some instant danger. And as fast as one flame was extinguished, another might break out anywhere, creating one more crisis that had to be dealt with by piecemeal measures.

Engaged in this six-week battle were the Eighth Army, with its four understrength divisions; the British 27th Brigade; all that remained of the ROK forces (five divisions); the 1st Provisional Marine Brigade, and all the combat aircraft the Marines, the Air Force, and the Navy could provide. When preparations were being made for the Inchon landing, the Marines were withdrawn, leaving Walker in a desperate fix for manpower and supplies. That he held on at all was a measure of his own dogged tenacity and of the fierce bravery of his troops. Although Walker privately felt, as did many of the officers of the Eighth Army, that the Army was being shortchanged by GHQ in favor of the X Corps, then preparing for the Inchon landing under command of General Almond, MacArthur's Chief of Staff, he never used his shortages as an excuse to temporize. He struggled manfully to concentrate his pitifully scanty forces where they were needed most and then tried to break out of the perimeter when the Inchon landing had supposedly put the enemy forces in mortal danger. But his battle-worn troops just were not up to the task of crossing the Naktong, without proper equipment. The enemy, although we bombarded his lines with news of Inchon, for some days just did not seem to know he had been beaten up north. Nor was there any evidence there that the Air Force battering had already "beat the NKPA to its knees"—a claim made in the Air Force official history. Still facing Walker across the Naktong—a wide and difficult barrier—was a disciplined, well-armed, and determined foe.

"We have been bastard children," Walker told GHQ by phone, referring to his failure to receive proper engineering equipment. ". . . But I don't want you to think I am dragging my heels." He was not. But the enemy was fighting just as fiercely as he had before the Inchon landing. Getting Walker's armor to the far shore of the river was simply beyond the general's present capability, he felt. He had been ordered to attack and break out on September 15, and had then been granted a one-day delay by MacArthur, so as to start his breakout the day after the landing. On the twenty-first, he still could not punch his way out, and the enemy showed no sign of withdrawing. MacArthur, deeply concerned by this hitch in his schedule, had his planners get to work planning a shorter end-run operation—a landing at Kumsan, on the west coast, a hundred miles due south of Seoul. Before this plan ever reached its final stages, however, the enemy at last began to show less appetite for the battle. The Inchon landing had succeeded and the NKPA was in danger of annihilation. On September 23, General Allen told GHQ in Tokyo by phone: "Something must be brewing. We haven't had a counterattack all day." Then the southernmost enemy units, those in greatest peril of being cut off, began to withdraw north. Walker at once ordered pursuit, directing all columns to forget their flanks and drive forward toward Seoul without delay. This they did, with all the vigor of embattled troops who finally smell victory.

On September 27, men of the 1st Cavalry Division, rolling northward, near Suwon, met forward elements of the U.S. 7th Division striking south. The jaws of the trap had been closed. Now the NKPA began to disintegrate, with tens of thousands of its men flowing into the prisoner-of-war cages hastily erected by the Eighth Army and the X Corps.

MacArthur reacted with his customary optimism, counting the victory complete before the prize was really in his grasp. On September 25 both he and General Almond announced that Seoul was "once more in friendly hands." But the X Corps units, particularly the Marine Division, could have told a different story. There was bitter street fighting ahead that lasted three days and cost added casualties among civilians as well as fighting men. It was

31

not until September 28 that the city was finally cleared. Then General MacArthur, in a brief and moving ceremony, officially turned back to President Rhee the capital of his nation.

There was glory for all the troops engaged in this operation. And there was particular glory for its brilliant author, General MacArthur, who, almost alone among our military leaders, saw what could be done and what could be won by doing it. But with the close of this first phase of the war, many hearts were filled with gratitude for the truly gallant performance of Task Force Smith, and the 24th Division, that tiny, meagerly armed, hopelessly outnumbered and nearly forgotten band of United States fighting men, too many of them young recruits without battle experience. They did indeed, as President Truman worded it in a tribute to their stand, "put up one of the finest rear guard actions in military history." Said the President: "A small band of heroic youngsters led by a few remarkable generals was holding off a landslide so that the strength for the counterpunch could be mustered."

While the incessant pounding given the NKPA by our air power did indeed make the stand possible, I believe that neither this pounding, nor the death of the NKPA's ablest leader, Lieutenant General Kang Kon (King Kong to the Americans), who was killed by a land mine, really did shatter the NKPA and make it easy meat for our ground forces, as some official sources insist. The men who faced the NKPA along the Pusan perimeter found it a fierce, a wily, a ruthless, and a determined enemy. And they had to outfight it on the ground.

CHAPTER THREE

THE UNITED NATIONS ON THE OFFENSIVE –
THE INCHON LANDING AND THE
BREAKOUT FROM THE PERIMETER

THE INCHON LANDING, Operation Chromite, the daring 5000-to-1 shot that restored the initiative to our forces in Korea and kept them from being pushed into the sea, was a typical MacArthur operation, from inception to execution. Almost before the rest of us fully comprehended that our nation was at war, MacArthur had begun to plan the amphibious enveloping movement, so characteristic of all his Pacific strategy, that would hit the enemy where he least looked for a blow, would sever his supply lines, and trap him between anvil and hammer. While others thought of a way to withdraw our forces safely, MacArthur planned for victory.

He did not, at first, have many on his side. I know that I was not alone in doubting the feasibility of his plan as it was outlined to the Joint Chiefs of Staff. There were some who were not reconciled until the success of the move was beyond denying. But General MacArthur was not merely a military genius. He was a brilliant advocate who could argue his points with so much persuasiveness that men determined to stand up against him were won to enthusiastic support.

Even while our bloodied and outnumbered forces were withdrawing into the Pusan perimeter, and while MacArthur was urging that more and more manpower and supplies be given him, there were sober and reasoned voices at home that warned against committing too much of our diminished military strength to an action that might prove only the opening skirmish in a war that would soon extend to Europe and quickly engage the whole world. We had other positions far more vital and more defensible than Korea to protect in other theaters and we had almost no force to spare as it was. In the Far East we had our major field command, the Eighth Army, an occupation force that had had practically no assigned responsibility for Korea. To accomplish its mission of occupation and internal security, it was dispersed throughout Japan and had access to few training areas where its units might keep themselves combat-ready. Indeed, training of these troops for combat-readiness had long since been reduced to second priority.

Despite MacArthur's warning that the danger in the Far East was real he had seen his command steadily whittled down. Every one of the Eighth Army's four infantry divisions (including one called the 1st Cavalry Division) was below its authorized makeshift strength of 12,500, a figure itself dangerously below the full wartime complement of 18,900. Every division was short 1500 rifles and all its 90-mm. antitank guns, missing three infantry battalions out of nine, lacking one firing battery out of every three in the divisional artillery, and all regimental tank companies. Only the 1st Cavalry Division had retained its organic medium tank battalion. There were no corps headquarters and no vital corps units such as medium and heavy artillery, engineer and communications troops.

The naval and air forces had been shortchanged too, the naval forces being below strength in combat ships, in amphibious craft of every type and in minesweepers and minesweeping equipment. The Air Force at the start had no jet fighters at all and too few combat and troop-carrying planes while its visual and photographic reconnaissance, as has already been noted, was severely handicapped by lack of trained personnel.

But it was not just in the Far East that our military might was threadbare. At home we had the skeletonized 3rd Division, sliced to its bare bones by the economizers, plus the 82nd Airborne Division, making up our entire General Reserve.

This was the state in which demobilization had left us. More than that, it had put us into a position where we had nowhere to reach for trained manpower but into the reserve, the just-discharged veterans of World War II, most of them newly settled into the good jobs and homes they had dreamed of through years of combat, and all of them understandably dismayed at having to go back, after having once made their contribution of toil, blood, and sweat, and make it all over again under the worst possible circumstances. The administration was reluctant to reactivate these men too. Yet where else was it to find what it needed? To draft many thousands of youngsters and make them combat-ready would take a year. And the battle was so urgent now that troops had to be dispatched by air. Nothing would do but to put the ex-soldiers back into boots.

It was into this atmosphere that MacArthur's hurried requests for larger and larger commitments were flung. He had first asked for authority to commit a Regimental Combat Team, then had estimated two full-strength divisions were needed. On July 7, he asked for four to four and a half full-strength divisions supported by an Airborne Regimental Combat Team and an armored group of four medium tank battalions. Two days later, he radioed the Joint Chiefs of Staff that he needed without delay an additional "field army of at least four divisions with all component services." He was, understandably, impatient with his superiors in the Pentagon and they, also understandably, were hesitant to commit all our current military muscle, and more that we had not yet developed, to a theater we had not selected, and perhaps a very secondary one at that.

There was doubt too whether the Far East requests for ordnance were not far out of line, and fear that we might be expending matériel already on hand and wasting our military substance beyond our ability to replace it in less than one to two years. It was not entirely clear, either, that Mr. Truman's policies—his urgent desire to do everything possible to avoid provoking a third world war in our lamentable state of unreadiness—were completely understood in Tokyo. It was decided therefore that the President's special representative, Averell Harriman, should travel to Tokyo to consult with General MacArthur. General Larry Norstad and I were ordered to go with him.

When we left Washington, there was a strong feeling in the Pentagon—a feeling that I shared—against granting MacArthur's request for the 3rd Division. It was tragically understrength, completely unready for combat, and its removal would reduce the General Reserve to a single major unit, the 82nd Airborne Division. As for dispatching the 82nd, or defusing it for the sake of supplying MacArthur with the airborne Regimental Combat Team he was requesting, I was prepared to dig my heels in against that. But I reckoned, as all of us did, without MacArthur's persuasiveness, his self-confidence, his eloquence, or his consummate skill in presenting a daring military plan.

The conference, which took place in Tokyo from August 6 to 8, was a personal triumph for MacArthur. Only Mr. Harriman, Generals Norstad and Almond, and I were with MacArthur when he, in a two-and-a-half-hour presentation, outlined his master plan for Korea and his needs for fulfilling it. When he had finished he had won us all over to his views. I know that after this brilliant exposition, and after I had studied the plans for Operation Chromite, the Inchon landing, my own doubts were largely dissolved. On the return flight, Mr. Harriman, General Norstad, and I agreed that we were prepared to support MacArthur's requests when we got home, for the alternatives seemed dangerous in the extreme.

MacArthur had argued the need primarily for speedy victory in South Korea before the winter set in and scored a victory of its own. Nonbattle casualties in a bitter Korean winter, he had urged, might exceed the expected battle casualties of a short campaign. By mid-November, he warned us, the snow and bitter winds would be upon us. Meanwhile, he was losing a thousand men a day and replacements were not even holding his forces even. Delay in achieving victory would also increase the danger of open intervention by Chinese and Soviet forces, he argued. But to achieve the destruction of enemy forces in South Korea, the offensive would have to be launched September 25—with adequate forces so that the operation would have every chance of success. Otherwise, with the enemy dug into his positions, and his armies reinforced, we faced the prospect of a far more difficult and costly operation at a time less favorable to us.

This summation, of course, does not do justice to the painstakingly detailed and persuasive arguments our Far East Commander presented.

Throughout this conference and the hour I had spent beside General MacArthur at the luncheon table the preceding day, his recognition of authority superior to him, of his channels of command, and of his sphere of responsibility was clear and unmistakable, and his loyalty to constituted authority was manifest.

I was so impressed in this respect that, at the first opportunity following this conference, when I was alone with Mr. Harriman and General Norstad, I said so in substantially the same language. They both stated their agreement.

Mr. Harriman added a conclusion of his own, that "political and personal considerations should be put to one side and our Government deal with General MacArthur on the lofty level of the great national asset which he is."

We all went home ready to argue for the prompt fulfillment of MacArthur's request, for the immediate release to him of the 3rd Division (its bones fleshed out to some extent by the inclusion of the 65th Infantry Regiment from Puerto Rico, plus a battalion from the 33rd Infantry Regiment then in Panama).

My notes of that Tokyo Conference, notes of which no copy was ever made and which are still in my possession, indicate that the talk was far-ranging and frank, covering not only the immediate situation in Korea but many of the Commander's private plans for meeting contingencies that fortunately never arose. He was especially ardent about Formosa. Were the Red Chinese so foolish as to launch an assault on that island he would, he promised, hasten down there, assume command, and "deliver such a crushing defeat it would be one of the decisive battles of the world—a disaster so great it would rock Asia, and perhaps turn back Communism." As for the possibility that the Red Chinese might commit themselves to such folly, he was doubtful. But, he said, "I pray nightly that they will—would get down on my knees." Whether this vision of himself as the swordsman who would slay the Communist dragon was what prompted his eventual reckless drive to the borders of Manchuria no one of course can now divine. But I suspect that it did add luster to his dream of victory.

At that time, however, I was particularly impressed, as I have said earlier, with MacArthur's recognition of authority superior to his own. His presentation did not reveal the slightest lack of loyalty to authority. Not a single portent then appeared of that clash of wills, bordering closely on insubordination, that would lead to this gallant old soldier's abrupt dismissal. He was confident, optimistic, proud, eloquent, and utterly without fear—yet he was completely a soldier, seemingly ready to implement, without cavil or complaint, whatever decisions his superiors communicated to him.

As for Inchon, the brilliance of this plan, the logic of its conception, and the extreme care with which the finest detail had been dealt with persuaded me quickly to support it. But this was not my decision to make; and before the operation could be approved there were doubting Thomases on the JCS who had to be won over.

The doubts of the plan's success were well-founded, for a combination of perfect timing, perfect luck, precise coordination, complete surprise, and extreme gallantry were all needed to spell victory here. It would have been difficult to find, on the entire tortuous Korean coastline, a spot more difficult to assault. Inchon's natural defenses rendered it nearly immune to hostile approach by sea. The thirty-foot tides, receding, left a tight and twisting channel through mile-wide mudflats that seemed ideally fashioned to ground our LSTs and turn them into artillery targets. What seemed to me an impregnable small island dominated the channel. And the channel itself, the only approach to the port, had surely been mined, as the island was most certainly fortified. In addition, the operation was timed for the typhoon season and there was at least an even chance that a howling storm might scatter our amphibious forces and lay them all open to destruction.

It is no wonder then that the Thomases continued to doubt. Veterans like Rear Admiral James H. Doyle, and Major General

Oliver P. Smith, both experienced in the amphibious operations of World War II, failed to warm up to the idea. A number of alternate plans were put forward, including a landing at Wonsan on the east coast or, well to the south of Inchon, at Kumsan, where the pressure might be more quickly felt by the enemy on the Pusan front. But MacArthur would have none of these, although he was later to be grateful that his staff had prepared a detailed plan for the Wonsan landing. Only Inchon would do, for only a landing at Inchon offered the opportunity for the climactic stroke needed if the enemy was to be destroyed before winter—a slashing of the enemy's main artery of supply and communications and an opportunity for a junction with the forces breaking out of the Pusan perimeter, to crush the enemy's forces in between.

To examine into the feasibility of this plan, which had so far been presented only in concept, the JCS, in the middle of August, sent Admiral Forrest P. Sherman, Chief of Naval Operations, and General J. Lawton Collins, Army Chief of Staff, to meet with MacArthur and his staff in Tokyo. All key officers were present at the meeting, including Admiral Doyle and General Smith. General MacArthur outdid himself, not only in presenting the arguments in favor of Operation Chromite (in addition to the military advantages, success at Inchon would, he pointed out, enable the South Koreans to harvest their rice crop and would provide the valuable psychological lift of liberating the new nation's capital city) but especially in conveying his own supreme confidence in early victory. Admiral Doyle, near the end of the conference, volunteered the remark that the operation was at least "not impossible." But Admiral C. Turner Joy found his own misgivings erased. Even Admiral Sherman, the most skeptical of all, was, according to Joy, "almost persuaded." It took the Commander in Chief another day, and a long private discussion with Sherman, to complete the persuasion. "I wish," said Sherman after his private session with MacArthur, "I had that man's confidence."

Confidence, of course, was not quite enough. Now the concurrence of the administration, the permission to strip our General Reserve bare and risk all on one daring throw of the dice, had to be won. All the pros and cons were solemnly weighed: There would be but two hours of high tide on September 15 (the date selected for the landing) before the landing craft would be left powerless on the mud; the 1st Provisional Marine Brigade would have to be withdrawn from the desperate Pusan beachhead to fill out the 1st Marine Division; there was a shortage of shipping; the envelopment would be so deep and so far to the north that it might not provide early relief to the southern front; a typhoon might be in the making—but *surprise,* the indispensable element in every operation of this sort, was almost certain. The North Koreans would never expect the Americans to lend themselves to such an "impossible and insane" undertaking. (It is ironical that MacArthur would himself, before the year was out, discount the chances of the Chinese commander's committing sizable forces across the Yalu—because "no commander in his right senses" would do that.)

Louis Johnson, Secretary of Defense, quickly approved the MacArthur plan. Operation Chromite, the 5000-to-1 gamble, was cleared for execution. Even while the beleaguered GIs in the Pusan perimeter were staving off disaster by a hairsbreadth every hour, the Theater Commander began to make ready the move that would completely rout the enemy, and assure our hold on Korea. It was a maneuver not unlike James Wolfe's assault on Quebec in 1759, an attack at the point where the enemy "knew" no attack could possibly come.

The first step in Operation Chromite was to scout the harbor islands, which commanded the straitened channel. A young Navy lieutenant, Eugene Clark, was put ashore near Inchon on the night of September 1 and worked two weeks, largely under cover of darkness, to locate gun emplacements and to measure the height of the seawall. So successful were his efforts that he actually turned on a light in a lighthouse to guide the first assault ships into Inchon harbor before dawn on September 15.

The action opened at dawn with a heavy bombardment by American destroyers, whose skippers gallantly steamed up the channel under the very muzzles of enemy cannons, and by British and American cruisers. The first task was to neutralize Wolmi-do, the little island that sat right athwart the channel, with all channel traffic within point-blank range of its guns. The island however was not nearly so strongly fortified as had been feared and its guns were quickly silenced by the naval bombardment. Marine Corsair planes strafed the island beaches and at half-past six the 3rd Battalion of the 5th Marines stormed ashore, scattering the dazed defenders and securing the island within forty-five minutes. Artillery was positioned on the island then to support the assault upon the seawall. In places the Marines used ladders to scale the wall, which stood four feet above the prows of the LSTs. Elsewhere the LSTs simply rammed holes in the wall, or Marines opened holes with dynamite, through which the assault troops poured. They had only too little daylight to work in. By dark the advance elements of the 1st Marine Division were securely dug in on their beachhead ready to repel counterattacks. But so complete and so devastating had been the surprise and so sudden the victory, that the counterattack never came. The next day, after a sharp tank battle, Kimpo Airfield, Seoul's airport, had been secured, and a day later the 7th Infantry Division landed unopposed at Inchon and sped inland to sever the main escape routes of the NKPA still fighting along the Naktong.

The battle to retake Seoul, however, was bitter. Although, as he had reported, MacArthur had the city safe "in friendly hands" by the twenty-fifth, the Marines still fought from house to house, from barricade to barricade, against enemy machine guns, antitank cannon, and sniper fire until the twenty-eighth, when the last North Korean was flushed out of his flaming refuge and smoke rose from every quarter.

For boldness in concept, for competence in professional planning, and for courage, dash, and skill in execution, this operation ranks high in military annals. Like every great military victory, the Inchon triumph brought sudden new problems—problems that had not been sufficiently reckoned with ahead of time. Before a major operation of this sort, it is customary to assemble all key commanders and staff officers and "war-game" the action on a map. Each commander is then called upon to outline his plan for meeting every possible situation, from complete failure to stunning victory. This time, there had been insufficient planning for the stunning victory, if indeed there had been any planning at all. The United Nations Command paid dearly for this failure. Because of it, large numbers of the North Korean People's Army escaped to fight again—either as organized units in the north or in large-scale guerrilla actions behind our lines in the south.

Washington too had been hesitant in laying out a detailed course of action for exploitation of a victory, deferring decisions pending the resolution of some of the major mysteries—what would the Chinese reaction to the victory be? How would Russia respond?

It was generally assumed by most of the staff planners, and by General Walker himself, that the X Corps, then under direct control of Tokyo, would, when firmly established ashore, pass to the control of Eighth Army so that it could be moved and supplied more efficiently. But MacArthur insisted on keeping the X Corps under his own control, and the feeling that the Eighth Army was being slighted again in favor of MacArthur's "pets" grew stronger still. While there was never any open expression of jealousy or unwillingness to cooperate, there was no mistaking the fact that the atmosphere of mutual trust so necessary to smooth cooperation was lacking.

A more subtle result of the Inchon triumph was the development of an almost superstitious regard for General MacArthur's infallibility. Even his superiors, it seemed, began to doubt if they should question *any* of MacArthur's decisions and as a result he was deprived of the advantage of forthright and informed criticism, such as every commander should have—particularly when he is trying to "run a war" from 700 miles away. A good many military leaders have recognized that it takes a special kind of moral courage (rarer I think than physical courage) to stand up to your military superior and tell him you think his plan is wrong. That is the time, as General George C. Marshall used to say, when you "lay your commission on the line." But every military leader, from the lowest to the highest, owes it to the men whose lives are at his disposal to speak out clearly when he feels that a serious mistake is about to be made.

Some few small voices were raised against MacArthur's new decision—a plan for an amphibious landing at Wonsan, on the east coast, another end-run in the Inchon style and in the Mac-Arthur tradition. Yet no one vigorously protested, even though some of the drawbacks to the plan were obvious and overriding. But this maneuver was the apparent reason why MacArthur wanted the X Corps to remain under GHQ direction. This made sense of a sort, although the plan itself had very serious flaws.

To accomplish the Wonsan landing, it was necessary to outload most of the X Corps at Inchon and Pusan (the 1st Marine Division pulling out through Inchon and the 7th Division traveling over-land by rail and road to Pusan) taxing the rail lines and the in-adequate facilities of these two ports, at a most critical time and severely interrupting the flow of supplies which the Eighth Army soon would sorely miss. (With the withdrawal clogging roads and rails, even artillery ammunition had to be brought to Seoul by air.)

Whatever the arguments in favor of another Inchon-type assault on Wonsan, they did not outweigh the importance of closing the trap quickly on the fleeing North Koreans. There was a good highway and a rail line—bombed and battered, it is true—overland from Seoul to Wonsan, through one of the relatively level stretches of the peninsula. The forces put ashore at Inchon could have moved with reasonable swiftness up this road, north and east to Wonsan, to link up with forces driving straight up the east coast. This would then have closed the gate on the rapidly fleeing enemy and have left him no time to regroup and refresh his forces.

Serious planning for exploiting the Inchon victory, however, did not begin until September 26, two days before fighting ceased in the streets of Seoul. At that time MacArthur asked for a plan to "destroy North Korean forces in another amphibious envelop-ment—coordinated with overland pursuit." Two plans were put forward. In one, the Eighth Army would drive north and north-west toward Pyongyang, the enemy capital, while an amphibious assault would seize the capital port, Chinampo, on the Yellow Sea. In the other plan, the Eighth Army would strike north and north-east along the Seoul-Wonsan corridor, while Wonsan would be the object of a similar amphibious assault. General Walker, as-suming the X Corps would be under his command, favored sending that force immediately overland to Wonsan. But this was not to be.

There was some talk, too, of cutting across the peninsula at the waist or narrow point, to put the UN forces astride the country from Pyongyang to Wonsan. This, in theory, seemed practical enough. But a quick study of the terrain—the indescribably rugged and narrow passes, the countless twists and turns and tunnels in the rail lines (which our own airmen had worked over unceasingly)—would have given a logistics expert nightmares. If there was any good argument in favor of keeping the X Corps under the direct command of GHQ it was the extreme difficulty of trying to feed its stomachs and its guns and its gasoline engines, with all supply matters under the control of a commander on the other side of a steep and almost trackless mountain range.

No one denied the need for a port like Wonsan through which the huge tonnages of food, ammunition, and gasoline could be carried to feed the combat armies who would be operating to the west and north. The real question was simply, should Wonsan be approached overland or by sea? General MacArthur decided in favor of the assault by sea. The naval authorities on the spot and the division commanders involved all opposed the amphibious envelopment but none strongly raised his voice, simply because at that time no one was questioning the judgment or prescience of the man who had just worked a military miracle. Had he suggested that one battalion walk on water to reach the port, there might have been someone ready to give it a try.

The plan for crossing the 38th parallel to destroy all the hostile forces on the peninsula had of course required prior approval from Washington, for the implications of such a crossing were manifold. Red China had been threatening by radio almost daily that it would come into the war if North Korea were invaded; and there was some feeling that the Soviet Union might also feel called upon to step in once the symbolic deadline had been crossed. It was clear enough, however, that if the NKPA were not destroyed quickly and if it were allowed to crawl back into a sanctuary and licks its wounds, another invasion might soon follow. So after some deliberation the Truman administration approved a JCS recommendation that MacArthur be authorized to operate in North Korea. There was one condition attached to this authority, and consciousness of this condition may just possibly have influenced MacArthur in his otherwise inexplicable refusal ultimately to admit that the Chinese had entered the war in force. For his authority to conduct operations north of the border, radioed to him on September 27, was contingent upon the proviso that "there has been no entry into North Korea by major Soviet or Chinese Communist Forces, no announcement of intended entry, nor a threat to counter our operations militarily in Korea." Beyond that, Secretary of Defense Marshall told MacArthur: "We want you to feel unhampered tactically and strategically to proceed north of the 38th parallel."

Complete victory seemed now in view—a golden apple that would handsomely symbolize the crowning effort of a brilliant military career. Once in reach of this prize, MacArthur would not allow himself to be delayed or admonished. Instead he plunged northward in pursuit of a vanishing enemy, and changed his plans from week to week to accelerate the advance, without regard for dark hints of possible disaster.

CHAPTER FOUR

NEAR DISASTER ON THE YALU – THE CHINESE ENTER THE WAR – FIGHTING WITHDRAWAL OF THE 1ST MARINE DIVISION

MacArthur's original plan for exploiting the Inchon victory with a two-pronged drive across the 38th parallel was sound and simple enough. But its effectiveness depended upon three unknown factors—the weather, the terrain, and the reaction of the Chinese. And, as it turned out, there were other developments that prompted the Commander in Chief to alter his basic plan beyond all recognition, until he had units of the X Corps scattered all over the rugged Korean landscape, unable to support or even communicate directly with each other, and highly vulnerable to harassment by guerrilla forces or encirclement by an enemy that far outnumbered them.

As for the intervention of the Chinese, MacArthur simply closed his ears to their threats and apparently ignored or belittled the first strong evidence that they had crossed the Yalu in force. The weather, he planned to outrace—he would close on the Yalu and bring hostilities to an end before the deep snows came. But the terrain, which he had not seen, proved to be an enemy whose strength he had never properly assessed. It made impossible even a tenuous liaison between forces on the left (west) and the right (east).

It might appear that, by keeping the X Corps, on the right, under his direct control, and leaving the left, or western sector, to General Walker and the Eighth Army, MacArthur had reckoned with the impassable ridges and roadless ravines that separated one force from the other. That he had not done so at all was made clear by his charging General Walker with logistical support of the X Corps troops as well as his own. Indeed, his placing this onerous burden on Walker while denying him tactical control of the X Corps (which would have added little to the load already awarded him) made his insistence on hanging on to the X Corps even more puzzling. Nor did it in any way mitigate the ill feeling between these two commands.

The plan as first presented called for the Eighth Army, on A-Day (October 17, three days before D-Day), to attack in the general direction of Pyongyang, to the northwest, and along the Kaesong-Sariwon-Pyongyang axis.

On D-Day the 1st Marine Division of the X Corps was to seize Wonsan in an amphibious assault and with that city invested the two forces were to attack toward each other along the east-west axis. Once they had joined hands the peninsula would be sealed off against the retreating NKPA. The two commands were then to make a coordinated advance to the Chongju-Yongwon-Hungnam line.

There were two obvious hitches to this plan. The first was the withdrawal of the X Corps from the Seoul-Inchon area and the consequent denial of port and transportation facilities to the Eighth Army, which suffered for weeks from the consequent choking off of supplies. The second hitch, equally obvious from a terrain study, was the impracticability of the two forces attacking along an east-west line until they joined. It still seems logical to me today, as it did then, that had one United States division been sent overland to Wonsan, carrying what supplies it needed and ignoring its flanks, as the Eighth Army had done on its advance from the Pusan perimeter, it would have had an excellent chance of seizing and clearing the Wonsan area far more efficiently and swiftly than actually was done. The nearest Chinese Communist Forces were then still north of the Yalu.

As matters turned out, there was one major and happy surprise that prompted further adjustments in the plan. The ROK I Corps, practically forgotten by the GHQ planners, sent its ROK 3rd Division streaking up the coastal road to seize Wonsan before the Navy had even opened a channel through the minefield for the 1st Marines. Had an immediate junction with an overland drive from Seoul been made, the whole area might have been cleared promptly and the northward movement could then have begun well ahead of schedule. The ROKs were in possession of the port by October 11, only nine days after MacArthur's plan had been approved and ordered put into execution by the JCS.

Nevertheless, it was October 26 before the Navy could complete its delicate and dangerous job of sweeping a channel through the 2000 mines the enemy had sown in Wonsan harbor. The 1st Marine Division then made what is known as an "administrative" landing, that is, one without opposition, and the ROK I Corps was free to range to the north and seize North Korea's vital industrial area, the Hungnam-Hamhung complex.

By this time, however, events had outrun the original plan and new objectives had been decided on. On October 17 MacArthur ordered a new goal set—a line some forty to sixty miles below the Manchurian border. Soon he was instructing his commanders to think of this as merely an intermediate goal. He was bound to get his forces to the Yalu, despite expressed State Department policy against using any except ROK forces close to the Manchurian border, and despite the obvious fact that, should the Chinese exercise their capability and cross the border in force, MacArthur's forces simply lacked the strength to hold that distant and sinuous line. Supply ports were distant eighty to 120 miles over tortuous, steep, narrow trails that were sometimes no more than goat-tracks. To spread his thin forces out along this far-flung line and try to keep them in food and ammunition, or to hold them firm against a determined enemy, who was fighting almost on his home base, would have been beyond the powers even of a MacArthur. Of course, had our planes been permitted to destroy the enemy's Manchurian bases, such a stand might have been a possibility. But were our Air Force to take on such a task it would have meant, in General Hoyt S. Vandenberg's view, the frittering away of our Air Force through natural attrition and combat losses, leaving our forces in Europe naked to the enemy as far as air strength was concerned for an estimated two years. The Pentagon had firmly decided against such a course. MacArthur knew of that decision. Yet he urged his troops to push on to the edge of Manchuria, without regard to Washington's prohibition against the use of U.S. troops that far forward.

When the ROK 3rd Division of the ROK I Corps took Wonsan, General Walker had flown there to appraise the situation and to make contact with these ROK forces, which were still under his command. At this time, the ROK II Corps, on Walker's right flank, had taken up positions near Chorwon, northeast of Kaesong, along the overland route to Wonsan. Walker immediately made plans for advancing this force toward Wonsan, to effect a link-up with the ROK I Corps, so that, once Pyongyang had been seized, a line could be extended, as first planned, across the peninsula from coast to coast. MacArthur, however, curtly overruled this plan and informed Walker that once the Marines had come ashore the ROK I Corps (the best in the ROK army) would be taken from Walker's command and placed under the X Corps.

At this point MacArthur set his new objective line, abandoning his original plan for a link-up across the waist of the peninsula. And when Walker's forces had taken Pyongyang, MacArthur established a boundary between the Eighth Army and the X Corps and ordered his commanders to think of the "objective line" as just an "initial objective." The only goal left now was the border.

On October 26, the very day the 1st Marine Division finally came ashore in Wonsan, the ROK II Corps had pushed advance elements of its 6th Divison all the way to the Yalu. On Walker's left flank, forward elements of the U.S. 24th Division had crossed the Chongchon and were pushing on toward the Yalu, then only seventy miles away.

Elsewhere UN forces were moving toward the Yalu along many different routes, incapable of mutual support or even of maintaining ground patrol contact. The U.S. 7th Division, first scheduled to follow the Marines ashore at Wonsan, was diverted to Iwon, some 150 miles up the coast, where they landed on October 29 and proceeded to Hyesanjin, on the Yalu. The ROK

I Corps was scheduled to advance up the coastal road toward the Soviet border. The Marines were to follow a narrow, single-track road up over the central plateau to Kanggye and then on to Manpojin on the Yalu. And the 3rd Division was to remain behind to guard the Wonsan-Hungnam-Hamhung area.

Before any of these maneuvers were well started, a chill warning blew down from the frozen ridges to the northeast. The 7th Regiment of the ROK 6th Division, first UN force to reach the Yalu, had turned south to draw back when they were struck by an overwhelming force of Communist Chinese, who rose as it were out of the ground and, in a vicious close-quarter fight, very nearly destroyed the regiment. It appeared later that this regiment had ventured unknowingly close to the staging area where the Chinese troops were massing for their offensive. The Chinese, not ready to open their drive, and determined to allow no discovery, practically wiped out this spearhead.

On October 26, far to the east, the 26th Division of the ROK I Corps, moving from Hamhung toward the Changjin (Chosin) Reservoir, met strong resistance at Sudong and took eighteen prisoners from two different regiments of the Chinese Communist 124th Division. When the Marines came up to relieve the ROKs a few days later they met and destroyed Chinese tanks (the only ones the X Corps was to encounter) and picked up prisoners from a fresh Chinese division, the 126th. Both the 124th and 126th Divisions belonged to the Chinese 42nd Army.

Yet all through this period, official reports shone with optimism. Washington was informed that there was "no confirmation" of the widely circulated press stories that 20,000 Communist Chinese troops had entered North Korea. On October 28, Washington was assured that there was still "no firm indication" of any open intervention by the Chinese. Two days later the Far East Command reported that it did not believe, despite reports to the contrary, that any elements of the Chinese 39th and 40th Armies, reportedly in Korea, had actually crossed the border. The presence of a few Chinese "volunteers" was accepted as just one more minor move in the diplomatic chess game that was of no immediate consequence to GHQ.

The Chinese themselves probed circumspectly to begin with, for of course they could not gauge what the United States response might be—whether we would attack Chinese territory or unleash the A-bomb against them. They sturdily maintained, right to the end, the fiction that these Chinese troops in Korea were volunteers serving at their own behest under the colors of the North Korean People's Republic. The Chinese troops kept their movements well concealed. They moved mostly at night, mostly on foot, avoiding the roads in the daytime, sometimes setting forest fires to provide a screen against air reconnaissance, and hiding in tunnels and mine shafts or in the villages. Each Chinese soldier going into action was a self-sufficient unit, equipped with cooked food (they wanted no fires to betray their positions) in the form of rice and beans and corn and sufficient small-arms ammunition to last him four or five days—after which he would either be relieved or would retreat to his main line and be replaced by fresh units, depending on the course of battle. Because the Chinese left no signs whatever of the presence of a moving army, there was some grounds for the skepticism of the High Command as to the presence of large enemy forces. But it was not just the High Command who refused to read the clear meaning of the mounting evidence.

Typical of the reluctance of all our troops, even the lower ranks, to take the Chinese threat seriously was the reaction of the forces positioned in and around the village of Unsan, just north of the Chongchon River, and about sixty miles south of the Yalu, at the end of October. Reports came in from several different quarters concerning the presence of large concentrations of Chinese troops. One Korean civilian reported there were 2000 Chinese in a valley nine miles southwest of Unsan, bent on cutting the main supply route that led south out of town. A member of the Korean Home Guard later reported there were 3000 Chinese six miles southwest of Unsan. At noon on November 1, an enemy column was observed eight miles southeast of town and was dispersed by air and artillery bombardment that left about a hundred horses and an undetermined number of men dead on the road. Still later our air observers reported large columns of

1. Bomb strikes on two of the three railroad bridges across the Han River near Seoul. The concrete highway bridge on the right was destroyed by TNT. On July 3, 1950, United States planes chose targets in this area to retard the North Korean build-up of supplies and units on the south side of the river. *Official U.S. Air Force Photo.*

2. An American Douglas C-54 military transport plane on fire after being strafed by North Korean fighter planes on June 28, 1950. *U.S. Army photograph.*

3. South Korean soldiers carrying 6.5-mm. Japanese rifles and wearing canvas-top shoes move forward to battle, July 5, 1950. *U.S. Army photograph.*

4. Army truck mounting a .50-caliber M2 HB Browning machine gun, camouflaged with rice straw. *U.S. Army photograph.*

5. Two North Korean prisoners, captured near the Kum River, being interrogated by a South Korean interpreter as Americans look on, July 16, 1950. *U.S. Army photograph.*

6. Landing craft shuttling from ship to shore, July 18, 1950. LSTs (landing ships, tank) at left. *U.S. Army photograph.*

7. Chaffee light tank M24 stops in a village between Andong and Yechon, July 24, 1950. *U.S. Army photograph.*

8. Foot-weary soldier cools his feet in a helmet full of water, August 19, 1950. *U.S. Army photograph.*

9. Lockheed F-80 Shooting Star, based in Japan, leaves on a mission against the North Koreans, passing over Japanese workers in a rice paddy. *U.S. Air Force photo.*

10. Cooks of the 25th Division moving chow in heavy rains, August 19, 1950. *U.S. Army photograph.*

11. Infantrymen scout along a highway as Sherman medium tanks M4 wait around the bend, August 13, 1950. *U.S. Army photograph.*

12. Tired Marines rest in bivouac area, August 16, 1950. Rocket launchers at the right, chemical mortar left foreground. *Defense Department photo, Marine Corps.*

13. Hillside positions overlooking the Naktong River. Marines are on the alert for enemy activity across the river, August 19, 1950. *Defense Department photo, Marine Corps.*

14. Aerial view of Pohang-dong two days after ROK units regained the town from North Koreans. August 20, 1950. *U.S. Army photograph.*

15. Corporal of the Signal Corps operates air-ground radio, maintaining contact with liaison planes, August 10, 1950. *U.S. Army photograph.*

enemy troops moving both above and below Unsan; an airstrike hit one of these columns and was reported to have destroyed twenty-one troop-carrying vehicles just nine miles from the village. In the afternoon an observer in an L-5 plane, directing our artillery fire, reported "two large columns of enemy infantry moving southward" along narrow pathways less than seven miles from Unsan.

Still the United States command was reluctant to accept this accumulating evidence. Chinese prisoners had been taken by the ROKs earlier but intelligence officials quite naturally hesitated to credit the prisoners' stories about Chinese strength and purposes in Korea, believing no private soldier would have such high-level information. And even when Colonel Percy Thompson, G-2 (intelligence officer) of the I Corps, warned troops of the 1st Cavalry Division, just committed to Unsan, that they might be facing Chinese forces, the men responded with disbelief and indifference. They had advanced on Pyongyang against stiff resistance and had taken that city in a sharp overnight engagement. Since then NKPA resistance seemed to have melted, with only sporadic outbreaks to slow their advance. Indeed the Eighth Army lacked the supplies to sustain a prolonged engagement against major forces of the enemy. And the men were in no mood to accept the fact that there might be anybody left in North Korea capable of giving them a fight. The staff of the 8th Cavalry Regiment, who were to hold the positions north and west of Unsan, likewise refused to pay heed to the stories told them by the troops and attached KMAG officers of the ROK 1st Division who had run up against the Chinese outside Unsan and had been unable to dislodge them. It was generally believed that what Chinese might be moving down from the north were merely reinforcements to be absorbed by the NKPA. A request by General Hobart R. Gay, commanding the 1st Cavalry Division, for permission to withdraw the 8th Cavalry Regiment to a position a few miles below Unsan, was denied by I Corps headquarters. Few indeed were the officers who took any of these disquieting reports to heart.

The troops charged with the security of Pyongyang had already begun to dream again of the joys of garrison life and by and large were far more concerned with the proper set-up for the planned "Homecoming Parade" in Tokyo than with these persistent stories of Chinese intervention.

Then the blows fell and fell with such devastating suddenness that many units were overrun before they could quite grasp what had happened. The Chinese struck first at the ROK 6th Infantry Division in the Onjong-Hunchon area, some fifteen to thirty miles east of Unsan, engulfing them so completely that by early afternoon of November 1st, General Walker notified General Frank W. Milburn, commanding the U.S. I Corps, that the ROK II Corps had ceased to exist as an organized force and that his right flank consequently was unprotected. When General Milburn hastened to the ROK II Corps headquarters at Kunu-ri, about twenty miles south of Unsan, the ROK II Corps commander told him that he had completely lost contact with his subordinate units and that there were but three battalions of the ROK 7th Division in the vicinity of Kunu-ri who were capable of any organized resistance.

Probing attacks against the 8th Cavalry Regiment, north of Unsan, began about 5 P.M., accompanied by mortar fire and by Russian Katusha rockets fired from trucks (a deadly new wrinkle in the war). The attack gathered strength as the dusk deepened, and spread gradually from east to west. This was the first time that many of the Americans had heard the wild clamor of Chinese horns—brass bugles that looked like oversize versions of the horns football linesmen used to use to signal infractions—and their barbaric notes, mixed with the frantic blowing of whistles, seemed to signal the opening of a new phase in the fighting. At least they helped make believers of the many who had told themselves that all this talk of massive Chinese intervention was so much fairy tale.

The fighting continued all night, often at close quarters and at a pitch unknown since the early days of the war. Before midnight a number of the United States units found themselves nearly out of ammunition. At 10 P.M., the U.S. I Corps, for the first time since the breakout from the Pusan perimeter, had gone on the defensive. Hostile troops that night were on three sides of the 8th Cavalry Regiment which was holding Unsan.

The ROK 15th Infantry Regiment held the ground on the east but the Chinese faced the U.S. troops in every other quarter. Until the order came to withdraw, however, U.S. forces did not realize that their escape route had been cut. A strong force of the CCF had blocked the main road before noon of that day and they held the position tight against subsequent efforts of the 5th Cavalry to dislodge them and go to the support of the 8th Cavalry in Unsan. In the early morning hours of November 2, the troops withdrawing from Unsan ran into an ambush on the main road that soon jammed the road with wrecked vehicles and sent tankers and infantrymen scattering in confusion.

The United States forces took to the hills, fighting singly or in groups of three and four, dragging their wounded. Some bypassed the roadblock to the east and then moved south into the hills. Others simply fled into the darkness to the south and found their way to the rear. Many were captured and no immediate accounting was possible of the killed and wounded.

Perhaps the most shattering surprise was achieved by the Chinese in their attack on the 3rd Battalion of the 8th Cavalry Regiment west of Unsan, where the men had been certain no enemy was operating. In the late afternoon of November 1, some of the troops had noticed airplanes strafing enemy positions somewhere south, near their main supply route, but no one had felt any concern. When the order to withdraw was relayed to their commander, the artillery was pulled out first and the 3rd Battalion was given the task of protecting the regimental rear. They were positioned at the north end of a bridge over the Nammyon River, with two squads charged with security of the bridge. About three o'clock in the morning a small column of men, whether a platoon or a company was never determined, approached the bridge from the south. The force charged with security of the bridge let the men cross over unchallenged. They had approached from the south and were taken for ROKs, so very little note was made of them. When the strangers had drawn up opposite the command post, one of their leaders sounded a wild blast on a bugle and, in response to the signal, Chinese attacked the command post from all sides, with small-arms fire and grenades. Chinese swarmed across the river to the south. On the southwest, along the river bank, other enemy forces engaged in bitter fighting with L Company of the 3rd Battalion. The Chinese who had first crossed the bridge immediately penetrated the headquarters area, shooting, bayoneting, hurling grenades, and tossing satchel charges into the standing vehicles, to set them on fire. Many of our men were awakened by the clamor of bugles blowing taps (this was a form of Chinese psychological warfare that was to become painfully familiar to us) or by the sound of unfriendly arms discharging almost in their ears. Having gone to sleep to await the signal for withdrawal, they crawled out of their foxholes into hand-to-hand fighting sometimes to wrestle the enemy to the ground in single combat, or to fight back at point-blank range with pistols. In cowboy-and-Indian style, the troops fought all over the area, crouching behind jeeps, running to give aid to a man locked in single struggle on the ground, trying to find centers of resistance, and finally, when mortar fire began to fall among them, fighting their way south across the stream and into the dark hills to find friendly lines. By twos and threes and half-dozens the men, many of them wounded, proceeded south and east, finding more and more stragglers as the night grew older.

The men left behind in the valley managed to draw together into islands of resistance, some of which held out until daylight, when air support gave them a respite. One group, beseiged in the command post dugout, lost fifteen out of twenty men to Chinese grenades during the night. When day came, there were only sixty-six officers and two hundred men still on hand and still able to fight. Major Robert J. Ormond, the battalion commander, had been mortally wounded by the first grenade hurled into the command post by the enemy force that had crossed the bridge. Within five hundred yards of the perimeter that had been set up around the dugout, 170 wounded men were found. No count was made of the dead.

Efforts to break through to rescue these remnants of the 3rd Battalion were vain. The enemy was too well dug in and friendly artillery support was lacking. Airstrikes were likewise unavailable for the thick smoke and haze concealed the targets. Nor could the remnants of the battalion, despite desperate and valiant efforts, break through the tight ring of Chinese. The Americans dug an elaborate trench system by daylight and managed thus to reach and conserve large quantities of supplies and ammunition. But they failed in every effort to escape from the trap. A division liaison plane finally dropped a message ordering the battalion to withdraw under cover of darkness. The relief forces had had to give up the effort and the 3rd Battalion was on its own. The infantry and the tank forces took counsel together and decided to try to hold out for another night in the perimeter, but heavy mortar fire first forced the tankers to take their vehicles out of the perimeter to draw the fire away, and finally decided them to try to make their own way to safety in the southwest. It was obvious, with each tank already having been hit two or three times, that they were of no use to the infantry, who wished them good luck and pulled in their necks to get ready for the next assault. The Chinese came at them in the darkness with a mortar barrage and an infantry attack. The entrapped men first set fire to the disabled vehicles around them to light up the area, then mowed down the advancing Chinese in large numbers. Six times, in strength of about four hundred men, the Chinese attacked the perimeter and each time were beaten back. Attracted by the racket of friendly fire, men of the 2nd Battalion, who had been hiding in the hills, broke through to join the defenders. Ammunition dwindled. Crawling out over heaps of Chinese dead, three deep in places, the men in the perimeter, after each attack, would retrieve enemy weapons and ammunition. The command post dugout at one point was overrun and many of the wounded were taken by the Chinese out of the range of fire. They too had to crawl to safety over mounds of Chinese dead.

Daylight brought no air support. What rations were left were divided among the wounded, who now numbered about 250, while but two hundred combat-fit troops remained. Early on the morning of November 4, the survivors decided they must try to escape, leaving the wounded to be surrendered to the Chinese. Captain Clarence R. Anderson, the battalion surgeon, volunteered to remain to look after the injured and effect their surrender. After a scouting party had found a way up roadside ditches, through a village to the north and thence to a river-crossing, the survivors started out to the east. Phosphorous shells, fired by the Chinese in preparation for an attack, gave them some accidental cover, and they were soon able to clear the perimeter and make their way through an open field, where the Chinese had not been able to take positions. They traveled all night through a drenching rain, to the east and north and finally south and southwest until they were almost in sight of Ipsok, where friendly forces awaited them. But before they could reach American lines, a Chinese force surrounded them and forced them to break up into smaller groups in hopes of escape. Only a few of this force ever reached our lines and no truly accurate reckoning was made of how many were killed, wounded, or captured. Some who were taken prisoner escaped to rejoin the regiment days later and some who were wounded, including Major Ormond, the battalion commander, died in captivity and were buried by the Chinese. For weeks afterward, men who had been hidden by friendly Koreans, or who had escaped their captors, straggled back to the lines. On November 22, the Chinese set free twenty-seven men, most of whom had been captured near Unsan, so losses were finally reckoned at about six hundred men, where first it had been feared more than a thousand had been lost.

The action of the Chinese in freeing the prisoners was in happy contrast to the treatment—often a bullet in the back of the head —prisoners had received from the North Koreans. At one point the Chinese actually set the severely wounded men on litters along the road, then drew back and held their fire while our medics in trucks came to retrieve the injured men. Moves of this sort by the Chinese in fact were prompted by the Chinese ignorance of Western life, ignorance rooted in their controlled upbringing. For the Chinese captors had sent the captured soldiers back to our lines after adjuring each to "tell his comrades" of the humane treatment he had received and to urge them all to "turn their guns against the officers" and thus free themselves from the oppression the Chinese had been taught to believe all the victims of capitalism suffered. Perhaps they confidently expected to see whole divisions of our troops responding to this invitation to flee the capitalist Hell and come sample the freedoms of the Red Paradise.

The Chinese, we were to learn, was a tough and vicious fighter who often attacked without regard for casualties. But he was a more civilized foe in some respects than we found the NKPA to be. In many instances he shared what little food he had with his prisoners and treated them with kindness, very likely to impress him with how much better he would live under Communism. When we retook Seoul we found he had not wantonly destroyed building materials we had brought in to repair the bombed city, but in his advance from Yongdong-po to Suwon he had systematically put the torch to houses in the villages.

Altogether the 8th Cavalry Regiment lost more than half its authorized strength at Unsan and a great share of its equipment, including twelve 105-mm. howitzers, nine tanks, more than 125 trucks, and a dozen recoilless rifles. It was determined later that, engaged with the ROK 1st Division and the U.S. 5th and 8th Cavalry Regiments at and near Unsan in this battle had been large elements of the 115th and 116th Divisions of the Chinese 39th Army as well as of the 347th Regiment. Although the enemy withdrew, Chinese fashion, some distance to the north after this engagement and the 5th and 7th Cavalry Regiments were able to establish and maintain, against light opposition, a shallow bridgehead north of the Chongchon River by November 11, General Walker well knew that he lacked the force and the equipment for a sustained offensive against an enemy whose numerical superiority now seemed clear. He sent a straightforward message to Tokyo acknowledging AN AMBUSH AND SURPRISE ATTACK BY FRESH, WELL-ORGANIZED, AND WELL-TRAINED UNITS, SOME OF WHICH WERE CHINESE COMMUNIST FORCES.

The eventual response from Tokyo was, however, one of irritation and impatience at Walker's failure to move forward on schedule. No matter how thoroughly convinced the 1st Cavalry Division might have become that the Chinese had entered the war in force, the Commander in Chief persisted in a mood of renewed optimism. He had spoken once of calamity, when, in a message protesting the countermanding of an order to bomb the Yalu bridges, he had warned the JCS that the movement of Chinese forces across the Yalu "threatens the ultimate destruction of the forces under my command." This was on November 8. By November 9, however, good cheer and optimism enveloped GHQ once more and messages to the JCS expressed confidence in the ability of the Air Force to keep enemy reinforcements from getting across the Yalu and in the ability of the United Nations Forces to destroy all armed resistance now before them. This was MacArthur's answer to a warning from JCS that Chinese intervention now seemed an accomplished fact. This wholly human failing of discounting or ignoring all unwelcome facts seemed developed beyond the average in MacArthur's nature. His own G-2, for example, had estimated that the CCF could put 200,000 troops across the Yalu per month. Not two weeks after he had himself informed the JCS that "a new and fresh army faces us, backed up by a possibility of large reserves and adequate supplies," MacArthur assured the JCS that complete victory was possible, that it would be "fatal" to abandon the original plan to destroy all resisting armed forces in North Korea. On November 24, MacArthur flew in from Tokyo to give the signal for the "jump-off" toward the Yalu and at that time, without ifs or buts, he averred that "the Chinese are not coming into this war" and that the war would be "over in two weeks." This gave to the advance its name of Home-by-Christmas offensive.

Although MacArthur described this movement toward the Yalu as an "attack" it was really no more than an advance to contact. It is not possible to attack an enemy whose positions are not known, whose very existence has not been confirmed, and whose forces are completely out of contact with your own. While many a field commander was convinced in his heart that strong forces of Chinese were lying in wait somewhere, and while one or two harbored definite doubts of the wisdom of moving blindly forward with flanks ignored and without liaison with friendly forces on either side, no one flinched at the job and many reflected the glowing optimism of the Commander in Chief. Even General Walker, who had good reason to appreciate the sort of opposition that might await him north of the Chongchon, hastened to assure GHQ that he was moving forward as soon as he could properly replenish his supplies, although he had by no means quelled his own misgivings.

There was no joy in the Pentagon at seeing our forces dispersed in the manner that MacArthur had now dispersed them, especially when the threat of massive Chinese intervention looked now so probable and so imminent. But in the Pentagon as well as in the field there was an almost superstitious awe of this larger-than-life military figure who had so often been right when everyone else had been wrong—who had never admitted a mistake in judgment, yet whose mistakes in judgment had been remarkably few. Then there were those who felt that it was useless to try to check a man who might react to criticism by pursuing his own way with increased stubbornness and fervor.

The Pentagon was soon aware that MacArthur had deliberately disobeyed a specific order from JCS, a directive issued on September 27, 1950, that instructed the Commander in Chief to use no non-Korean forces in the provinces bordering on the Soviet Union or along the Manchurian frontier. In the final advance toward the Yalu and Tumen Rivers, MacArthur directed removal of all prohibitions against the use of non-Korean troops and had told the JCS when they questioned him that his decision had been prompted by military necessity. Later General Collins told a Congressional committee that the Pentagon had been concerned at that time lest MacArthur might later disobey another order with more serious results.

But whatever the private attitude of MacArthur's superiors might have been, no voice was raised against him. I say no voice, because I do not include my own, which did express private protest and had no right to do more. I well remember my impatience on that dreary Sunday, December 3, as we sat through hours-long discussions in the JCS War Room, reviewing the ominous situation in North Korea. Much of the time the Secretaries of State and Defense participated in the talks, with no one apparently willing to issue a flat order to the Far East Commander to correct a state of affairs that was going rapidly from bad to disastrous. Yet the responsibility and the authority clearly resided right there in the room, and my own conscience finally overcame my discretion. Having secured permission to speak, I blurted out—perhaps too bluntly but with deep feeling—that I felt we had already spent too damn much time on debate and that immediate action was needed. We owed it, I insisted, to the men in the field and to the God to whom we must answer for those men's lives to stop talking and to act. My only answer, from the twenty men who sat around the wide table, and the twenty others who sat around the walls in the rear, was complete silence—except that I did receive from a Navy colleague sitting behind me a hastily scribbled "proud to know you" note that I acknowledged with an appreciative note of my own.

The meeting broke up with no decision taken. The Secretaries of State and Defense left the room and the Joint Chiefs lingered to talk among themselves for a few moments. I approached Hoyt Vandenberg, whom I had known since he was a cadet and I an instructor at West Point. With Van I had no need for double-talk.

"Why," I asked him, "don't the Joint Chiefs send orders to MacArthur and *tell* him what to do?"

Van shook his head.

"What good would that do? He wouldn't obey the orders. What *can* we do?"

At this I exploded.

"You can relieve any commander who won't obey orders, can't you?" I exclaimed. The look on Van's face is one I shall never forget. His lips parted and he looked at me with an expression both puzzled and amazed. He walked away then without saying a word and I never afterward had occasion to discuss this with him.

This was not the first time I had let my emotions overcome my discretion in these protracted discussions. Once before I had asked why action could not be substituted for talk and that time I had also received no reply but silence. General Wade H. Haislip, however, my immediate boss as Army Vice-Chief of Staff, had come into my office grinning and told me: "That was wonderful.

But one of these days, you'll find yourself thrown out of here on your donkey in a snowstorm."

All the same I felt no regrets at these outbursts and I have never regretted them since. It has always seemed to me that a commander has as deep a duty to the men with whose lives he is temporarily entrusted as they have to him—and part of that duty is to see that those lives are not needlessly squandered.

Several field commanders in Korea were themselves thoroughly aware of the dangers ahead as they sought to close on the Yalu and they did what they could, while still obeying MacArthur's orders to the letter, to forestall disaster. Indeed, had it not been for the foresight—and in one instance the deliberate feet-dragging —of some of these commanders the subsequent defeat might have been what some of the newspapers tried to make it into—a complete debacle.

General Walker was perhaps more alive than any of his colleagues to the fact that Chinese Communist forces in vastly superior numbers possibly stood between him and the border. While others were uneasy, they were partially lulled into optimism by the fact that the Chinese forces, after the first bloody clashes, had broken contact and seemed once again to have disappeared into the ground, showing no campfires, no tracks in the snow, no supplies moving on the roads. Yet our intelligence reports were not really wanting. In retrospect, they turned out to be remarkably close to the mark. The failure lay once more in the interpretation of the facts rather than in the gathering of them. As early as November 10, GHQ G-2 had reported that the CCF buildup in the area of the reservoirs on the plateau north of Hamhung "even now may be capable of seizing the initiative and launching an offensive which might take the form of a concerted drive to the south—to cut off UN forces north and northeast of Hungnam."

But MacArthur, like Custer at the Little Big Horn, had neither eyes nor ears for information that might deter him from the swift attainment of his objective—the destruction of the last remnants of the North Korean Peoples Army and the pacification of the entire peninsula.

The Eighth Army was, in MacArthur's phrase, to complete

a "massive compression envelopment" and "close the vise" after the X Corps had "reached a commanding enveloping position cutting in two the northern reaches of the enemy's geographical potential." In executing his orders, General Walker moved with both courage and discretion. He had already had to justify his withdrawal south of the Chongchon River as being due to his lack of sufficient equipment and proper reserve. Having rebuilt his strength to a marginal but acceptable level, he moved his forces northward on phase lines, always conscious of his open flank on the right, where the wild mountain terrain vitiated any hope of mutual support with the X Corps, and more than conscious of the existence of a strong enemy force between his forward elements and the Yalu. In brief, he knew his own weakness and enemy strength too well to drive forward in the Patton manner without regard for his flanks. In the light of his relations with MacArthur, I do not see how he could have done any better than he did. It was Walker's intent to keep the Eighth Army always under close control. His Order of Battle comprised the U.S. I Corps, consisting of the U.S. 24th Division, the British 27th Brigade, and the ROK 1st Division; the U.S. IX Corps, including the U.S. 2nd and 25th Divisions and the Turkish Brigade; the ROK II Corps, including the ROK 6th, 7th, and 8th Divisions; and the 1st Cavalry Division in Army reserve.

The Korean peninsula widens considerably toward the north, which meant an increasingly wide dispersal of Walker's thin forces and the opening of a broader and broader gap between the Eighth Army and the X Corps, on the right. Walker's dangerously exposed right flank therefore could only become increasingly imperiled. The fact that this flank was manned entirely by the ROK II Corps, perhaps the least reliable of all the troops under his command, added nothing to Walker's peace of mind. That Walker was deeply disturbed over his relationship with GHQ at this time was revealed in private conversations just before his untimely death. He was eager to explain, in talking privately with a newspaper correspondent, that his deliberation in advancing once more across the Chongchon—deliberation that had brought him sharp messages from his superior—had been occasioned by his efforts to prepare for the retirement he felt might become necessary. Those preparations, he was convinced, had enabled him to save most of the Eighth Army so that it might fight again. At this time, he told his interviewer he was convinced that he was about to be relieved of his command because of the retreat of the Eighth Army in the face of the Chinese assault.

Well to the right of Walker, the 1st Marine Division, under General Oliver Smith, had been ordered to advance up on to the roof of Korea north and northwest to Kanggye and Manpojin on the Yalu. The only road over which the Marines could advance was a single-track dirt-and-gravel path, narrow, winding, crawling through forbidding cliffs and ridges and climbing up over terrain as wild and inhospitable as any in all of Korea. One section, known as the Funchilin Pass, was a ten-mile stretch that climbed 2500 feet along a narrow, frightening shelf with an impassable cliff on one side and a chasm on the other. This road ended at the woebegone village of Yudam-ni on the southwest corner of the Changjin Reservoir, that bleak and wind-blown stretch of ice that nearly marked a major disaster to our forces. But before it reached Yudam-ni, the road wound agonizingly up over 4000-foot Toktong Pass, where temperatures resembled those in Alaska.

General Smith was as alive as Walker was to the dangers that lay before him and he started this advance with the conviction that he had neither the supplies nor the forces he needed to accomplish his mission. So he moved ahead with constant concern for the safety of his forces, regardless of the urging from the X Corps headquarters that he speed up his forward movement. Before jump-off, while not knowing the full measure of the disaster, Smith had learned of the collapse of the ROK II Corps, on Walker's right wing, near Tokchon, some seventy miles southwest of Smith's forward elements, which was the 5th Regimental Combat Team at Yudam-ni, itself some fifty-five miles short of the division's first objective—the village of Mupyong-ni. All the terrain in between, from Yudam-ni to Tokchon and from Yudam-ni to Mupyong-ni, was wild, rugged, and nearly trackless. Now Smith's wide open left flank was in a more perilous fix than before.

Nevertheless, Smith dauntlessly set forth toward his objective, despite all the misgivings occasioned by his judgment of the enemy's capabilities and his knowledge of the distances to be covered over almost impassable terrain. With some bitterness, he reported to the Commandant of his Corps that he had "concentrated his Division into a reasonable sector"; that he had "taken every feasible measure to develop and guard the Main Supply Road" (there was only one!); that he had prepared an airstrip at the south end of the Changjin Reservoir for air supply of critical items and for the evacuation of wounded; and that he had "ensured that at all times he had possession of the high ground along the route of his division's advance." As it turned out these textbook precautions were all that enabled this magnificent fighting force to battle its way out of entrapment in one of the most successful retrograde movements in American military history.

Further to the right, in the northeast sector of Korea, the 7th Division was to proceed from Iwon toward Hyesanjin on the Yalu, while the ROK I Corps, the cream of the ROK army, was to advance up the coastal road to the Soviet border. Major General David G. Barr, commanding the 7th Division, had the same sort of steep, narrow, winding, one-way road to follow that lay before the 1st Marine Division, although he did not, as it developed, run into the sort of savage opposition that faced General Smith. But between these forces, there was nothing but impassable mountain country, making mutual support impossible and preventing even patrol contact.

While MacArthur's intense eagerness to complete his mission with dispatch is understandable, it is difficult to justify his plan and orders in the face of all that was known about the enemy's strength, his own supply situation, the terrain, and the manner in which his own forces were dispersed—even had they been adequately equipped and at full strength, which was far from the case.

Possibly not typical but at least a memorable example of what the government "economizers" had done to our armed forces was the condition of the 17th Regimental Combat Team of the 7th Division, by no means at the lowest levels of men and supplies. It had been first planned to move this unit to the Wonsan-

Hungnam area by sea and send it westward to make contact with the Eighth Army. Unquestionably it would have found the terrain fierce and inhospitable and the roads scanty and treacherous—but no more so had they moved laterally across the peninsula than had they moved, as they were finally ordered to, northwest to the Yalu. The 17th RCT, under the command of Colonel H. B. Powell (who eventually became U. S. Ambassador to New Zealand) was put ashore at Iwon, on October 29, ready to join the advance to the Yalu, but completely ignorant of the roughing-up the ROKs had received along that river in the distant northwest sector, three days before. The men of the 17th wore leather combat boots, but only a few had arctics. None had insulated footwear and many had no gloves, while the clothing supply generally was short of winter gear. Ammunition supplies seemed suitable to accomplishment of their mission, although some shortages did develop later. Food supplies were just barely sufficient. The regiment itself was at 85 percent strength.

Their goal was Hyesanjin, on the Yalu, some one hundred miles away, along another wretched dirt road, up and up through mountain country where low scrub afforded the only cover and where the bitter wind out of Manchuria took the thermometer down to 32 degrees below zero Fahrenheit. At one point along the march a four-man patrol volunteered to search out a crossing place for their battalion in a swift-running stream. Despite the merciless cold, the men waded into the nearly waist-deep river, and they were almost immediately encased in ice. They had to be put promptly into a warming tent and have all their clothing cut off.

Fortunately, Chinese resistance, as contrasted to what the 1st Marine Division would encounter, was light and sporadic, so the regiment, despite cold that froze up vehicles and turned perspiration to ice inside the men's boots at night, despite the almost constant suffering from improper clothing, frostbitten fingers, and scanty meals, succeeded in attaining the Yalu on November 21, the only United States troops ever to reach that stream. They had but a few days to look out over the endless icy wastes of Manchuria. Then the X Corps, fearful for the safety of the regiment, as the military situation everywhere began rapidly to deteriorate, ordered an immediate withdrawal.

The retirement to escape a trap was made in haste but not in panic. Moving night and day, with all the resourcefulness, ingenuity, initiative and tactical skill typical of our best leadership, the regiment extricated itself smoothly and with only minor damage. At one point they seized a narrow-gauge railroad in their zone and used it to get men and equipment swiftly down from the high ground. At another point they bridged a ten-mile roadless gap in the mountains by making ingenious use of an overhead ore-bucket line, built by the Japanese before the World War, to carry the regiment's heavy equipment.

Small guerrilla forces of Chinese Communists harried their retreat but constant close air support by Marine aviation held the enemy in check. For the first time in their combat service, the battalion commanders were able to talk directly to the leaders of the flights that zoomed overhead and to call them in promptly for pinpoint strikes that broke up enemy concentrations. It is true that the pressure of the Chinese Communist Forces was largely concentrated on other zones. But with less gallant, skilled, and imaginative leadership, the regiment might have suffered heavy loss to both weather and enemy action. As it was they withdrew into a beachhead area with relatively few casualties and with most of their equipment intact.

The 1st Marine Division and two battalions of the 7th Division endured a far more bitter experience. But again, thanks to courageous leadership and the extreme forethought of General Smith, complete disaster was averted. Smith, as I have explained, despite the pressure from the X Corps, took the time to keep his line of retreat open and secure, as he moved his forces up into the barren plateaus near the Changjin Reservoir. He stockpiled ammunition, gasoline, and other supplies along the way, held what high ground it could, prepared an airstrip for evacuation of wounded and pushed ahead only when he felt reasonably certain of what lay beyond. There was intermittent hit-and-run resistance all the way and it was all Chinese, to judge from the prisoners taken. According to the doctors at the sickbays, the sudden, intense cold, more than enemy fire, was the shocker. Smith felt certain now that a strong force of the enemy lay somewhere in his path and he suspected he was being drawn into a trap. The X Corps headquarters, however, under the whiplash of Mac-Arthur's known wishes, urged him on toward his objective—a group of mud-thatched huts on the western edge of the Changjin Reservoir. When he reached there, it was late November, the bitter Korean winter had already moved in, and the Chinese Communists, as their radio broadcasts had long been threatening, were ready to strike their mightiest blow.

In the west, along the Yellow Sea, the Eighth Army had advanced once more north of the Chongchon River, for the first two days against moderate resistance. GHQ's optimism seemed justified. But Walker was still opposed to any reckless advance to the border, and his fears were quickly realized. On November 26 the Chinese Communist Forces fell upon the Eighth Army again with full power and ferocity. Attacking first on the right, against the ROK II Corps, they practically destroyed Walker's flank, sweeping aside the remnants of the ROK forces in a matter of hours. Howling American profanity, and blowing endlessly on their bugles, the Chinese troops then struck the U.S. 2nd Division and in subsequent action this gallant division lost over 4000 men and much of its artillery, signal, and engineer equipment. Only Colonel Paul Freeman's 23rd Regimental Combat Team, withdrawing with his division commander's permission westward toward the sea, escaped intact. There were, Walker reported to Tokyo, an estimated 200,000 Chinese attacking, and the situation was close to desperate. This was not a counterattack, Walker warned, but a major offensive, and he knew it would be necessary for UN forces to pull in their necks.

Across the granite cliffs and dismal gorges to the east, the 1st Marine Division, stretched out along the twisting road from Yudam-ni, through Hagaru and Koto-ri, forty miles to Chin-hung-ni on the south, heard the news of the collapse of the Eighth Army's right wing. Lieutenant Colonel Raymond Murray's 5th Marines, which had led the advance from Koto-ri, followed by Colonel (later Lieutenant General) Homer B. Litzenberg's 7th

Marines, were ordered to attack to the west in a futile attempt to take pressure off Walker. Smith ordered them to proceed with caution and to watch out for ambush. As these two regiments moved out, they were rapped hard by the long-concealed Chinese. It was then that Murray and Litzenberg decided on their own, without consulting Smith, to call off the attack and go on the defensive, disregarding Almond's orders, as they figured the show was hopeless.

The Marines had been looking for such a blow and despite it they managed to hold on to the high ground near the village. An attack by two assault battalions from the CCF 79th and 89th Divisions, supported by mortar fire, developed in the night into an all-out drive by three Chinese divisions attempting to overwhelm the two Marine regiments, Raymond Murray's 5th and Litzenberg's 7th. By advancing in the dark, the Chinese avoided our air power, and were able to send overwhelming numbers against the Marines. They attacked along a narrow front, in column formation, then deployed widely once they were within hand-grenade range. Resourcefulness, fighting spirit and superior fire power of the Marines helped balance the scales, but the fighting was bitter in the extreme. The 18-below-zero cold made many of the carbines and BARs unusable, although most of the M-1s and Browning machine guns resisted the freeze-up and stayed in action. At half-past two in the morning, one Marine platoon set fire to a native hut and lighted all the nearby ground, so they were able to wreak terrible slaughter upon the attacking Chinese. But with one formation cut to pieces, there would be a fresh one to clamber on up over the corpses and continue the assault.

This, and the subsequent attacks upon Marine units stretched out through the villages to the south, were among the bloodiest battles of the war. They cost the Division dearly. But there was no rout and no disaster. At Hagaru, at the foot of the reservoir, the commander had arranged to stockpile six days' supplies and these were supplemented by air-drops of small-arms ammunition, weapons, medical supplies, food and even drinking water. But the embattled Marines were most grateful of all for the doughty men of Company D of the 1st Engineer Battalion, who labored all night under floodlights to hack an airstrip out of the frozen earth from which the wounded could be evacuated. They completed the job in twelve hours, stopping sometimes to take up rifles in support of the ground troops out in front of them. The fighting grew more intense, but the bulldozers roared and banged along until the job was done.

So desperate was the situation, with nine Chinese divisions available for an assault upon the Marines, that General Almond urged General Smith to speed his withdrawal, just as he had a few days earlier been pressing him to hasten his advance. Almond authorized Smith to abandon any equipment that might slow him down. But Smith was not going to abandon anything he might need. The speed of his withdrawal, he said, would be governed entirely by the dispatch with which he was able to take out his wounded. As he intended to fight his way free, he would need all his equipment and he intended to bring most of it back. He did too, and carried out in trucks all the men who were wounded along the way. He left behind only those who had been killed in the fighting at Yudam-ni. For the eighty-five officers and men who lost their lives there, a field burial service was conducted before the withdrawal began.

The Marines pulled back in order, followed by a number of refugees. An apron across a hydroelectric-plant spillway, hanging on a cliffside above a chasm, had been destroyed by the Chinese, but General Smith had foreseen this danger and had a Treadway bridge air-dropped in sections in time to get his forces across, bulldozers and all. Two companies of the 1st Marines coming from Chinhung-ni seized and held the high ground commanding the crossing and fought off all attempts to cut the column off.

It was a long and tortuous retreat, seeming to move inch by inch with fighting all the way. When the advance elements were entering Chinhung-ni, the southernmost village on the route, the last units were still in Koto-ri, ten miles to the north.

Actually the retirement was more of an attack then a retreat, for it was necessary for each unit to battle its way back against superior force to join the Marines in the village to the rear. This meant attacking often to take commanding heights, so that enemy artillery could not zero in on the retreating columns along the road. The force at Yudam-ni slugged its way back to Hagaru at the lower end of the Changjin Reservoir. Here the Marines had to fight out on the ice of the reservoir to rescue the remnants of Task Force MacLean from the 7th Division, a force that had been split in two and nearly demolished by a sudden Chinese attack. Here, Lieutenant Colonel Don C. Faith, Jr., 32nd Infantry Regiment, won the Congressional Medal of Honor while gallantly trying to extricate his truck convoy filled with more than five hundred wounded, but losing his life in the attempt.

Back through Koto-ri and Chinhung-ni the Marines, with some infantrymen and a few British Commandos, crept, clawed and fought their way, smashing roadblocks, beating off attacks from either side of the road, attacking and seizing hills along the route. Marine Aviation and the Fifth Air Force gave them constant close support and dropped needed supplies. The airstrip at Hagaru saw more than 4000 wounded or severely frostbitten men flown out to safety.

By December 11, the ordeal was over and General Smith had brought his tough, battle-tried, and half-frozen troops, still in possession of most of their equipment and all of their fighting spirit, clear of the final defile into the beachhead area near Hungnam, and into a defense perimeter they could have held, with help from the Navy and Air Force, for as long as they had been ordered to stay.

On November 28, at a conference with the Commanders of the X Corps and the Eighth Army at Tokyo, MacArthur had given General Walker permission to withdraw as he felt necessary to prevent his being outflanked on the east. The Eighth Army had taken a severe pounding. The U.S. 2nd Division, whose losses along the Chongchon River had been so heavy, was declared combat noneffective by the end of November and withdrawn to South Korea to refill its ranks and re-equip.

The Eighth Army withdrew now behind the Chongchon River and then southward without interruption, and by steady stages, in good order. By December 5, Walker had abandoned the North Korean capital of Pyongyang and cleared the area. The Chinese broke contact and showed no immediate appetite for pursuit, perhaps because they habitually supplied their troops for only a few days of combat at a time, but kept coming at about six miles a day. Their own supply lines were lengthening now and were of course receiving the unremitting and savage attention of our own air power.

The Eighth Army was pulling back toward the 38th parallel, while the X Corps began its withdrawal from its beachhead positions around Hungnam. News reports at this time, or at least news headlines, gave the impression that the UN forces had suffered a major catastrophe, when actually they had performed a magnificent withdrawal in the face of unremitting attacks by overwhelmingly superior forces—and thanks to some extremely gallant fighting, particularly by the 1st Marine Division and the U.S. 2nd Division, had kept their losses to a minimum.

That there had been severe defeats along the way, particularly of the ROK II Corps, and that some units had been nearly decimated, there was no denying. But by early December, when General Collins, Army Chief of Staff, made a personal survey of the troops in Korea he found them "calm and confident," with the Eighth Army ably executing its planned withdrawal and the X Corps evacuating the beachhead area without panic or confusion.

The Navy, at Hungnam, performed with spectacular skill, although they received no banner headlines for their evacuation by sea of the entire X Corps and its equipment. But to take out, from unfriendly territory, 105,000 troops, 91,000 Korean refugees, more than 17,000 vehicles and several hundred thousand tons of cargo was in itself a military triumph of no small dimensions. Equipment and supplies that could not be outloaded were destroyed on the beach, so nothing was left for the enemy.

It should be remembered too that the U.S. 2nd Division, badly mauled as it was in holding the Chongchon River so the balance of the Eighth Army could cross, was back in combat in central Korea in less than a month. The 1st Marine Division, which received severe punishment from a force of at least six Chinese divisions as it fought its way down off the Korean roof, was also back in action in less than thirty days.

Still the defeat was severe and the losses tragic, doubly so because they might have been greatly minimized. It is easy enough from this distance to look back and say that the Commander in Chief was at fault in this respect or that, or that this decision ought not to have been allowed to stand, or that this or that order should never have been issued. There are some too who argue that all might have turned out better had MacArthur's hands not been tied and had he been permitted to destroy the Yalu bridges and bomb the enemy's bases in Manchuria. But I do not believe there is much profit in assessing blame unless it can be done so as to help our nation and its leaders to avoid similar mistakes in the future.

As I said earlier, it is easy to understand MacArthur's eagerness to accomplish his assigned mission—a mission for which he had pleaded—the destruction of all hostile armed forces on the peninsula. And too much blame cannot be attached to his superiors and his colleagues who, after the blazing success at Inchon, hesitated to question MacArthur's military judgment or even the obviously hazardous disposition of his forces. MacArthur was surely one of our greatest generals—far more than a military figure, for almost by the power of his own personality he brought defeated Japan from feudalism to democracy and set her on the road to early resumption of her rightful place in the family of free peoples. His brilliance, his persuasiveness, his diplomatic skills, his personal courage all belonged to a man of heroic mold.

But MacArthur's all-too-human weaknesses, which marked him as a man rather than a demigod, seemed occasionally to have been granted him in overgenerous proportion too. No military commander is immune to mistakes, and many commanders at one time or another have perhaps made errors that cost our nation dearly—any wasted lives being too dear a price. But it is still the part of a soldier to accept responsibility for blunders and to examine honestly into their origin. This is one role MacArthur refused to play. Yet it should have been clear to anyone that his own refusal to accept the mounting evidence of massive Chinese intervention was largely responsible for the reckless scattering of our forces all over the map of Korea.

Perhaps there was some justification for his apparent assumption that China was a paper tiger and that her radioed warnings were bluff, even that the appearance of a few volunteers was part of that bluff. But how could any man, not obsessed with his own reputation, have persisted in misinterpreting detailed intelligence reports and actual events on the battlefield—not merely the taking of large numbers of Chinese prisoners, clearly belonging to units known to be in the CCF order of battle, but the brutal mauling of a U. S. Regimental Combat Team, and the near-annihilation of a ROK Division? And how could the Commander in Chief not have realized that his forces were too meager, and too thinly supplied, to have held the line of the Yalu and the Tumen—even had he reached it—against an enemy known to be concentrated there in great numbers? Later, in extenuation, it was argued that, had he been set free to bomb Manchurian bases, his forces would have been adequate for the job. It is not at all certain that that is so, but assuming it were, he knew before the jump-off that he would not be allowed to risk total war by bombing those bases. And it would not have been difficult for him to determine General Vandenberg's view that for us to carry the war to China this way and to engage her air force (and perhaps part of Soviet Russia's too) would have, through combat losses and natural attrition, stripped our air power to a point from which it would have taken us two years to recover. Meanwhile our commitments in other parts of the world could not have been fulfilled.

Some commentators have forgotten that we had nearly complete air superiority in Korea through a sort of unwritten agreement that left our airfields in Korea and Japan immune from attack by the Chinese. So we too had our "privileged sanctuary"—without which the Korean War could have been a far more tragic story.

As a matter of fact we had in Korea a prime example of how mistaken it is to imagine that an enemy's supply lines can be "interdicted" through air power alone. We had almost no opposition in the air over the battlefields in North Korea and we were free to attack the enemy's supply lines without hindrance except from ground fire, and not even that during the first year. As a result we did indeed destroy much of the enemy's equipment and

75

supplies on the road and undoubtedly we hampered him severely and cost him a high price in lives and machinery. Yet the enemy still remained strong on the ground, where we had to fight him, and he still kept his armies intact and the vital real estate in his possession.

It has always been tempting for men removed from the conflict to envision cheap and easy solutions, through naval blockades and saturation bombing. But any man who has fought a war from close up must know that, vital as are the sea and air arms of our combat forces, only ground action can destroy the armed forces of the enemy—unless, of course, resort is had to obliteration attacks with nuclear weapons. There is simply no such thing as "choking off" supply lines in a country as wild as North Korea, or in jungle country either. And when the enemy soldier is self-sufficient, as in Asia, where he carries his supplies and his weapons on his back and where he can move at night or travel by day along foot trails not visible from the air, it is self-delusion to think that he can be defeated by dropping bombs on him. Even were he to be rendered quiescent for a time by endless bombardment, it would still be necessary to meet him face to face on the ground to subdue him and to keep him subdued.

There is of course the school that argues for immediate use of nuclear weapons when a stalemate threatens, that talks of "reducing the enemy to the Stone Age" by blowing his homeland to dust. This to me would be the ultimate in immorality. It is one thing to do this in retaliation, or as a measure of survival as a nation. It is quite another to initiate such an operation for less basic reasons. We have not, it may be argued, advanced too far from the jungle, over the ages; but what little advance we have made, whatever margin still exists between us and the beasts, I believe we should cling to. If we put "victory" at any cost ahead of human decency, then I think God might well question our right to invoke His blessing on our Cause.

But let us return to Korea. In looking over the stubborn way in which MacArthur clung to his determination to push on to the Yalu, despite all evidence that prophesied disaster, I cannot help drawing a parallel with Custer's behavior at the Little Big Horn,

16. Supplies being dropped by parachute over green rice paddies. They were flown over enemy-held territory and dropped for isolated troops. *U.S. Air Force photo.*

17. American soldiers duck while firing 60-mm. mortar M2 at enemy boats trying to cross the Naktong River during the night of August 26–27, 1950. *U.S. Army photograph.*

18. Grief-stricken American infantryman whose buddy has been killed is comforted by another soldier. Medical corpsman fills out casualty tags. August 28, 1950. *U.S. Army photograph.*

19. Chow in style near the front lines near Masan, August 28, 1950. *U.S. Army photograph.*

20. ROK troops in a rice paddy await orders to move forward in the Masan area, September 6, 1950. *U.S. Army photograph.*

21. South Korean refugee waits to board a boat at Masan, to be evacuated from the fighting area to a small island near Pusan, September 13, 1950. *U.S. Army photograph.*

22. Marines mopping up fire-swept Wolmi Island during the Inchon invasion, September 15, 1950. *Defense Department photo, Marine Corps.*

23. Marines head for the beaches in amtracks during the Inchon landings. The first units landed on Wolmi Island at six-thirty in the morning of September 15, 1950, and had overcome the light resistance by eight-seven. *U.S. Army photograph.*

24. Marines with bazooka and machine gun guarding the causeway from Wolmi Island to the mainland, September 15, 1950. *Defense Department photo, Marine Corps.*

25. LSTs (landing ships, tank) unload men and equipment on the beach at Inchon, September 15, 1950. *Official U.S. Navy photo.*

26. North Korean prisoners captured in the Inchon area, awaiting medical treatment and clothing. September 17, 1950. *Defense Department photo, Marine Corps.*

27. LSTs grounded by the receding tide off Wolmi Island after unloading during the Inchon landing. September 17, 1950. *U.S. Army photograph.*

28. American infantrymen use a cow to carry ammunition and equipment as they move through Waegwan, September 21, 1950. *U.S. Army photograph.*

29. Marine lieutenant firing an M1 sniper rifle. In the background is the Seoul Railroad Bridge across the Han River. September 23, 1950. *U.S. Army photograph.*

when the commander's overriding belief that he alone was right closed his mind to all counsel. It simply cannot be argued that MacArthur was unaware of the enemy's presence or his capabilities. He himself at one point, in pushing for permission to take out the Yalu bridges and bomb Manchurian bases, warned the JCS that the Chinese forces along the Yalu "threatened the destruction of my command." Nor can it be argued that he did not grasp the difficulties of the terrain that made it impossible for the separate commands in North Korea to render each other mutual support. While he did earlier propose a solid line across the waist of Korea, and while the X Corps, which he kept under GHQ control, was expected at one point to attack west to relieve pressure on the Eighth Army's right flank, it was MacArthur himself who, after the Chinese intervention could no longer be denied, argued that it was impossible to link up the Eighth Army and the X Corps across North Korea.

The JCS had suggested, after the mauling of the Eighth Army and the X Corps by the Chinese, that MacArthur consider a junction of his two commands, to close the gap between them, and to establish a continuous line. MacArthur objected strongly. He gave as his reasons all the reasons that might well have served to restrain him from plunging toward the Yalu: his forces were too weak to cover so extensive a front; the distances were too great; it was impossible to supply both commands from one port; the Taebaek Range, cutting the peninsula in two sections, was well-nigh impassable.

On December 3, he informed the JCS that, unless positive and immediate action were taken (to bolster his forces or occupy the enemy elsewhere) hope for success "cannot be justified and steady attrition leading to final destruction can reasonably be contemplated." That he had hoped, as some of his critics whispered, to force the administration's hand by getting us into a position where only an attack on mainland China would salvage the situation, is not, I think, a reasonable supposition. Rather I prefer to believe that, with the prize within his grasp, holding tight to his conviction that Red China was a paper tiger, MacArthur had simply closed his ears to all counsel save his own. He had won a 5000-to-

1 wager just a few months earlier. Now he meant to do it again, where the stakes were even greater.

To me one of the final ironies is that MacArthur, who had so often silenced his critics by chiding them because they simply "did not understand the Oriental mind," should have been so completely misguided in his own attempts to read enemy intentions.

Of course, in making these comments I have the advantage of being able to look back and read the course of events, such as no man could have done in those bitter days of late November and early December 1950. At the time, while I shared the uneasiness of those few who felt our forces were dangerously dispersed, and while I had little patience with the reluctance of the JCS to give MacArthur a direct order, I had the deepest respect for MacArthur's abilities, for his courage, and for his tactical brilliance. I had first known him in the 1920s when I was a young captain at West Point and he was Superintendent. Ever since those days I had profound respect for his leadership, his quick mind, and his unusual skill at going straight to the main point of any subject and illuminating it so swiftly that the slowest mind could not fail to grasp it. He was, despite any weakness he may have shown, a truly great military man, a great statesman, and a gallant leader. And when Fate suddenly decided that I would serve directly under him in Korea I welcomed the chance to associate once again with one of the few geniuses it has been my privilege to know.

CHAPTER FIVE

CHANGE OF COMMAND – I TAKE
OVER THE EIGHTH ARMY –
REBUILDING THE FIGHTING SPIRIT –
RETURN TO THE OFFENSIVE

EVERY SOLDIER LEARNS in time that war is a lonely business. All your study, all your training, all your drill anticipates the moment when abruptly the responsibility rests solely on you to decide whether to stand or pull back, or to order an attack that will expose thousands of men to sudden death.

My own direct involvement in the Korean War came with the suddenness of a rifle shot. I was sipping an after-dinner highball at the home of a friend, talking about something so trivial, I am sure, that it is useless to try to recall it, when my host told me General J. Lawton Collins (then Army Chief of Staff) wanted me on the phone. The news General Collins delivered to me turned my evening upside down. General Walton Walker had been killed in a jeep accident and in keeping with a stand-by selection made long before (without my knowledge) by General MacArthur, I was in line to succeed Walker as commanding officer of the Eighth Army. I was to report without delay. There would be little time to plan and hardly any for saying goodbye. My host and hostess, both Army people, knew better than to question the nature of the phone conversation, and to allay my wife's quite natural curiosity I rejoined the group in the living room, finished my drink, and then took my leave with her.

My wife, from long habit, waited for me to volunteer the reason for Joe Collins' call so late at night, but while my mind was racing with plans for the many things I must quickly do, I decided that announcement of the assignment could wait for the few hours of night remaining. She could get some sleep even if I couldn't. At seven, when I had brought the coffee upstairs, I told her, and like the courageous thoroughbred she is, she accepted it with the characteristic fortitude of an Army wife.

There were routine tasks I had to complete, regardless of exigencies. And there was one duty I knew I must take time for. That was to express to General Walker's widow, in the pitifully small degree I was capable of, the deep sympathy of those who had served with her husband in battle and the devotion of all those who had long been his comrades. Until I had done this, I could not take up my duties with a quiet heart.

I made a quick trip to the Pentagon to pick up some papers from my office and to check in with any of the Joint Chiefs who might be there that Saturday morning. Only Forrest Sherman was in, and I had a few pleasant and profitable minutes with him and more with the Army Vice-Chief of Staff, my dear friend Ham Haislip. Up until this time I think my wife had clung to the hope that I would still have part of Christmas at home, this being the twenty-third, and I did not know myself just when my plane would take off. I now learned that it would be that same evening. I hadn't the heart to phone and tell her that, so I asked General Haislip if he would do it for me.

"That will be a hard thing to do, Matt," he said, "but I shall." Deep gratitude welled up in my heart.

Always in moments of sudden stress, as this was, the most trifling details seem to cling to your memory. There were half a hundred important matters that occupied me in the few hours between the time I received my assignment and the moment I boarded the plane that was to fly me to Tokyo, via Tacoma and Adak. Most of them I completed, thanks to the brother officers who hastened to lend me their hands, brains, and time. Some I had to postpone, or complete on the plane. Very few of them do I recall now. But I do remember vividly how pleased I was with myself for having had the forethought to rescue from the attic the precious track flannels that had served me so well in the Ardennes and lay them out ready to be packed in my bedroll. And I recall, too, my dismay when I unpacked in Korea to discover that I had left them, arms and legs outspread, lying uselessly behind me at home. But at least this oversight did give me an opportunity for the first few days to share the leading edges of a Korean winter as some of our incompletely outfitted troops knew it.

Because a day was lost on the way East, it was December 25 when I touched down at Haneda Airport in Tokyo, just short of midnight. At home I knew it was still Christmas morning, and one of the last things I did before turning in was to arrange for the PX to let me select a Christmas present for my wife in the morning. After hastily putting together the notes I would need for the next day's meeting with General MacArthur, I went to bed with a feeling that I had at last completed all my Stateside missions and was ready for whatever might await me across the dark Tsu Shima Strait.

My meeting with MacArthur began at nine-thirty the next morning in the Commander in Chief's office in the Dai-Ichi Building. Only Doyle Hickey, who had courageously led Task Force Hickey of the 3rd Armored Division in my Corps in the first days of the Battle of the Bulge, sat with General MacArthur and me. But, delighted as I was at his genial presence, I found my whole attention focused on the dramatic figure of Douglas MacArthur. Of course I had known MacArthur since my days as a West Point instructor but, like nearly everyone who ever dealt with him, I was again deeply impressed by the force of his personality. To confer with him was an experience that could happen with few others. He was a great actor too, with an actor's instinct for the dramatic—in tone and gesture. Yet so lucid and so penetrating were his explanations and his analyses that it was his mind rather than his manner or his bodily presence that dominated his listeners.

My notes indicate that our talk that morning was detailed, specific, frank, and far-ranging. Some weeks before my arrival

MacArthur had informed the Department of the Army that his current planning provided for "a withdrawal in successive positions to the Pusan area." When he met with me, his immediate instructions were to hold as far as possible "in the most advanced positions in which you can maintain yourself." I was to hold on to Seoul, largely for psychological and political reasons, as long as possible but not if it became a citadel position. The possibility of holding Seoul against a full-scale attack had already ceased to exist, although I did not know it at the time.

Supply discipline in the U.S. forces, he told me, was not good—a fact I was soon to confirm by firsthand observation. The troops, said MacArthur, were taking inadequate care of themselves in cold weather. It is interesting to recall that at this conference MacArthur decried the value of tactical air support. It could not, he flatly stated, isolate the battlefield or stop the flow of hostile troops and supply. This is perhaps a point some active-duty officers and their civilian superiors have yet to learn.

His chief concern at this conference seemed to be the fact that we were then operating in a "mission vacuum," as he termed it, while diplomacy attempted to feel its way. "A military success," he said, "will strengthen our diplomacy."

He noted that Communist China was wide open in the south and that an attack by forces already on Formosa would greatly relieve pressure on our forces in Korea. He had already recommended such an attack, he told me, but Washington had not approved. Yet in telling me this he expressed no criticism whatever of Washington, nor was any implied. It was simply a decision by higher authority that he had accepted as a soldier.

He urged me especially not to underestimate the Chinese. "They constitute a dangerous foe," he warned me. "Walker reported that the Chinese avoid roads, using the ridges and hills as avenues of approach. They will attack in depth. Their firepower in the hands of their infantry is more extensively used than our own. The enemy moves and fights at night. The entire Chinese military establishment is in this fight."

As for his own goal, the maximum he had in mind, he said,

was "inflicting a broadening defeat making possible the retention and security of South Korea."

"Form your own opinions," he told me in closing. "Use your own judgment. I will support you. You have my complete confidence."

It was my turn then to ask some questions but his presentation had already covered most of those I had been prepared to ask. Just a few remained. What calls might I expect him to make on the Eighth Army in the improbable event that the USSR should enter the fight? In that case, he said, he would withdraw the Eighth Army to Japan, even though this might take several months.

Then I wanted to know if he felt that, in the event of further southward advance by the enemy, there was danger the South Koreans might defect. There was he said indeed a distinct danger that, under those circumstances they might. But there was no such danger now. And he agreed when I suggested that, if we made any further material rearward movement, we should strongly reassure the South Koreans that we meant to stand by them. My final question was simply this: "If I find the situation to my liking, would you have any objections to my attacking?" And his answer encouraged and gratified me deeply:

"The Eighth Army is yours, Matt. Do what you think best."

All that was left now was to sit down with the men who could give me specific details of the job that faced me and fill in all I needed to know of the state in which all our forces stood. Doyle Hickey had the Chiefs of all the GHQ General Staff Sections gathered at a table awaiting me, along with Vice-Admiral C. Turner Joy, commanding the Naval Forces in the Far East, and Lieutenant General George E. Stratemeyer, commanding the Far East Air Forces. Before noon I had soaked up answers to all the questions I could think of, and whatever information they felt I might require. By twelve o'clock I was on my way to Haneda Airport to take my plane for Korea, and at four that afternoon I stepped out on the apron at Taegu, shivering just a little in the bright winter sun, to greet a colleague and friend of many years, Major General Leven C. Allen, Eighth Army Chief of Staff.

Prior to leaving Tokyo, I had prepared two messages, both for the Eighth Army. The first was despatched from there and was limited to an expression of my respect for General Walker, whose death I deplored. The second, which was to be issued immediately upon my arrival, dealt with the single fact that I was thereupon assuming command.

There were several important errands to be completed on that first day, many petty details to give heed to, and messages to send. Then I was determined to make a personal inspection of the troops under my command and to determine how quickly we could return to the offensive. But even before that, I had to find some way of reassuring our ROK Army allies* that we were not going to pull out suddenly and leave them to cope with the Communists alone. I knew that would mean a wholesale slaughter, and I could not blame a South Korean for contemplating a change of coat if he had any reason for believing he would be left to try to live out his life under Red rule.

It was my duty to pay an immediate courtesy call on both Ambassador Muccio and President Rhee, where I would have an opportunity to talk of this problem. Ambassador Muccio shared my uneasiness, for he too had been much concerned with the effect upon South Korean officialdom of our new withdrawal. When I called on Syngman Rhee, therefore, it was my first concern to try to impress this staunch old warrior that I had not come to lead the Eighth Army back to Japan. He greeted me rather impassively but I extended my hand at once and said, right from the heart, for I had no time to sort over ceremonial phrases: "I'm glad to see you, Mr. President, glad to be here, and I mean to stay."

That was the one word the old gentleman seemed to have been awaiting. His face broke into a smile as warm as the Eastern sun, his eyes grew moist and he took my extended hand in both of his. He led me then to meet his charming wife and we shared a cordial cup of tea, while I endeavored as best I could to impress him with our determination not to be driven from the peninsula, and to go on the offensive again as soon as we could marshal our forces.

* My letter to Lieutenant General Chung Il Kwon, ROKA Chief of Staff, appears in Appendix 3.

Earlier I had held a conference with the two U. S. Army Corps Commanders, Generals Frank W. Milburn and John B. Coulter, and with the Eighth Army Deputy Chief of Staff, Colonel William A. Collier. My concern in this conference was to devise every means we could to make an immediate improvement in the Eighth Army's combat potential, for I was determined to return to the offensive just as quickly as our strength permitted. We discussed the use of mines, both antitank and antipersonnel, the proper employment of searchlights for battlefield illumination, the improvement of lateral communications between Corps, and particularly between the IX Corps and the ROK III Corps on its right, the availability of bridging material, and the maintenance of a two-division bridgehead north of the Han. I said I would expect the utmost in coordinated planning and action between the two U. S. Corps.

But before the Eighth Army could return to the offensive it needed to have its fighting spirit restored, to have pride in itself, to feel confidence in its leadership, and have faith in its mission. These qualities could not be assessed at secondhand, and I determined to make an immediate tour of the battlefront to meet and talk with the field commanders in their forward command posts and to size up the Eighth Army's spirit with my own eyes and senses. Fighting spirit is not something that can be described or spelled out to you. An experienced commander can feel it through all his senses, in the posture, the manner, the talk, the very gestures of the men on the fighting front.

In going over the tactical situation with Ambassador Muccio, for whose courage and competence I came to have the highest regard, I had found our right flank dangerously exposed to an enemy thrust south through Wonju and southwest then to sever our Main Supply Route and the rail line to Pusan. I knew the U.S. 2nd Division, after its mauling on the Chongchon, was still in the process of rehabilitation, but the situation struck me as so urgent that I ordered it to move to Wonju without delay and to block those avenues of approach to our right rear. (As it turned out, we just barely anticipated the enemy's move and halted his thrust just in time.) Except for this, however, I occupied myself for the next several days entirely with an assessment of the Army's readiness for offensive action.

Using a light plane, a helicopter, and a jeep I visited the Commanders of the U.S. I Corps, the British 29th Brigade, and the U.S. 25th Division, the U.S. 27th Infantry Regiment and the ROK 1st Division. Within forty-eight hours I had met with every Corps Commander and all but one of the Division Commanders— the ROK Capital Division on the distant and quiet east coast being the exception—and had learned from their lips their feelings about a major offensive—that any such effort by our armies at this time would fail and perhaps cost us heavily. And for my own part I had discovered that our forces were simply not mentally and spiritually ready for the sort of action I had been planning. Their courage was still high and they were ready to take on any mission I might have assigned. But there was too much of a looking-over-your-shoulder attitude, a lack of that special verve, that extra alertness and vigor that seems to exude from an army that is sure of itself and bent on winning. The first MP I came upon as my jeep toured the forward zones, immediately impressed on me the sharp contrast between this army and those I had known in other actions in Europe. He was correct in posture and in gesture—correct in every way, except in spirit. That extra snap to the salute, that quick aggressive tone and gesture, that confident grin that had always seemed to me the marks of the battle-seasoned American GI, all were missing.

The men I met along the road, those I stopped to talk to and to solicit gripes from—they too all conveyed to me a conviction that this was a bewildered army, not sure of itself or its leaders, not sure what they were doing there,* wondering when they would hear the whistle of that homebound transport. There was obviously much to be done to restore this army to a fighting mood. Some of it I could begin to do at once. I listened to their complaints— offered not in the classic griping style of a victorious and high-spirited army but in a tone of dissatisfaction and uncertainty: the food was often insufficient, not always on time, and not always

---

* On January 21, 1951, I told them, in a communication I directed to every man in my command. "Why Are We Here?" appears in Appendix 4.

hot; there was no stationery for a man to write home on; clothing was not suited to the weather. These were matters I could get prompt action on: I had stationery brought in by helicopter, ordered those kitchens brought close to provide hot food a-plenty; requested immediate increase in the quantity and quality of rations. (Local food products, much of it alive with gastro-intestinal disasters for those who had not built an immunity, was forbidden to the troops.) I had taken note myself that many of the troops were without gloves, their hands red and chapped, in the raw December wind, and I knew from personal experience how easy it is to leave a glove behind or to drop it to fire a weapon and then not see it again. In Europe it had been my practice to travel with an extra supply of gloves in my jeep to give to the men I came across who needed them. I now made an immediate effort to have gloves enough supplied to warm the fighting hands.

Every command post I visited gave me the same sense of lost confidence and lack of spirit.* The leaders, from sergeant on up, seemed unresponsive, reluctant to answer my questions. Even their gripes had to be dragged out of them and information was provided glumly, without the alertness of men whose spirits are high. I could not help contrasting their attitudes to that of a young British subaltern who had trotted down off a knoll to greet me when he spotted the insignia on my jeep. He saluted smartly and identified himself as to name, rank, and unit. Knowing that the British Brigade had hardly more than a handful of men to cover a wide sector of the front line, with a new Chinese offensive expected almost hourly, I asked how he found the situation.

"Quite all right, sir," he replied quickly. Then he added with a pleasant smile: "It *is* a bit drafty up here." Drafty was the word for it, with gaps in the line wide enough to march an army through in company front.

I could not condemn our own troops, however, for I knew they had good reason for their state of mind. It was not their doing that had brought them far understrength to this unfortunate country with major shortages in weaponry and insufficient clothing

* It should be noted that the X Corps, with its three divisions, the 3rd, 7th, and 1st Marine, had not then joined.

87

and food, and had spread them across an area far too wide for them to maintain an effective front. Nor were they at fault in wanting to know why they were here and what they were expected to do. If any war that our country ever engaged in could have been called a forgotten war, this was it. If ever we were unprepared for a war, we were on this occasion. The primary purpose of an army—to be ready to fight effectively at all times—seemed to have been forgotten. Our armed forces had been economized almost into ineffectiveness and then had been asked to meet modern armor with obsolescent weapons and had been sent into subarctic temperatures in clothing fit for fall maneuvers at home. The people in the States, I knew, were often too preoccupied with the essential task of making a living to concern themselves with faraway battles, unless one of their immediate kin was involved. As for the men themselves, a good many had been reactivated after making considerable sacrifice in a war that seemed hardly over, while the workings of Selective Service had sent into action young men who often wound up in uniform simply because they were people of little influence at home.

In view of all this, it was a miracle, and a credit to those who had bred them, that our soldiers had fought so magnificently against such brutal odds and still retained their courage and the dogged willingness to go where their leaders sent them.

The leadership I found in many instances sadly lacking, and I said so out loud. The unwillingness of the army to forgo certain creature comforts, its timidity about getting off the scanty roads, its reluctance to move without radio and telephone contact, and its lack of imagination in dealing with a foe whom they soon outmatched in firepower and dominated in the air and on the surrounding seas—these were not the fault of the GI but of the policymakers at the top. I'm afraid my language in pointing out these faults was often impolite.

What I told the field commanders in essence was that their infantry ancestors would roll over in their graves could they see how roadbound this army was, how often it forgot to seize the high ground along its route, how it failed to seek and maintain contact in its front, how little it knew of the terrain and how

88

seldom took advantage of it, how reluctant it was to get off its bloody wheels and put shoe leather to the earth, to get into the hills and among the scrub and meet the enemy where he lived. As for communications, I told them to go back to grandfather's day if they had to—to use runners if the radio and phones were out, or smoke signals if they could devise no better way.

I knew well enough that our forces were too thin to man a solid line across the peninsula, yet I saw no reason why these could not be mutually supporting, division-to-division and corps-to-corps. Our howitzers had a range of several miles, so that in many cases each unit could support the next to a considerable extent, and the units on the flanks, particularly, could tie in together well enough to offer each other some artillery support when it was needed.

The enemy, it is true, traveled light, traveled at night, and knew the terrain better than we did. He was inured to the weather and to all kinds of deprivation and could feed himself and carry what weapons and supplies he needed by whatever means the land offered—by oxcart, by pony, even by camel, a number of which had been brought in by the Chinese, or on the backs of native workmen, even on the backs of the troops themselves. There was nothing but our own love of comfort that bound us to the road. We too could get off into the hills, I reminded them, to find the enemy and fix him in position. I repeated to the commanders as forcefully as I could, the ancient Army slogan: "Find them! Fix them! Fight them! Finish them!"

The pressing problem, once I had abandoned hope of an immediate return to the offensive, was to make ready for the Chinese offensive that was almost certain to begin on New Year's, the offensive that had been expected on Christmas but that had not yet begun. The Chinese outnumbered us. But our armor was far superior now and of course we had control of the air. We lacked the manpower to halt the night attacks. But by buttoning up tight, unit by unit, at night and counterattacking strongly, with armor and infantry teams, during the day, we had an excellent opportunity to deal out severe punishment to the hostile forces that had advanced through the gaps in our line. I urged upon our commanders, therefore, the importance of occupying suitable hill masses and positioning our troops so as to invite enemy penetration at night. Then with our superior firepower and air support we could destroy the enemy by daylight.

There was no question in my mind that we would have to give some ground but I wanted the withdrawal to be orderly, on phase lines, with rearward positions properly reconnoitered and prepared. Here the native labor battalions assigned to me by President Rhee would help us immensely, by preparing ground to which we could withdraw. I also knew it was vital, in restoring the fighting spirit in the troops, to make clear to all of them that the leaders were concerned for their safety, would not risk their lives needlessly, nor abandon any units that were cut off. I made strong efforts therefore to drive home to Corps and Division Commanders that no unit was to be left to be overwhelmed and destroyed; that units which were cut off were to be fought for and brought back unless a major commander, after personal appraisal, should decide that their relief would result in the loss of equal or greater numbers.

To illustrate these efforts: I learned that a certain Corps Commander, in a directive to a Division Commander, had ordered a specified position held "at all costs." I ordered the immediate rescinding of that portion of the directive. The use of this phrase to a major unit is the prerogative of the Army Commander in person. It was my resolve, I told them, never to issue such an order unless I had personally reconnoitered the terrain, had observed the situation on the ground and had decided such a measure was necessary.

Corrective measures could not be confined to Korea alone, however, for some of our major weaknesses had their roots in failures at home. The lack of aggressiveness in our Corps and Division Commanders reflected a failure to pour on the heat in America. I wrote Joe Collins, urging him to do what he could to wake up the people at home to the urgency of our problem. What was needed, I told him, was a toughness of soul as well as body, to cope with a ruthless foe who acknowledged no rules in warfare, who fought over a wild and difficult terrain, and who would even drive helpless civilians before him as a shield against our fire. The people at home needed to be told the truth about this war, I insisted. Once they knew the truth they would support us in toughening our training, in demanding more manpower, more armor, more sacrifice to keep our armies fed and cared for. Above all, we had to learn to be ruthless with our general officers or we would never develop the aggressive and resourceful leadership this army required.

The Corps and Division Commanders had made a show of complying with my instructions concerning the positioning of strong forces to permit powerful daylight counterattacks, but I found their efforts inadequate. Consequently we had lost many opportunities to inflict heavy losses on the foe, and I knew I was going to have to bear down hard to make sure no more such opportunities were wasted. While there was certainly no air of real defeatism in our ranks, there may have filtered down some of the feeling in GHQ, and in Washington too, that we might have to pull out of the Korean peninsula altogether. At the end of December the JCS informed MacArthur of their conclusions that the CCF were strong enough to force the United Nations out of Korea if they chose to apply their full strength. MacArthur, after the success of the Chinese New Year's offensive, agreed that if the JCS decisions stood unchanged—that we were to receive no major reinforcements, that there was to be no blockade of the Chinese coast, nor any air attack upon mainland China, no permission to bomb Manchurian bases, no "unleashing" of the Chinese Nationalist forces in Formosa—then, in the absence of overriding political considerations, "the command should be withdrawn from Korea just as rapidly as it is tactically possible to do so."

At no time did I agree, either that the enemy was capable of driving us out of Korea, or that we should withdraw. I was ready of course to lead the army wherever it might be sent—back to Japan, or across the 38th parallel once more. But whatever the decision was to be, I felt it should be made sufficiently in advance so that, if a retirement was ordered, we could prepare for it properly, withdraw in good order, and outload our forces through an unimpeded port. I knew too well what the price of sudden, unplanned withdrawal might be, without time to collect ships enough to effect the move smoothly and swiftly, without a carefully prepared perimeter of defense, without proper scheduling and fixing of priorities. I knew too what the effect might be on the ROK government if such a decision was made and prematurely disclosed or even rumored, and I urged that the greatest possible care be taken to prevent leaks if such a decision seemed probable. Beyond this, there was what I considered the really crucial question of what to do about the ROK armies, civilian officials, and prisoners of war. Surely we could not contemplate leaving behind us, to the savage attention of the enemy, the outnumbered and poorly equipped soldiers who had fought gallantly at our side through these past bitter months, or President Rhee and his government? I had no solution to offer, except to insist upon our obligation to provide for the safety of these men—and all those in government and civilian service who had assisted us, a total that I estimated and reported would not be far from one and a half million.

The prisoner of war question was a sticky one. What to do with them if we should withdraw was a problem for which I had no ready solution. But I felt I had to bring it up now and stress the complexity of it, with so many troops and so much food and other freight being diverted to their confinement and care. Just how villainously difficult the question would eventually become, I then, of course, had no premonition of.

The issue of pulling out was settled quickly. With his customary incisiveness, President Truman decided that the United States would evacuate the peninsula only if we were forced out by military necessity. He left with MacArthur the authority to withdraw his forces if he felt he must, either to insure the safety of his command or to accomplish his basic mission, the defense of Japan.

We still had to prepare, however, for a deep retirement that might even drive us back upon Pusan. Our knowledge of enemy strength was still incomplete and he was boasting daily on his radio that he meant to push us into the sea. This time I wanted no makeshift perimeter nor porous defense. So I assigned Brigadier General Garrison H. Davidson (later Lieutenant General and

Superintendent of West Point), an engineer officer before pro-
motion to general's rank, to the job of laying out a defense line far
to the south, covering the Pusan port area. Using many thousands
of Korean labor, Davidson then undertook to mark out a deep
defensive zone, dig much of the trench system, select artillery
positions, and actually erect barbed wire. I had flown the chosen
trace at a low altitude and was satisfied that we could hold fast in
that zone in the event we ever had to occupy it. A few weeks
after my first examination of the area I flew the "Davidson Line"
once more and was deeply impressed with the speed and effectiveness with which the job was being completed. We never did have
to occupy those positions nor test those defenses, some two hundred miles to our rear. But I cannot say the work went for
naught. After my first irritation I found a certain wry satisfaction
in the fact that the impoverished peasantry thereabouts had filched
nearly all the sandbags to bolster their own walls and dikes and
had "liberated" most of the barbed wire, a precious commodity to
them, as anything marketable was bound to be.

Most of these matters concerned me only after the Chinese
offensive had forced us to pull back over the Han. In my first
days in command this forthcoming action by the enemy occupied
my mind almost completely. It jumped off as expected, on New
Year's Eve after extensive artillery preparation, and amid the wild
sound of Chinese bugles and screaming threats in makeshift and
ribald English. The reports that came to me through the night
clearly indicated that the attack was in great strength and that we
might not be able to contain it. Fortunately, we had our rearward
positions organized and at this time I still had hopes that we
would be able to inflict severe punishment on the enemy by
strong counterattacks.

On New Year's morning I drove out north of Seoul and into
a dismaying spectacle. ROK soldiers by truckloads were streaming
south, without order, without arms, without leaders, in full retreat.
Some came on foot or in commandeered vehicles of every sort.
They had just one aim—to get as far away from the Chinese as
possible. They had thrown their rifles and pistols away and had

abandoned all artillery, mortars, machine guns, every crew-served weapon.

I knew the futility of trying to stop a mass flight of frightened men when I could not even speak their language. But I had to make the effort. I leaped out of my jeep and stood in the middle of the road waving my arms over my head to flag down an approaching truck. The first few dodged by me without slowing down but I did soon succeed in stopping a group of trucks all carrying ROK officers. The group in the advance truck listened without comprehension and would not obey my gestures. Soon the whole procession was rolling again. The only effective move now was to set up straggler posts far to the rear, manned by our own MPs under officer command, to try to regain control. This method worked. The routed forces were reorganized into units, rearmed, fed, and sent off under their own officers to occupy new sectors. Most of them, thereafter, fought well, as do most courageous men when they are well-trained and properly led. (I never could blame the untried ROKs who fled the enemy armor in the first few days of the war. There are few things more monstrous or more terrifying on first view than a hostile tank, its gun smoking and seeming to point right at your head, roaring and banging through every obstacle to overtake and destroy you. I have even seen American troops throw down their rifles and flee to the woods when tanks roared down on them—in *maneuvers* on friendly soil, and the tanks armed only with blanks.)

A battalion of the U.S. 19th Infantry had also been caught up into an untidy retreat when the ROKs next to them had broken. I interviewed some of the wounded of this battalion in the Divisional casualty clearing station that morning and found them thoroughly dispirited, without the eagerness to rejoin the unit that American fighting men, when not too severely wounded, usually show. We were obviously a long way from building the will to fight that we needed.

In general the Eighth Army had fallen back in good order and with almost all its equipment. But our situation now was dangerous indeed. At our backs we had the Han, an unfordable river, choked with huge cakes of floating ice, which might tear loose the pontoons of our only two bridges, particularly when acted on by the strong tides that still controlled the river at a point above Seoul. Jammed into a tight bridgehead on the north bank of the Han, we had more than a hundred thousand UN and ROK troops with all their heavy equipment including British Centurion tanks and U.S. 8-inch howitzers. And pressing upon us was the imminent possibility that panic-stricken refugees by the thousands might overwhelm our bridge guards and hopelessly clog our bridges—while enemy artillery, if resolutely pushed forward at night, might soon have the crossings within range.

In discussions with our two U. S. Corps Commanders, with the ROK Army Chief of Staff and with the Chief of KMAG, it became clear that a combination of enemy frontal attack and deep envelopment around our wide-open east flank, where the ROK had fled in panic, could soon place the entire army in jeopardy. I had not yet found sufficient basis for confidence in the ability of the troops to hold their positions, even if they were ordered to. Consequently I asked our ambassador, on January 3, to notify President Rhee that Seoul would be once more evacuated and that withdrawal from our forward positions would begin at once.

I also informed the Ambassador and what part of the ROK government still remained in Seoul that from 3 P.M. on, the bridges and main approach and exit roads would be closed to all but military traffic. All official government vehicles would have to clear before that hour and there would be no civilian traffic permitted from then on.

It is, of course, one thing to issue an order and quite another to have it obeyed. I could take no chances of failure to execute this order, so I undertook to bolster the ordinary Military Police control. Having great faith in the Assistant Division Commander of the 1st Cavalry Division, Brigadier General (later General) Charles D. Palmer, I placed him in personal charge at the bridge site with full authority to use in my name whatever measures were needed to keep the Eighth Army traffic flowing. Just how these hundreds of thousands of frightened refugees would react when told to get off the only road and bridge that led to safety no one could predict. My specific orders to General Palmer therefore

95

were to instruct his MPs that if civilians refused to stay clear of the highway, the MPs were to fire over the heads of the refugees, and if this failed to stay the tide, the MPs were, as a last resort, to use their weapons directly against the offenders.

The Koreans, being a docile people who had long before learned to live with hardship, obeyed the orders quietly and there was never a need for even a threat of force. But I have often shuddered to imagine what might have happened had this pitiful horde, hundreds of thousands of them, some with their entire household packed in A-frames on their patient backs, yielded to the terror that must have gripped them. The scene is one that shall always live in my mind: men, women and children, patriarchs with storybook beards, grandmothers carried on their sons' backs like children, stolidly waiting their turn in the dusk and the near-zero cold, without a destination except some spot far away from the Chinese, with nothing left to them beyond what they could carry, a terrible procession of the meek and the disinherited bound only to escape the terrors of Communism and to cling to the freedom so briefly known.

I stayed on the scene, at the north end of the main bridge, until dark, watching the long slow parade of foot soldiers, trucks, tanks, self-propelled weapons, and carriers of every sort. When the big 8-inch howitzers and the Centurion tanks came along my heart rose into my throat and remained there while the bridge sagged deep in the rushing water. A combat-loaded Centurion tank, I knew, exceeded the rated tonnage capacity of the bridge. But the bridge held and the last of the heavy armor moved safely to the south bank. It was full dark, and behind me the patient swarm of refugees had begun to stir like a legendary beast come alive, when I crossed the bridge in my own jeep, squeezed in among vehicles of every type, to proceed to a temporary overnight CP at Yongdong-po.

South of the Han, the Eighth Army, its equipment intact and with room for maneuver, took up strong defensive positions, with two of the Army's three U. S. Corps (the X Corps was still assembling in the south) and two ROK Corps holding a line on good defensive ground. Soon X Corps' strength would be available. The

1st Marine Division, and the U.S. 2nd, 3rd, and 7th Divisions would all be back at fighting strength too and ready to help deal out severe punishment to any hostile forces attempting a further advance.

But before going on the offensive, we had work to do, weaknesses to shore up, mistakes to learn from, faulty procedures to correct, and a sense of pride to restore. GHQ in Tokyo, the entire military establishment at home, and the Japan Logistical Command were all working at forced draft now to meet our needs. Gradually our armor and artillery were strengthened and our ranks began to fill up with well-trained replacements. More and better rations were delivered. Field medical and surgical services were raised to top level, and became the finest any army had ever owned in the field. Selected superior officers took over command of regiments and battalions and soon corrected the basic weaknesses in our training.

I was still much concerned with restoring the Army's fighting spirit, a quality that cannot be imposed from above but that must be cultivated in every heart, from private on up. It is rooted, I believe, in the individual's sense of security, of belonging to a unit that will stand by him, as units on both sides and in the rear stand by all other units too. Good training should help a soldier get rid of that awful sense of alone-ness that can sometimes overtake a man in battle, the feeling that nobody gives a damn about *him*, and that he has only his own resources to depend on. Americans, I think, are often more self-sufficient than soldiers of other nations. But still they need help in cultivating that assurance that they belong to a group that will return their loyalty no matter what danger threatens.

When I took over the Eighth Army, the Forward Command Post was, for reasons undoubtedly sound at the time the site was chosen, situated in a large city on the extreme west flank while the Eighth Army Main was 150 miles behind the zone of fire. A Battle CP does not belong in a large building in a city, for such a location tends to separate the headquarters men and the men in troop units—mentally as well as physically. Officers and men at higher headquarters then find it almost impossible to identify with the troops they are there to serve. As a consequence it is impossible ever to attain that mutual respect and confidence which is so vital an ingredient of military success.

In those first few weeks after we had been forced out of Seoul, I kept my personal forward command group at an absolute minimum. There were my two splendid aides: Walter Winton, with whom I had shared service throughout World War II and later in the Caribbean Command; and Joe Dale, whom I was lucky enough to have found already in Korea. Then there were my one orderly, a driver for my personal jeep, and a driver and operator for my radio jeep. I knew it was no source of joy or comfort to General Milburn of the I Corps to have the Army Commander under foot at all times; but I felt as a stopgap arrangement it was best for my small group to camp and bivouac with his forward CP. And he was patient and generous with us. This arrangement meant we did not need to take a single additional man from the already too thinly populated combat units under my command. We were able to dispense with security guards and mess personnel and we had instant access to Corps' communications and intelligence nets.

In about six weeks after that afternoon when I watched the last Centurion tank inch its perilous way across the Han, we had telephone cables and other tele-communications facilities all in place and I opened up the Army forward CP on a bare bluff at Yoju, about one-third of the way across the peninsula, generally behind the U.S. IX Corps, and equidistant from the advance CPs of the U.S. I Corps in the west and the U.S. X Corps, by then in the line, in the east. This in a sense became my home for the remainder of my period of command of the Eighth Army.

My living arrangements were simple indeed and we owned few comforts not available to all troops except those in actual contact with the enemy. There were two small tents, each about 8′ by 12′, placed end to end to create a sort of two-room apartment. One tent held my cot and sleeping bag, a small table, a folding chair, a wash basin, and a small gasoline heater stove where I often sought comfort for half-frozen hands and feet after a day in the jeep. The other tent held another small table, with two folding chairs drawn close to it and the plywood panel that held the excellent relief map of the battle area, a priceless asset that had been prepared for me by the Army Map Service of the U. S. Corps of Engineers.

I am sure that any man who has ever been at war in a cold climate, or who has ever worked long hours outdoors in wild country can understand the attachment I developed for this primitive little hideout. Great horror as war itself is, every honest soldier knows that it has its moments of joy—joy in the fellowship of one's fighting comrades, joy and pride in the growth of a fighting spirit and the conviction of invincibility that shines out of the faces of well-led and well-disciplined troops; and the small but treasured joy of a warm fire and a plain hot meal at the end of a cold and difficult day. I never think of Korea now without recalling a freezing day in an open jeep, where the cold had seeped into my toes from the steel flooring and inched up through my socks until my feet had turned into wooden clogs loosely hinged to my ankles—and then the welcome panting warmth of my little stove and the feeling as I gratefully took that cup of steaming tea in both hands and lifted it to my lips. It would be a whole minute often before my lips drew back blood enough so I could do more than mumble my appreciation.

The spot itself was as pleasant as any spot in a war-scarred country can ever be. My tents had been pitched on the bare banks of the Han above the nearly dry stream bed, with only the sound of small living creatures around me, when the planes and the guns were still. There was no city traffic, no village near to enrich the air with the thick and fruity smell of spoiled cabbage and human excrement. I could sit there undisturbed, poring over my map, reading reports, and concentrating with my aides entirely on the job of plannning tactical operations and working to improve the lot and the spirit of the men who were fighting the war. On the wide gravel shoulder of the river's flood bank we soon had a light-plane landing strip, which the engineers later enlarged so my four-engined B-17 could land, pick me up, and fly me on the longer hops, such as the one to the Eighth Army Main at Taegu, where that CP remained during the whole period of my command of the Eighth Army.

Perhaps the chief advantage I derived from the isolation of my new command post was the opportunity provided for quiet hours of intense map study and for uninterrupted concentration on tactical plans for the Eighth Army. It has long been my conviction that a conscientious commander must understand precisely what the circumstances are under which his command must operate, and particularly what obstacles or advantages the terrain offers. To that end I spent many hours before my relief map, supplemented by low-level flights over the disputed area, until I felt that I could find my way around the territory in the night. Every road, every cart track, every hill, every stream, every ridge in that area where we were fighting or which we hoped to control—they all became as familiar to me as the features of my own backyard. Thus, when I considered sending a unit out into a certain sector I knew if it involved infantrymen crawling up 2000-foot ridges with their weapons, ammunition, and food on their backs or whether they could move heavy equipment in, could ford the streams, or could find roads where wheeled vehicles could advance.

Never in all my career had I held a position comparable to the one I now found myself in, as far as responsibility was concerned. In my combat service in Europe, my unit had always been part of a still larger command. In the Normandy invasion, the greatest single military operation of all time, I was a Division Commander in Joe Collins' VII Corps, which was in turn a part of Bradley's First Army. In the Battle of the Bulge, I was commanding a Corps, yet mine was only one of several Corps in General Courtney H. Hodges' First Army, and that in turn was successively a part of Field Marshal Montgomery's 21st Army Group, or of General Omar Bradley's Twelfth Army Group. There was plenty of room for local initiative in both campaigns, yet there was always some higher commander immediately in the rear, with greater resources, with the authority to use them to further the effort of the team as a whole. If I found myself in trouble in those circumstances, there was always a higher-up to whom I could turn for immediate help.

In Korea, there was a higher-up of course—General MacArthur.

30. Marine fires on enemy during street fighting in Seoul, September 20, 1950. *U.S. Army photograph.*

31. U.S. tanks move through a street in Seoul during an offensive against the North Koreans, September 25, 1950. *U.S. Army photograph.*

32. Left to right, Major General Doyle O. Hickey, Deputy Chief of Staff, GHQ; Syngman Rhee, President of the Republic of Korea; General of the Army Douglas MacArthur, Commander in Chief, UN Command; Mr. John Muccio, United States Ambassador to Korea; Vice Admiral Arthur D. Struble, and Major General Edward M. Almond confer in the Capitol building, Seoul, after ceremonies restoring the capital of Korea to its president, September 29, 1950. *U.S. Army photograph.*

33. The USS *Missouri* bombarding Chongjin with her 16-inch guns, October 21, 1950. The *Missouri* was an element of a powerful naval task force that moved up the north coast of Korea and shattered the Chongjin area, only thirty-nine miles from the Chinese border. *Official U.S. Navy photo.*

34. Railroad yards and docks at Pusan, South Korea. *U.S. Army photograph.*

35. Fairchild C-119 Flying Boxcars drop troops and supplies to intercept the north-ward retreat of North Korean troops forced out of the enemy capital of Pyongyang. The drop was made between the North Korean cities of Sukchon and Sunchon on October 20, 1950. *U.S. Air Force photo.*

36. North Korean prisoners, guarded by ROK soldiers, waiting at Wonsan airfield to be evacuated. *Official U.S. Navy photo.*

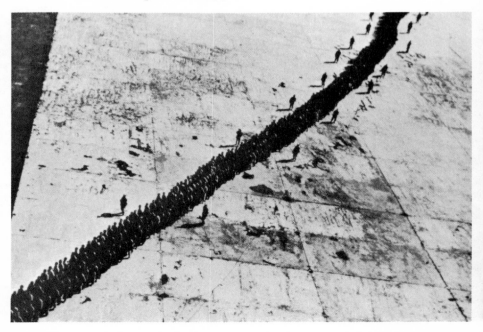

37. Rocket men of the U.S. Marines fire a 3.5-inch launcher M20 against enemy units dug in on the hills in North Korea, November 3, 1950. *Defense Department photo, Marine Corps.*

38. Marine units along a road near Yudam-ni, just west of the Changjin (Chosin) Reservoir. The Marines, who had hurled back a surprise onslaught by three Communist divisions, have just heard that they are about to withdraw. In five days and nights, from November 28 to December 3, with the temperature dropping to twenty-five degrees below zero, they fought their way through masses of Chinese troops to Hagaru-ri, on the southern tip of the reservoir, where they regrouped for the epic forty-mile fight through snow and ice down mountain trails to the sea, burying their dead, carrying out their wounded, and retaining their equipment. *Defense Department photo, Marine Corps.*

39. Marines assemble before starting their withdrawal from the Changjin (Chosin) reservoir area. *Defense Department photo, Marine Corps.*

OPPOSITE
40. Marines guard a road against enemy attack as others of the unit prepare to evacuate the Koto-ri area. *Defense Department photo, Marine Corps.*

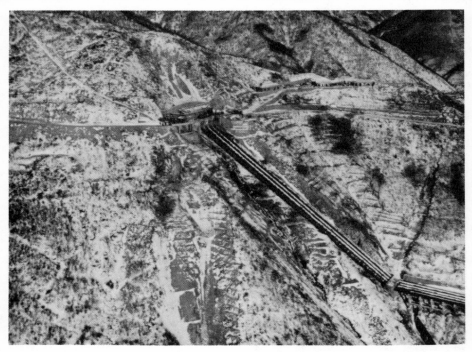

41. Area near the Changjin (Chosin) Reservoir, showing the narrow, winding road and the electric power station, where Marines were delayed until a parachuted bridge was assembled and put in place. On December 11, after a thirteen-day fight, the UN forces broke out of the Communist trap and emerged from the hills of northeast Korea onto the plains of Hamhung. *Defense Department photo, Marine Corps.*

42. Houses burning near Sibyon-ni as UN forces evacuate under heavy assault by Chinese forces, December 10, 1950. *U.S. Army photograph.*

As Commander in Chief of the United Nations Forces he had full authority over my ground forces and over the sea and air forces in the Pacific Theater. But he had no additional troops with which to come to my aid, should I request reinforcements. And he was in Tokyo, 700 miles away. At first, with so much to do and so little time to accomplish it in, I had no time to stand back and look at my situation. It was only after several breathless weeks that I realized the full import of MacArthur's remark to me on December 26: "The Eighth Army is yours, Matt. Do what you think best."

The Navy, I knew, would continue to dominate the sea lanes all around us. The Air Force and Navy and Marine aviation would retain mastery of the skies. But in good weather and in bad, in daylight and in darkness, come success or disaster, the responsibility for the safety of the ground forces—U.S., UN, and ROK—was mine alone. There were no reserve forces that might be deployed to help me, no higher authority to bring in new strength from another theater. All that I had was what was already at hand. There would be no more.

General MacArthur had given me full tactical control, which he never abridged, and all the authority a military commander could ask for. It was the sort of challenge—and opportunity—that I suppose every dedicated military man dreams may some day be his. Conscious as I was of the honor such an assignment carried with it, I could not allow my pride to blind me to the full weight of the responsibility.

The very first task I set myself was restoring the fighting spirit of the forces under my command. This meant, in addition to developing confidence in the commander's concern for the safety of every individual soldier, the recruitment of confidence in the soundness of the top commander's decisions. In combat, every unit commander is absorbed in the accomplishment of his own mission. Be he in command of a squad, a platoon, a company, or any unit all the way up to Corps, his assigned task requires all the professional competence, all the physical energy, and as much strength of spirit as he possesses. He has no time to concern himself with how the higher-ups are carrying out their assignments. And it is often natural that the commanders of the smaller units—from squad up through battalion—should feel that the higher commanders have a relatively simple task—that they just draw lines on a map with a broad black crayon, to mark out objectives, zones of action, boundaries, and phase lines; and that they issue their orders with no understanding of the difficulties provided by weather, terrain, problems of supply and communication, or strength of the opposing forces. The higher-ups, they may sometimes suspect, just press the buttons and leave the commanders of the smaller units to figure out how the impossible may be accomplished.

But in truth, the larger the command, the more time must go into planning; the longer it will take to move troops into position, to reconnoiter, to accumulate ammunition and other supplies, and to coordinate other participating elements on the ground and in the air. To a conscientious commander, time is the most vital factor in his planning. By proper foresight and correct preliminary action, he knows he can conserve the most precious element he controls, the lives of his men. So he thinks ahead as far as he can. He keeps his tactical plan simple. He tries to eliminate as many variable factors as he is able. He has a firsthand look at as much of the ground as circumstances render accessible to him. He checks each task in the plan with the man to whom he intends to assign it. Then—having secured in almost every instance his subordinate's wholehearted acceptance of the contemplated mission and agreement on its feasibility—only then does he issue an order.

The flow of battle may sometimes change conditions or create new tasks no amount of advance planning could have allowed for. Then the success or failure of the entire mission may well depend on the resourcefulness, the training, the alertness, the decisiveness of the leaders of even the smallest units. The ability to make prompt decisions and to execute them vigorously is best bred in men who, through confidence in their troops and in their superiors, have persuaded themselves that they are unbeatable. Unrelenting attention to detail, concern for the well-being of every member of every unit, painstaking checking out of each assignment with the men charged with performing it—all these help instill that self-confidence, that sense of belonging to a tightly organized and well-led organization, the feeling that can give momentum to a whole force and make it truly unconquerable.

I concerned myself with petty matters too, some of which may seem at a distance to be trifling in the extreme but all of which have a cumulative value in building esprit. For instance, when I first took a meal at the Eighth Army Main, I was shocked at the state of the linen and tableware—bedsheet muslin on the tables, cheap ten-cent-store crockery to serve the food in. Not that I personally fretted over whether I ate off linen or linoleum. But this sort of thing, at the mess where VIPs from all over the world were sure to visit, struck me as reflecting a total lack of pride in the whole operation—a confirmation that this was indeed what it was sometimes called at home: the Forgotten War. I promptly got that dreary muslin swapped for serviceable linen and that crockery changed for presentable chinaware.

I made an effort, too, hampered though it was by more overriding considerations, to develop among the arms of the service a better understanding of what the other fellow was up against in getting his part of the job done. Civilians, conditioned by the headlines often given to some of the home-front quarrels among the branches of the service, may have believed there was a permanent petty war going on among the Army, Navy, and Air Force, erupting daily in jealous bickerings. It is true that there are deep-rooted interservice differences that break out occasionally in seemingly bitter exchanges. But they are the product of honest convictions by honorable men of broad experience and lifetime service, each to his own arm, and manifestations of a deeply justified pride in all that their respective services have contributed to the growth and the security of the country. These apparent "differences" emanate almost entirely from the widely published headlines often given to the remarks of men at the highest levels of command. They are endemic in Washington. But in an overseas combat zone these "differences" almost never arise. Had I ever been tempted to believe otherwise, I would have been corrected every day, for not a day went by during my service in Korea when General Earle E. (Pat) Partridge, commanding the Fifth

Air Force, did not call me to ask, "What can we do for you today?" And Admirals Thackrey, Doyle, and Struble would make the same inquiry whenever opportunity offered.

My plan, which was carried out in some degree, was to effect an interchange of senior noncommissioned officers and petty officers, with sailors joining the ground forces for a spell to see what it was like to carry your supplies all on your back up a rugged hilltop under enemy fire, to hang on to a forward position throughout a freezing night; with soldiers observing at firsthand the business of patrolling a wintry sea, every wave offering to knock you loose from your hand hold; or discovering the perils of trying to clean a flight deck of snow in the pre-dawn darkness with the rough sea keeping the deck continually aslant; or what perils our airmen faced as they flew their missions of interdiction or armed reconnaissance in every kind of weather. We did not do as much of this as we hoped, for we had a great deal of fighting to do that interfered with our plans. But those who did participate in this project developed a strong mutual respect that added its bit of strength to the over-all esprit de corps.

But it was not merely in the ranks that the winning spirit and the urge to take the aggressive needed to be cultivated. I was shocked, some time in late January, at the results of a Staff study I had requested concerning "the desirable location of major elements of the Eighth Army for the period February 20 to August 31, 1951." You must understand that I was thinking as I had right from the start, in terms of attack. The worst of the winter would be over by March and the heavy rains and heavy cloud cover normally expected in June, July, and August would turn large areas into mudholes, make many roads impassable, wash out culverts and bridges in the mountains and reduce the effectiveness of close air support. We would need to improve our positions markedly to enable us to move back toward the 38th parallel.

But the recommendations I received in a G-3-authenticated document, reported as having been cleared with G-2, G-4, the Engineers, and a representative of COMNAVFE and the Weather Section, Fifth Air Force, were for phased redeployment to positions south of the Sobaek Range. In effect, the study (still in my possession) urged that we should abandon all thought of going on the offensive, that we should hold our present positions until the winter was over, and then, before the summer rains came, withdraw to the very lodgment area from which the Inchon victory had set us free—the old Pusan perimeter. To have approved it would have been to surrender all initiative, an unthinkable course of action. I disapproved it at once.

Aware that I would not be reinforced, and conscious of the extreme difficulty of defending at this time a position north of the Han River, I made my immediate plans for a coordinated phased advance by both U. S. Corps—the I and the IX—for the purpose of developing the enemy situation on their front. (The U.S. X Corps had not yet come into the forward zone.) They were to be ready to advance to the Han if so ordered, and there to hold.

There were supposed to be 174,000 Chinese in front of us at that time, but where they were placed, in what state of mind, and even that they were there at all was something we could not determine. All our vigorous patrolling, all our constant air reconnaissance had failed to locate any trace of this enormous force. Dissatisfied with the meagerness of the intelligence that reached me, I felt that I must make a determined effort to detect the presence of large concentrations of hostile forces, if they existed, before I ordered the Eighth Army into its first offensive operation since its setback. Pat Partridge offered me a slow AT-6, an old advance trainer, with himself at the controls and a seat for me in back. We proceeded then to search the area from our own advance elements to a point some twenty miles deep in enemy-held territory. We flew at times at tree-top level and frequently below the barren ridges. Hardly a moving creature did we spot, not a campfire smoke, no wheel tracks, not even trampled snow to indicate the presence of a large number of troops. Obviously the only way we were ever going to remove the question mark from the goose egg was to advance into it. But this advance would be far different from the reckless and uncoordinated plunge toward the Yalu. Now all ground forces would be under a single command, with all major units mutually

105

supporting, and the entire Army under tight control. We started rolling forward on January 25 and the Eighth Army soon proved itself to be what I knew already it could become: as fine a fighting field army as our country had yet produced.

I received about this time a number of commendatory messages from Tokyo and Washington. But none I received gave me any deeper satisfaction than the comment of my own intrepid pilot, Eugene M. (Mike) Lynch, in one of our daily flights. Beneath us we watched the long columns of foot soldiers, artillery, tanks, trucks, and jeeps as they flowed back north once more to support the men on the fighting front. "You've certainly got this army fighting for you, General," he said. And they were indeed fighting again, but not for me. They were fighting for themselves, with pride rekindled, and with a determination that they would never again take the sort of licking they had accepted a month before. They were back in the traditional American role of dishing out more punishment than they had to take.

As it developed, we had bitter fighting ahead. About Lincoln's Birthday, the CCF began their fourth-phase offensive, with the aim, announced daily on their radio, of driving us into the sea. We had to give more ground and once more the U.S. 2nd Division took the full brunt of the Chinese blow, suffering heavy losses, particularly in its artillery, losses they sustained largely as a result of the panicky retreat of the ROK 8th Division, which collapsed in the face of a night assault and left the 2nd Division flank wide open. The ROKs, having suffered severely at the hand of the Chinese, were inclined to view the Communist soldiers with deep awe, bordering on superstition, and it took them a long time to cultivate a faith in their ability to stand off these night assaults. The sudden appearance right inside their positions of the sneaker-shod Communist soldiers would send many of the ROKs into headlong flight.

During the period January 31–February 18 the 2nd Division performed in the finest traditions of its service in both World Wars. Among the many tough engagements fought in those three weeks, none was conducted with greater skill, gallantry, and tenacity than that fought by the 23rd Regimental Combat Team (with the intrepid Monclar's* French battalion attached), Colonel (now General) Paul L. Freeman commanding. Operating throughout this CCF offensive in the "twin tunnels"-Chipyong-ni area some twenty miles northwest of Wonju, it was surrounded by five Chinese Communist divisions, which attacked repeatedly in an effort to break through its perimeter and annihilate it. It smashed all attacks, inflicting extremely heavy losses, with 2000 enemy dead reported to have been counted in front of its position. Immediately after an armored task force of the 1st Cavalry Division had forced its way in, and the Chinese had broken off their attacks, I flew into the position by helicopter and saw hundreds of the still-unburied enemy dead.

Despite the ferocity of the fighting and the apparent determination of the enemy, I never had the slightest doubt over the outcome of this battle. Whether I was on the ground with the forward elements or flying over them for a more comprehensive picture, I felt confident they would hold. And I believe the troops shared my conviction that this time the enemy attack was going nowhere.

Once this enemy effort had been contained, my next project was a powerful, limited-objective attack with two divisions forcing a crossing of the Han east of Seoul, with the aim of cutting enemy supply lines and enveloping hostile forces massed to the west. Originally I had seen no military advantage in the recapture of Seoul, as I did not feel we could operate effectively with an unfordable river at our backs. But General MacArthur had pointed out to me the value of recovering the use of the Kimpo Airfield and the port facilities of Inchon, to strengthen our air support and ease our supply problems. While General MacArthur agreed that the military value of Seoul was practically zero, he did remark to me the great psychological and diplomatic victory that would be ours if we could retake the city. I agreed with his criticisms

* The Battalion Commander, Lieutenant Colonel Ralph Monclar, as gallant and distinguished a combat soldier as France had ever produced, with every decoration his country could confer and seventeen times wounded in battle, had asked to be reduced in rank from lieutenant general to lieutenant colonel so that he could command this French Army unit.

and incorporated these suggestions into my planning. But my fundamental concept remained the same, that territory, as such, meant nothing to me except as its occupation might facilitate destruction of enemy forces and the protection of our own.

Between the end of January, when we were in full swing forward, and February 20, General MacArthur honored my command three times with personal visits, expressing each time complete satisfaction with our performance and our tactical plans. On February 20, at the time of his third visit, we met at Wonju, where I showed him an EYES ONLY memorandum that I had prepared that day to send to all Corps Commanders and to the ROK Chief of Staff, in which I outlined the facts upon which our planning was based, and the underlying purpose of all our operations, and particularly of the action then under consideration, the recrossing of the Han by two divisions. As to the facts: The strength, equipment status, morale and intentions of the four CC armies reported to be in the Pyongyang area remained undetermined. But reinforcements from this area might easily have been flowing south for some weeks to strengthen the forces with which we were now in contact, and could appear on the battleline almost any day. Beyond that, we had no intelligence, nor did I have any information not available to the commanders themselves. As for our purpose: It remained the infliction of maximum damage on the enemy with minimum to ourselves, the maintaining of all major units intact, and a careful avoidance of being sucked into an enemy trap—by ruse or as a result of our own aggressiveness— to be destroyed piecemeal. We were to pursue only to the point where we were still able to provide powerful support or at least manage a timely disengagement and local withdrawal.

This was the thinking upon which I had based my plan for the forthcoming offensive, which had been given the code name Operation Killer. I had planned this action personally on Sunday evening, February 18, two days before the visit of the Commander in Chief, and had outlined it to the Commanding Generals of the U.S. IX and X Corps and of the 1st Marine Division. It may be noted that this resumption of the offensive was the final implementation of the plan I had nourished from the time of my taking command of the Eighth Army—and had done so it may be said in the face of a retreat-psychology that seemed to have seized every commander from the Chief on down.

You can imagine my surprise then and even my dismay at hearing the announcement General MacArthur made to the assembled press correspondents on February 20, the eve of the target date. Standing before some ten or more correspondents met at the X Corps Tactical Command Post, with me leaning against a table in the rear, MacArthur said calmly: "I have just ordered a resumption of the offensive." There was no undue emphasis on the personal pronoun, but the implication was clear: He had just flown in from Tokyo, had surveyed the situation, discussed it with his subordinates, and had then ordered the Eighth Army to attack. There had, of course, been no order at all concerning any part of the operation from CINCFE or from the GHQ staff in Tokyo. Naturally MacArthur had been informed in detail of my intentions, but neither he nor his staff had had any part in the conception or in the planning of Operation Killer.

It is not so much that my own vanity took an unexpected roughing up by this announcement as that I was given a rather unwelcome reminder of a MacArthur that I had known but had almost forgotten. It undoubtedly did me good on both counts. Very soon afterward I was obliged to make note of another of the Commander in Chief's efforts to keep his public image always glowing. This time I felt called upon to interfere, for there was definite danger connected with it. It had long been MacArthur's habit, whenever a major offensive was about to jump off, to visit those elements of his command that were involved and, figuratively, to fire the starting gun. In general this is an admirable practice. The over-all commander's personal presence has an inspiring effect upon the troops. And invariably the best impressions of the temper of the men under his command are gained through the commander's own eyes and ears. Normally such visits by commanders are made with little or no chance of their becoming known to the enemy until well after they have taken place.

But in this instance, the pattern of MacArthur's flight from Tokyo and appearance at the fighting front every time a major operation was to be initiated had been well established. And the flights themselves were made with such ceremony that knowledge of them was almost certain to reach the enemy. Whether such knowledge would reach the enemy in time for him to react became a major concern of mine when we were about to jump off on the second general offensive, Operation Ripper, which, if successful, would take us back to the 38th parallel and beyond. I well understood that a protest on my part could be considered an act of disrespect, a withdrawing of the welcome mat, or an intrusion upon my superior's prerogatives. Yet I felt I had to speak up and so I put in a long session of carefully choosing my words, then sent a lengthy message that conveyed my views. Here the Commander in Chief showed another side of his remarkable character. He accepted the message with quick understanding, with no mistaking of the spirit in which it was sent, and at once postponed his next visit until after the offensive was well under way.

Before proceeding, I should like to offer an interesting footnote to Operation Killer that will give a hint of how varied are the political pressures under which a major war is waged. When the code name Operation Killer, which I had chosen, was imparted to the Pentagon, there was a quick but courteous protest from Joe Collins, Army Chief of Staff, pointing out that the word "killer" was deemed to have struck an unpleasant note as far as public relations was concerned. I did not understand why it was objectionable to acknowledge the fact that war was concerned with killing the enemy. Years later I was told that the objection had been prompted by Republican charges that the Truman administration had no other aim in Korea but to kill Chinese. (How reminiscent of Korea are the counts of enemy dead that appear every day in our newspapers.) In view of heavy United States casualties, it was felt that such a goal lacked political "sex appeal." Another explanation offered me was that while the killing of Chinese might be an aim of considerable appeal to the Eighth Army Commander, it would not, from a strategic point of view, forestall future aggression by Peking. That could be done, MacArthur had propounded before the Senate Hearings, only by "destroying its power to wage war now." Behind this theory was the concept that "The index of modern war is not manpower but material."

But even now I am not convinced that the country should not be told that war means killing. I am by nature opposed to any effort to "sell" war to people as an only mildly unpleasant business that requires very little in the way of blood.

The Eighth Army spent a good deal of blood in fighting its way back to and across the Han, and in reinvesting the capital of Seoul, never to be dislodged again. But it spent far less than it might have, had we not stuck to our precepts of inflicting maximum casualties at minimum cost and of avoiding all reckless, unphased advances that might lead to entrapment by a numerically superior foe. Actually some of the actions were remarkable for the low casualty figure. One or two advances, in battalion strength or better, were made with no casualties at all, thanks to good planning, well-timed execution, close cooperation among units and above all to old-fashioned coordination of infantry, artillery, and air power.

The Chinese greatly outnumbered the UN forces, and could reinforce their front-line troops extensively. But our superior firepower more than redressed the balance. Heretofore we had not been taking advantage of this superiority, through lack of intensive training, through use of pursuit tactics that scattered our forces, or from allowing ourselves to grow roadbound. By February 1951, Field Artillery battalions that had been undergoing intensive training in the States and had long been earmarked for our use began to join the I and IX Corps, enabling those forces to return to normal old-fashioned tactics of coordinated action.

The really terrifying strength of our firepower, when used in concentrated fashion, was strikingly exemplified by the success of the IX Corps in clearing enemy forces from the Hoengsong-Wonju area, as a part of Operation Killer. These two centers, about halfway across the peninsula, and northeast of the Han, sit astride major highways and rail lines that provide important north-south links. The IX Corps fought from a line between Yang-pyang and Hujin. Within seven days an estimated 5000 Chinese had been killed in this area and we held undisputed possession.

A feature of the renewed offensive was the greatly improved performance of the ROK forces, certain elements of which fought as well as any troops in the Eighth Army command. There was still much lacking in the Korean leadership, for which we would have to pay dearly. But where the troops were well-led, their accomplishments spoke for themselves. During Operation Ripper, which opened on March 7, 1951, the 1st Battalion of the ROK 2nd Regiment annihilated an enemy battalion without losing a single man. A patrol having discovered an enemy concentration in front of the 1st Company, Major Lee Hong Sun, commanding the ROK battalion, ordered a surprise attack that was to be a double envelopment. The first company was to attack from the front while the second attacked from the left and the third from the right. The enemy detected the maneuver and attempted to withdraw, whereupon Major Sun ordered an immediate attack. The ROK troops themselves were astonished at the swiftness of their advance. Inexorably, they pushed ahead, mowing the enemy down unmercifully and sustaining no casualties of their own. When the fighting was over, 231 enemy dead lay on the field and the ROK battalion had taken a great store of functioning equipment, including four artillery pieces and seven mortars.

More striking successes lay ahead, although there was much small-unit action and the advance was often inch-by-inch. In mid-March the Eighth Army succeeded in making a surprise crossing of the broad Han River east of Seoul and seized a mountain ridge facing west across and dominating the valley where ran the main supply and communications route for enemy forces in the Seoul sector. I had personally planned and ordered this tactical operation and I was on hand to observe its jump-off, at first on the ground with the forward infantry elements of the U.S. 25th Division and later from my light L-19 plane, piloted as always by the intrepid and indefatigable Mike Lynch.

As our infantry worked its way up the valley of the Pukhan River, Mike and I flew up and down until we spotted a place in the dry gravel flood plain of the river where we could set the plane down. Then I stepped out and walked among the men who were leading the attack. This never failed to provide me with a deep inner satisfaction and I believe it always had a heartening effect too upon the troops, who were always glad to see the "old man" up with them when the going was rough. It also gave me a chance to judge the progress of the operation and to learn at firsthand what I might do to help.

The operation met with swift and complete success, with hardly a single casualty. And it brought just the results I had hoped for— and which I had outlined to the gathered war correspondents the night before: By pointing a dagger at the enemy's heart-line, actually at the brain of the enemy commander, it forced him to choose between attacking us at tremendous disadvantage to himself (inasmuch as we controlled the high ground) or abandoning the South Korean capital. On March 14, a patrol from the ROK 1st Division was sent across the Han River west of Seoul to feel out the defenses of the city. It moved north for several miles before it drew any hostile fire. That night another patrol probed the outer defenses of the city and found them nearly abandoned. On the morning of March 15, the Eighth Army moved in and once more raised the ROK flag over the ancient and battered city. The remnants of the population, ragged, hungry, sick, and scared, were there to greet us—perhaps 200,000 of what had been originally a population of a million and a half. The shopping district had been demolished by air and artillery fire, all the lights were out, the light poles down and the wires dangling, and the streetcars had long since ceased to move. Yet before two weeks were out, a new city government had been established and the city throbbed with life again. (In General Eisenhower's book, *Mandate for Change,* he reports that Seoul was recaptured after General James A. Van Fleet had taken over the Eighth Army. This is untrue. General Van Fleet did not assume command until more than a month after we had retaken Seoul, which thereafter remained in our hands.)

The aim of Operation Ripper, however, was not merely to recover the capital city or to occupy new ground. It was primarily to seize or destroy enemy personnel and equipment. In this respect it was not wholly successful, for the enemy fought delaying actions only, as he pulled his forces rapidly northward. Weather and terrain gave us more trouble than enemy action, particularly in the central zone, where mountain peaks thrust into the clouds and precipitous slopes dropped into valleys hardly wide enough for a cart road. Enemy strong points, perched high on the barren summits, had to be enveloped and carried by assault.

The spring thaws and rains made roads into rice paddies, so that supplies had to be hauled on soldiers' backs or in their arms. Front-line troops made do with the bare essentials, until air-drops were able to supply them. Helicopters were useful too in lifting out wounded men who would otherwise have been carried in stretchers for two days before reaching jeep ambulances that could move them to the hospital.

Activity in the rear areas slowed our advance too, for remnants of the North Korean 10th Division still managed to operate in the rugged Chungbon Mountains some twenty-five miles behind our lines. Throughout mid-March, groups from this division would enter our positions from the rear, fight their way through, and flee to the north.

A special prize in Operation Ripper was the town of Chunchon, an important supply and communications point in the center of a basin that is laced with good roads. Our intelligence reports had led us to believe that the enemy had built up a large store of supplies in this town, which lay just behind the main muscle of his February offensive against our center. We expected a bitter fight for this town and we got it. In contrast to his actions at other points along the front, where we often encountered only light screening forces well ahead of the main line of defense, the enemy here fought from bunkers dug deep into the hillsides, and almost impregnable against aircraft and artillery attack. The U. S. Marines often had to pry the enemy loose from his hold with bayonets. We first planned a drop by the 187th Airborne Regimental Combat Team to take the city, but as Operation Ripper moved forward swiftly on other fronts, the enemy pulled back rapidly and we soon decided that the air-drop would gain us little. Our patrols began to move into Chunchon on March 19 and Mike Lynch and I flew over the city just as the patrols were entering. Chunchon, while battered, seemed in fairly usable shape, its streets not cratered and only a little debris cluttering the ways. Mike and I circled until we found a street that seemed long and straight enough for a landing strip. The only problem was provided by some still-hanging telephone lines on high poles at one end of the street. After two or three passes, Mike decided he could come in under the wires without trouble and set the plane down safely. In we coasted and came to a stop in the deserted town. We had spotted a jeep patrol as we were circling and I set out immediately on foot in search of it. It turned out to be a 1st Cavalry Division Engineer patrol which, when I approached, was checking a major bridge to disarm any demolition charge the enemy might have placed. They were surprised to find the bridge undamaged and unwired. But when they looked around to discover the Army Commander peeking over their shoulders they were really astonished, hardly knowing how to react. Mike and I enjoyed their confusion for a while, were disappointed to discover that the enemy had left the cupboard utterly bare, and took off finally without having drawn any hostile fire.

The original objective of Operation Ripper had been the Idaho Line, which created a wide bulge east and north of Seoul, while the I Corps on the left flank and the ROK units on the extreme right largely maintained their positions, with the IX and X Corps crossing the Han and getting into a position to envelop the capital city. With the attainment of this objective and our failure to destroy a sufficient number of the enemy, I enlarged the operation to include a move to the west by the I Corps, with the Imjin River as its objective. This river, which flows south until it reaches the 38th parallel, runs a meandering course to the southwest at that point and empties into the Yellow Sea. In this move, the 187th RCT and two Ranger companies were dropped into zones near Munsan-ni, a town about twenty miles northwest of Seoul, in the hope that we might trap large enemy forces by blocking their movement along the Seoul-Kaesong road. An armored task force from the I Corps had been sent forward to provide the

hammer that would demolish the enemy against the anvil provided by the airborne troops. The enemy, however, had already
withdrawn and the advance to the Imjin River was made almost
without bloodshed. The next move then was to send the airborne
troops to the east to seize high ground behind the enemy troops
that faced the U.S. 3rd Division, in another effort to trap sizable
forces between hammer and anvil. This time it was the weather
that frustrated us. Heavy rains and melting snows mired our tanks
so that they could do nothing but pull out and return to Seoul.
And by the time the 187th RCT reached the commanding heights,
the enemy had pulled back still farther to the north.

Our advance had now brought us close to the 38th parallel
and we were faced once more with the decision as to whether
that mystic line—which was neither defensible nor strategically
important—should be crossed again. This time, Washington
deemed the decision a tactical one and, with General MacArthur's
approval, I chose to continue the advance. I was still not satisfied
with the destruction we had wrought upon the enemy, and I
wanted to leave him no time to regroup and recruit his strength.
It had become clear from all signs that the enemy was making
ready for a spring offensive and was engaged in a buildup far
to the rear of his current positions. Under the circumstances it
was better to keep him off balance than to sit and wait for him
to move. Consequently, we undertook a new attack, named Operation Rugged, to take us to a new objective—the Kansas Line,
which would run generally parallel and to the north of the 38th
parallel, except on the left, where it would follow the twists and
turns of the Imjin River to the sea.

This new line was to include the ten-mile water barrier of
the Hwachon Reservoir, formerly a source of water and power
for the city of Seoul and a serious threat, because of the possibility
of blowing the dam and overflowing the banks of the Pukhan
River, to our positions downstream. The enemy resistance was
uneven as we advanced toward this new line. Where the terrain
favored him, he dug in and fought. Where we could move rapidly,
he faded quickly away. The ground on the right was especially
difficult, with few roads and many rocky cliffs. But our forces

advanced steadily in every sector. On April 9, all the units on our left flank had reached the Kansas Line. On the right, the U.S. X and the ROK III Corps, struggling to overcome the difficulties of terrain and the lack of supply routes, were still moving toward the objective when the enemy opened several sluice gates on the dam at the foot of the Hwachon Reservoir. At first this seemed as if it might do us severe damage. The river rose several feet within an hour, washed out one engineer bridge, and forced us to swing a second one back to the shore to keep it from breaking up. We immediately sent a task force to seize the dam and immobilize the gate-opening machinery, but poor visibility, rugged terrain, tenacious enemy resistance and a lack of landing craft spelled failure for this attempt. We decided at last that bombing the penstocks would lower the level of the reservoir enough to minimize the threat. Destroying the dam itself would have been a major engineering job. It seemed most unlikely that the enemy had either the time or the explosives to manage this. All the same it was a relief to watch the 1st Marine Division and some of the 1st Cavalry cross the wide reservoir in assault boats, powered by outboard motors. The craft had been painfully trucked up to the reservoir to put the Marines back in their proper element after weeks of fighting far from the water's edge. But it was not until April 16, after Van Fleet had arrived to take command, that the dam fell to us.

As we advanced to the Kansas Line we found the enemy everywhere in a defensive mood. But there were hints nonetheless that an offensive might be close at hand. Consequently it was my serious concern to keep the Eighth Army under close control, to prevent unphased advances that might lead to the mousetrapping of any of our forces. Our troops were confident and aggressive and in some sectors they moved forward so swiftly that there was a danger of their becoming victims of their own aggressiveness. I constantly reminded the field commanders of our essential aim— to deal out maximum damage at minimum cost.

I found occasion earlier, at the command conference just before Operation Ripper had been completed, to emphasize to all Corps and Division Commanders that official reports to the Army Commander should be specific in giving the locations and movements of all friendly units. Vague and carelessly worded reports, without dates, without times, without circumstantial details—weather, number of observers, etc.—could lead to foul-ups as serious as any that might be caused by enemy action. As an instance, I told the conference of observing a heavy attack by friendly planes upon a hill mass just north of Uijongbu that lasted all the time I was in the air in the vicinity—about fifteen or twenty minutes. Yet when I returned to my command post, I found a report by the I Corps that the 187th Airborne had been in possession of that hill all afternoon.

I recalled too a report from the IX Corps, 25th Division, to the effect that "Elements of the 5th Infantry were counterattacked and withdrew." No details at all. And when I did learn the facts, it developed that what had really happened was not a counterattack but merely an advance by a company-sized unit of the 5th Infantry against a hill and a withdrawal under fire, on the personal order of the Division Commander, who wanted to put artillery and airstrikes on the hostile forces there.

This sort of slipshod reporting, indicative of complacency, or inadequate supervision, or insufficient staff visits to front-line units was unforgivable in my book. If I was to maintain proper control of this army, reports to my headquarters were to be complete, truthful, and specific, with no glossing over of unpleasant facts and with sufficient details included to enable me to draw swift and proper conclusions.

I also bore down hard on the need for prompt launching of attacks, and for immediate reporting of when attacks were launched. Maximum coordination meant maximum adherence to official time table and direction. Like the football coach who drills his linemen to charge Together! Together! Together! I insisted that my commanders adhere strictly to schedule and maintain the direction of the attack. I knew that more attacks failed from neglect to maintain direction than from all other reasons combined. Power applied in the wrong direction could vitiate the whole effect of the action, as a wrongly directed drive by one wrestler against another can do the attacker himself more damage than it does the man attacked.

Communication was also accorded a top importance in all my planning. I wanted no more units reported "out of communication" for any extended period. We had liaison aircraft, with personnel specifically trained to pick up and drop messages. I once more urged a return to the methods of our ancestors: using runners, or smoke signals. I ordered my commanders to make a careful study of their instructions concerning the relaying of messages.

We also had to remain ready and alert in the event of an enemy parachute drop into our rear areas—a very real danger and a move of which the Chinese were entirely capable. This was a form of attack each unit commander had to be prepared for, within his designated area, just as he was responsible for meeting any kind of ground attack in a carefully marked out section of the area assigned to his Corps or Division. I ordered each major unit to divide up its area, right back to the rear boundaries, so that every unit commander knew exactly what ground was his to defend against attack of any sort.

Preparations like this were to pay priceless dividends in coming operations. The system of maintaining close contact with supporting units, of advancing on phase lines, and of buttoning up at night to prevent infiltration, kept us from falling into traps the enemy laid for us and enabled us to blunt the power of his final massive assault when it came. I urged upon each unit commander the importance of learning to strike a balance between boldness in moving to destroy the enemy forces and caution in conserving his own. As in every forward movement, there were always occasions for rapid exploitation of sudden successes. To seize these opportunities, while taking care never to render our forces unable to meet sudden serious threats from enemy action or weather changes—that was a problem requiring imagination and forethought.

In our first Korean successes, there had been insufficient thought given to the exploitation of sudden success, so valuable time was lost while we decided how best to move to cut off and destroy the fleeing North Korean army. From now on I wanted our major advances planned so thoroughly that each commander knew not only what he might do to cope with sudden disaster but how he might take maximum advantage of sudden success.

We did meet a number of successes as we pushed toward the Kansas Line in Operation Rugged, so much so that I became concerned with the elimination of overconfidence in the troops. The manner in which the Eighth Army had pulled itself off the ground, shaken itself, and struck back at the enemy had awakened a tremendous surge of confidence at home, where some optimists were seeing total victory around the corner. I wanted to quiet this feeling among the troops, lest another "Home-by-Christmas" (or Home-by-Fourth-of-July) type of spirit leave the front-line troops unprepared for the blows I knew still might fall. It was our job to keep self-confidence from mushrooming into foolhardiness. To this end, I met with two of the three U. S. Corps Commanders and with the Chief of Staff of the other Corps on April 1 to share with them my conviction that the hardest fighting and the most serious crisis that the Eighth had yet faced still lay ahead. Considering the enemy's immediate capability and declared intention, I felt that for several days it would take the utmost stoutness of heart and the deepest spiritual strength on the part of every soldier. Such spirit had to originate with the field commanders and find its way through the chain of command down to the troops. A fight against Communism might develop untold dimensions and our army had to be ready to face even greater dangers than any it had so far known. Our immediate task was to keep pressing the enemy so that he received no opportunity to reorganize until we had reached a line from which we could sustain our strongest fight.

Having reached the Imjin so easily, I had first thought to press on into the wide coastal plain that lay between the Imjin and the Yesong, the river that flowed down into the Yellow Sea west of the Imjin, just beyond Kaesong. New intelligence reports, however, indicated that this area held far fewer enemy forces than I had hoped. Only one North Korean Division remained there, while to the north of Kaesong two fresh Chinese Armies, the 63rd and 64th, not previously engaged, had been identified. These fresh armies would provide an extreme threat to my right flank if I did advance across the Imjin. Consequently I informed the Commander in Chief of the change in my original plan, to move instead, using I Corps and left-flank units of the IX Corps, in the direction of Chorwon, a town at the southwest corner of the Iron Triangle—the center of enemy strength, marked out by Pyonggang in the north at the apex, Kumhwa in the southeast and Chorwon in the southwest.

This meant a new objective line north of the Kansas Line— the Utah Line, really no more than a northward bulge in the Kansas Line to put us in a position to strike at the Iron Triangle. As we moved forward, the enemy fought more stubbornly. He set fire to brush and forests all along his front to screen his movements and to interfere with air support of our ground troops. But after the Hwachon Dam was seized, and the Korean I Corps had taken the town of Taepo-ri on the east coast, enemy resistance seemed to melt and we advanced to the Utah Line virtually without opposition.

Despite the inability of many of our front-line units to make contact with the enemy, evidence persisted that the Chinese were making ready to attack. Artillery and air observers reported a four- or five-thousand-man enemy force moving southeast, north of the line held by the IX Corps. The Chinese were preparing no further defense lines to the north and they were filling in the tank-traps that they had dug astride our advance.

I had no real fears that the Chinese would make good their boast to drive us into the sea or defeat us in the field. We now had a tested, tough, and highly confident army, experienced in this sort of fighting, inured to the vicissitudes of the weather, and possessed of firepower far exceeding anything we had been able to use on the enemy heretofore. The only development that could possibly cause us to withdraw from the peninsula was, I felt sure, massive intervention by the Soviets. In the spring of 1951, such intervention was not altogether an impossibility. Indeed an ominous report was furnished me by GHQ in late March that seemed to confirm some of the field intelligence that had reached me through the questioning of prisoners taken in our recent operations. The report passed on by GHQ was said to have originated with a former ambassador of a European nation to Turkey, a man of high integrity who insisted he had reliable information to the effect that a Soviet Far Eastern Committee, with the redoubtable Vyacheslav M. Molotov at its head, was planning a large-scale offensive in Korea toward the end of April. Extensive use would be made, according to this report, of Soviet aircraft and of regular Soviet troops of Mongolian extraction, under the guise of volunteers, while the Soviet Far East Command was under instructions to render all necessary assistance to insure victory, regardless of the risk of full-scale war.

It was impossible for me to confirm intelligence of this sort and I recommended to GHQ that Theater and National Intelligence agencies should intensify their efforts to ascertain the facts. I also urged that the Soviet Union be given solemn and unequivocal warning that any intervention in Korea, no matter how it was disguised, would be deemed an act of war. What came of my recommendations I never learned. On the other hand, we never found any evidence, when the fifth-phase offensive finally started, that Soviet forces were participating in any form.

But I wanted no looking over the shoulder on the part of this army and so I made clear, at the command conference already mentioned, that no retrograde movement was to be considered or discussed except by those who had the actual responsibility for advance planning to meet recognized enemy capabilities. I informed the Corps and Division Commanders present that I personally would direct instant initiation of a withdrawal *only* under the following assumptions:

(a) that the Soviets intervene with their military forces to their current capabilities;

(b) that the CCF and NKPA exercise their full capabilities at the same time;

(c) that all these efforts are timed to take maximum advantage of weather.

I had no doubt that under such circumstances a withdrawal would have the full approval of our government, which would in fact order it if we did not. An outline plan, drawn up by the

Army Staff in consultation with the Navy and the Air Force, was already in existence to face these contingencies and would be initiated, on my approval, on the flash dissemination of a single code name. The plan, once tentatively approved, was to be submitted to Corps Commanders for further development and at that time the Corps Commanders would be authorized to include in their deliberations the Division Commanders and a specified list of Divisional Officers, so that they too might be prepared to initiate their parts. But discussion of the plan or even knowledge of its existence was to go no further than the officers specifically designated.

If ever word were to leak out that withdrawal was even contemplated, defections on the part of ROK forces could be looked for. Nor could anyone blame them for making ready to live with a situation to which we might consign them. It was my feeling, too, and MacArthur agreed with me, that in the event of direct Soviet intervention and a decision to evacuate Korea, the evacuation order should be withheld until after the Eighth Army was south of the Sobaek Range. Otherwise ROK defections might leave us with both flanks exposed at a point where we could be enveloped and severely damaged.

Meanwhile of course we did not merely pull in our necks and wait for the blow to fall. We pushed on to the north and east, first to the Utah Line and then to an eastward extension of this bulge, designated the Wyoming Line. The next step would be to seize the high ground overlooking Chorwon. But before ever that move was made, the enemy came to life and halted the swift push forward. The fifth-phase offensive was ready to begin. Meanwhile, however, political developments suddenly overshadowed all the doings on the battlefield.

MAPS

Trans-Pacific Distances in Nautical Miles
North Korean Peoples Army Invasion and Exploitation
Landing at Inchon
UN Breakout and Link-up
Drive to Seoul
Chinese-North Korean Intervention Attack:
    First, Second, and Third Phase Offensives
The Chinese Intervene in the West
The Eighth Army Disengages
1st Marine Division Fights Its Way Out
UN Attack: Repulse of Chinese Fourth Phase Offensive
Chinese-North Korean Fifth Phase Offensive
Chinese and American Airfields

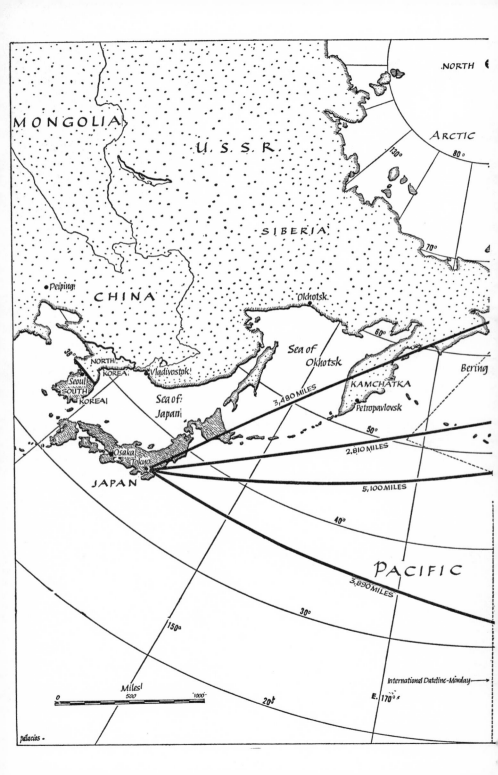

POLE

OCEAN

CANADA

UNITED
STATES

ALASKA
Fairbanks
Juneau
Anchorage

Seattle
Portland

San Francisco

1,540 MILES

1,960 MILES

2,360 MILES

Sea

Dutch
Harbor

ALEUTIANS

2,780 MILES

2,410 MILES

OCEAN

150°

MIDWAY

International Dateline-Sunday

HAWAII

Honolulu

170° W.

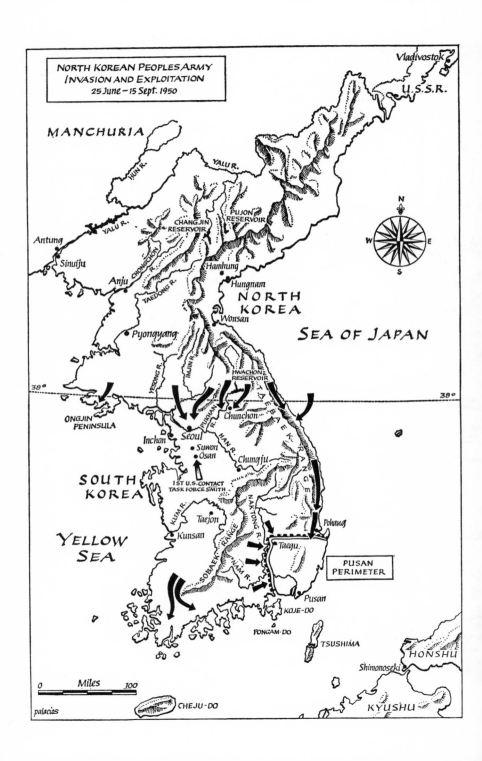

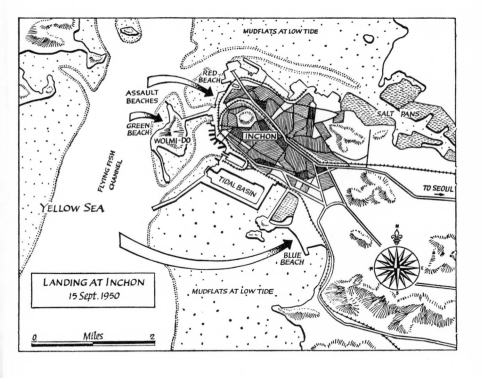

MUDFLATS AT LOW TIDE

RED BEACH

ASSAULT BEACHES

GREEN BEACH

WOLMI-DO

INCHON

SALT PANS

FLYING FISH CHANNEL

YELLOW SEA

TIDAL BASIN

TO SEOUL

BLUE BEACH

LANDING AT INCHON
15 Sept. 1950

MUDFLATS AT LOW TIDE

0   Miles   2

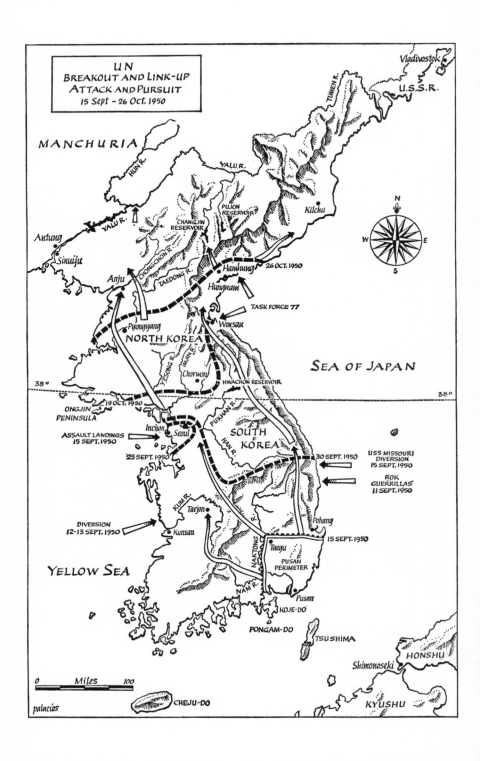

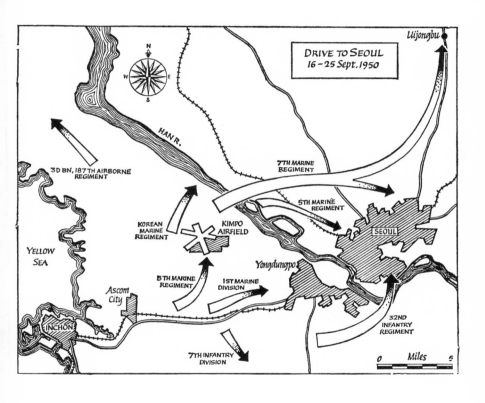

DRIVE TO SEOUL
16-25 Sept. 1950

Uijongbu

HAN R.

YELLOW SEA

3D BN, 187TH AIRBORNE REGIMENT

KOREAN MARINE REGIMENT

KIMPO AIRFIELD

7TH MARINE REGIMENT

5TH MARINE REGIMENT

SEOUL

Yongdungpo

5TH MARINE REGIMENT

1ST MARINE DIVISION

Ascom City

INCHON

7TH INFANTRY DIVISION

32ND INFANTRY REGIMENT

0   Miles   5

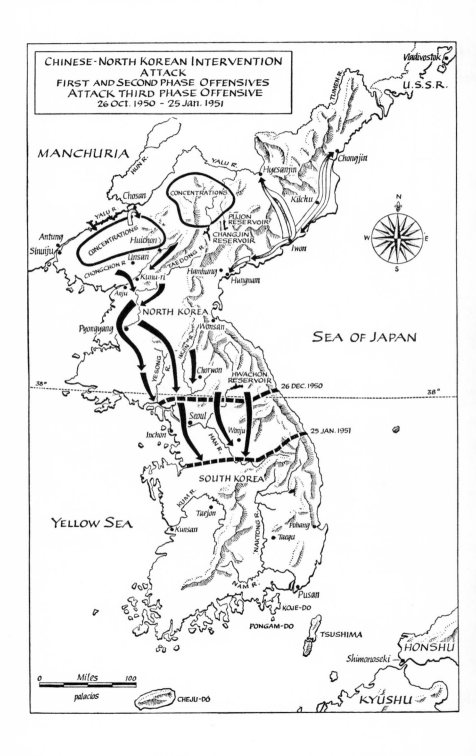

CHINESE-NORTH KOREAN INTERVENTION
ATTACK
FIRST AND SECOND PHASE OFFENSIVES
ATTACK THIRD PHASE OFFENSIVE
26 Oct. 1950 - 25 Jan. 1951

Vladivostok

U.S.S.R.

MANCHURIA

TUMEN R.

YALU R.

HUN R.

Chongjin

Hyesanjin

Chosan

CONCENTRATIONS

Kilchu

YALU R.

PUJON
RESERVOIR

CHANGJIN
RESERVOIR

Antung

CONCENTRATIONS

Huichon

Iwon

Sinuiju

CHONGCHON R.

Linsan

TAEDONG R.

Hamhung

Kunu-ri

Hungnam

Anju

NORTH KOREA

Pyongyang

Wonsan

SEA OF JAPAN

IMJIN R.

YESONG R.

Chorwon

HWACHON
RESERVOIR

38°   26 DEC. 1950   38°

Seoul

25 JAN. 1951

Inchon

Wonju

HAN R.

SOUTH KOREA

KUM R.

YELLOW SEA

Taejon

NAKTONG R.

Pohang

Kunsan

Taegu

NAM R.

Pusan

KOJE-DO

PONGAM-DO

TSUSHIMA

HONSHU

Shimonoseki

0   Miles   100

palacios

CHEJU-DO

KYUSHU

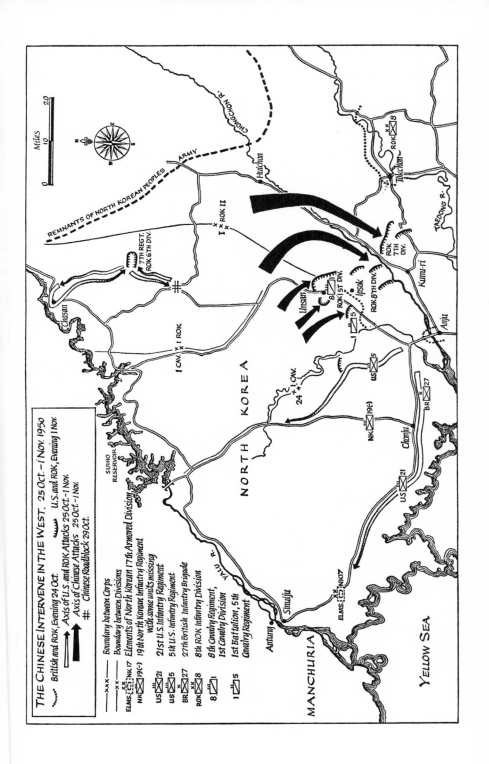

THE CHINESE INTERVENE IN THE WEST. 25 Oct.–1 Nov. 1950

········· British and ROK, Evening 24 Oct.
━━━ Axis of U.S. and ROK Attacks 25 Oct.–1 Nov.
➤ Axis of Chinese Attacks 25 Oct.–1 Nov.
Chinese Roadblock 29 Oct.

U.S. and ROK, Evening 1 Nov.

—xxx— Boundary between Corps
—xx— Boundary between Divisions
ELMS.⌷NK17 Elements of North Korean 17th Armored Division
NK19(−) 19th North Korean Infantry Regiment with some units missing
US 21 21st U.S. Infantry Regiment
US 5 5th U.S. Infantry Regiment
BR 27 27th British Infantry Brigade
ROK 8 8th ROK Infantry Division
8 1 1st Cavalry Regiment, 1st Cavalry Division
1 5 1st Battalion, 5th Cavalry Regiment

MANCHURIA

YELLOW SEA

Antung
Sinuiju
ELMS.⌷NK17

US 21

Chonju
NK19(−)

24 ⚬ 1. CAV.

US 5

BR 27

Ariju

Kunu-ri

ROK 7TH DIV.

ROK 8TH DIV.

Ipsok

ROK 1ST DIV.
8 1
Unsan
1 5

I CAV. xx I ROK

#

7TH REGT.
ROK 6TH DIV.

Chosan

CHONGCHON R.

REMNANTS OF NORTH KOREAN PEOPLES ARMY

Huichon

I xx I ROK II

TAEDONG R.

ROK 8

NORTH KOREA

SUIHO RESERVOIR

YALU R.

Miles
0   10   20

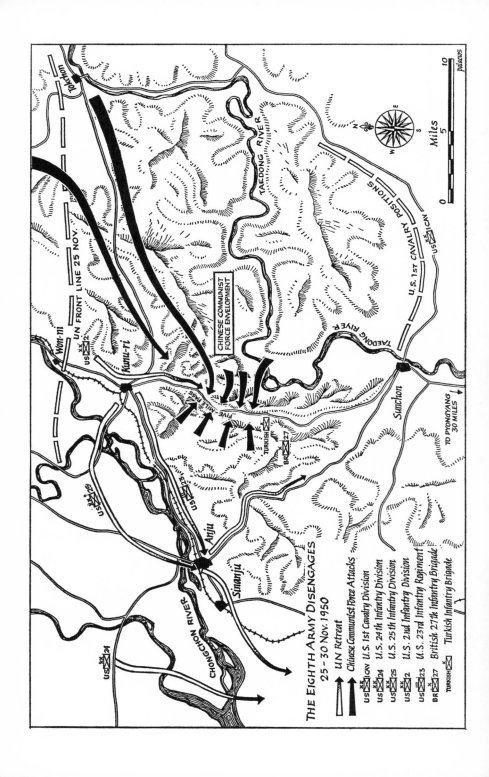

THE EIGHTH ARMY DISENGAGES
25–30 Nov. 1950

UN Retreat
Chinese Communist Force Attacks

US | ICAV | U.S. 1st Cavalry Division
US | 24 | U.S. 24th Infantry Division
US | 25 | U.S. 25th Infantry Division
US | 2 | U.S. 2nd Infantry Division
US | 23 | U.S. 23rd Infantry Regiment
BR | 27 | British 27th Infantry Brigade
TURKISH | | Turkish Infantry Brigade

Miles

CHINESE COMMUNIST
FORCE ENVELOPMENT

U.S. 1st CAVALRY POSITIONS

TAEDONG RIVER

TAEDONG RIVER

UN FRONT LINE 25 NOV.

Tokchon

Won-ni

Kunu-ri

Sunchon

TO PYONGYANG
30 MILES

FIVE MILE

TURKISH

BR 27

US 25

Anju

Sinanju

CHONGCHON RIVER

US 24

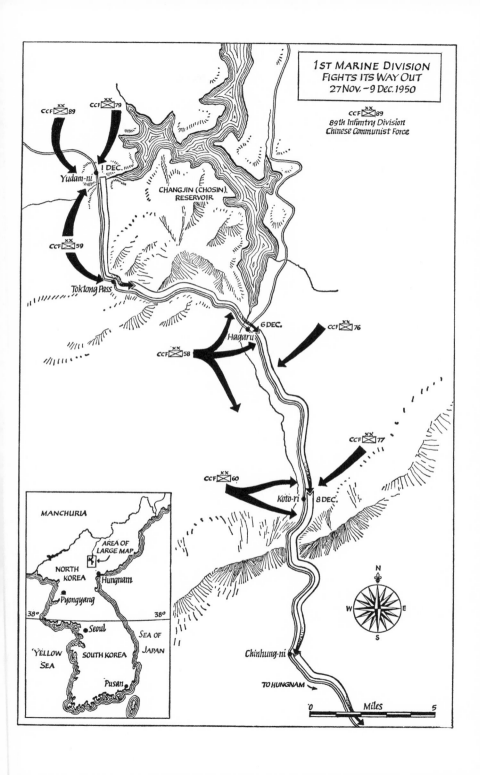

1ST MARINE DIVISION
FIGHTS ITS WAY OUT
27 Nov. – 9 Dec. 1950

CCF 89
89th Infantry Division
Chinese Communist Force

CCF 89
CCF 79
CCF 59
CCF 58
CCF 76
CCF 77
CCF 60

Yudam-ni
1 DEC.
CHANGJIN (CHOSIN) RESERVOIR
Toktong Pass
Hagaru
6 DEC.
Koto-ri
8 DEC.
Chinhung-ni
TO HUNGNAM

MANCHURIA
AREA OF LARGE MAP
NORTH KOREA
Hungnam
Pyongyang
38°
38°
Seoul
SEA OF JAPAN
YELLOW SEA
SOUTH KOREA
Pusan

N
W   E
S

0   Miles   5

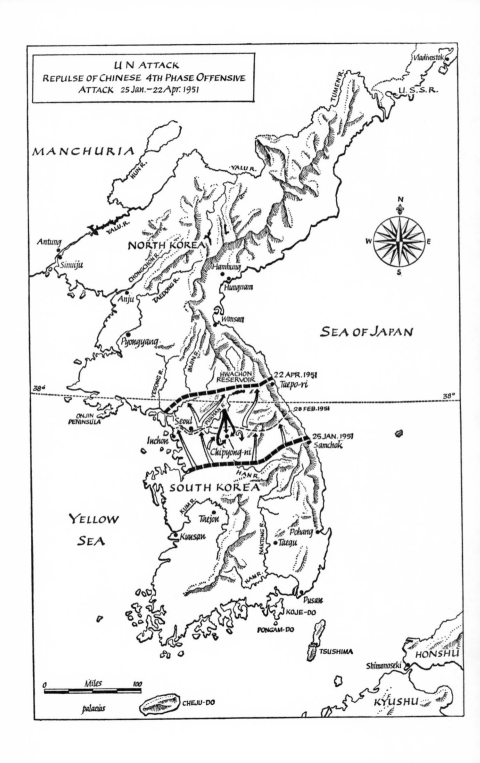

UN ATTACK
REPULSE OF CHINESE 4TH PHASE OFFENSIVE
ATTACK 25 Jan.–22 Apr. 1951

MANCHURIA

NORTH KOREA

Antung
Sinuiju
Anju
Pyongyang

HUN R.
YALU R.
YALU R.
CHONGCHON R.
TAEDONG R.

Hamhung
Hungnam
Wonsan

SEA OF JAPAN

Vladivostok
U.S.S.R.
TUMEN R.

N
W   E
S

38°   38°

HWACHON
RESERVOIR

22 APR. 1951
Taepo-ri

28 FEB. 1951

ONJIN
PENINSULA

Seoul
Inchon

IMJIN R.
YESONG R.
PUKHAN R.

Chipyong-ni

25 JAN. 1951
Samchok

SOUTH KOREA

H. AN R.

YELLOW
SEA

Taejon
Kunsan

KUM R.
NAKTONG R.

Pohang
Taegu

NAM R.

Pusan
KOJE-DO
PONGAM-DO

TSUSHIMA

HONSHU

Shimonoseki

KYUSHU

0   Miles   100

palacias   CHEJU-DO

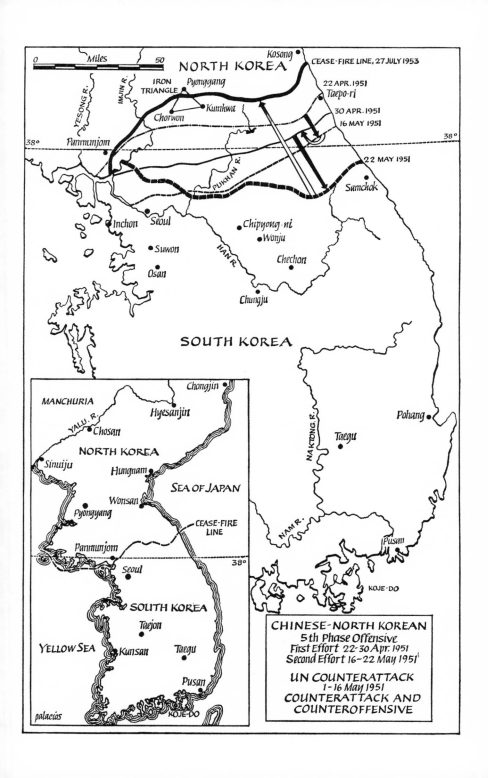

Miles 0 50

NORTH KOREA

Kosong

CEASE-FIRE LINE, 27 JULY 1953

IRON TRIANGLE
Pyonggang

22 APR. 1951
Taepo-ri

Chorwon Kumhwa

30 APR. 1951
16 MAY 1951

YESONG R. IMJIN R.

38° Panmunjom

22 MAY 1951

Samchok

PUKHAN R.

Inchon Seoul

Chipyong-ni
Wonju

Suwon

Chechon

Osan

HAN R.

Chungju

SOUTH KOREA

Chongjin

MANCHURIA

Hyesanjin

YALU R.

Chosan

Pohang

NORTH KOREA

Taegu

NAKTONG R.

Sinuiju

Hungnam

SEA OF JAPAN

Wonsan

Pyongyang

Panmunjom

CEASE-FIRE
LINE

38°

Seoul

SOUTH KOREA

Taejon

NAM R.

Taegu

Pusan

YELLOW SEA

Kunsan

Taegu

KOJE-DO

Pusan

palacios

KOJE-DO

CHINESE-NORTH KOREAN
5th Phase Offensive
First Effort 22-30 Apr. 1951
Second Effort 16-22 May 1951

UN COUNTERATTACK
1-16 May 1951
**COUNTERATTACK AND
COUNTEROFFENSIVE**

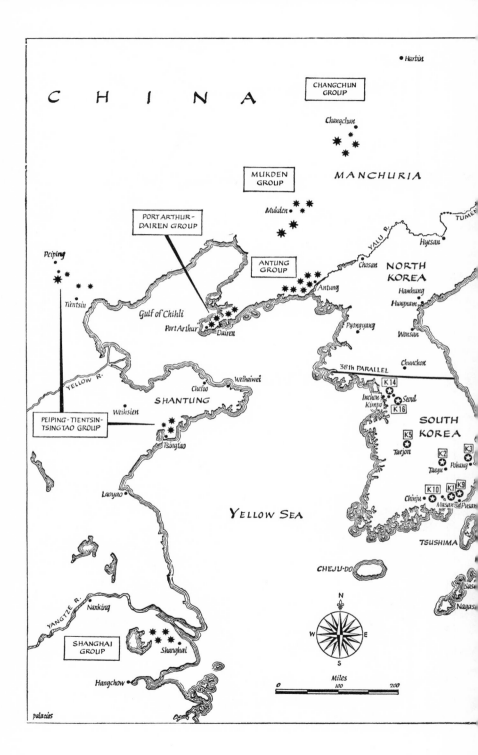

Harbin

CHINA

CHANGCHUN
GROUP

Changchun

MANCHURIA

MUKDEN
GROUP

TUMEN

PORT ARTHUR-
DAIREN GROUP

Mukden

YALU R.

Hyesan

Chosan

NORTH
KOREA

ANTUNG
GROUP

Antung

Hamhung

Hungnam

Peiping

Tientsin

Gulf of Chihli

Port Arthur   Dairen

Pyongyang

Wonsan

Chunchon

YELLOW R.

38th PARALLEL

Chefoo   Weihaiwei

SHANTUNG

Weihsien

Inchon   Seoul
Kimpo

K14

K16

SOUTH
KOREA

PEIPING-TIENTSIN-
TSINGTAO GROUP

Tsingtao

K5

Taejon

K2   K3

Taegu   Pohang

Laoyao

YELLOW SEA

K10   K1 K9

Chinju   Masan Pusan

TSUSHIMA

CHEJU-DO

Sasu

Nagasu

YANGTZE R.   Nanking

N

SHANGHAI
GROUP

Shanghai

W   E

S

Hangchow

Miles
0   100   200

palacios

U.S.S.R.

HOKKAIDO

Vladivostok

Otaru

Chongjin

Hakodate

SEA OF JAPAN

Aomori

Hachinohe

Akita

Morioka

Sendai

Niigata

Takaoka

HONSHU

Kanazawa

Tokyo

Yokosuka

Shizuoka

Kyoto

Nagoya

Matsue

Okayama

Kobe

Hiroshima

Osaka

Takamatsu

Ube

Otake

Kokura

Matsuyama

Tokushima

Fukuoka

Beppu

Oita

KYUSHU

SHIKOKU

Korea Strait

Kagoshima

Miyazaki

PACIFIC OCEAN

CHINESE COMMUNIST AIRFIELDS
IN NORTH CHINA AND MANCHURIA
✹ Possible Heavy Bombers
✱ Medium and Light Bombers and Fighters
✲ Light Bombers and Fighters   • Jet and Piston Fighters

AMERICAN AIRFIELDS
IN JAPAN AND SOUTH KOREA
✪ Fifth Air Force Tactical Units

THE PRESIDENT AND THE GENERAL – DISMISSAL OF MACARTHUR – CAUSES AND CONSEQUENCES – THE CHINESE ARE DRIVEN BACK

THE DISMISSAL OF General MacArthur—so abrupt, so irrevocable, and offering so needless an affront to the General's pride by the crude manner of its execution—produced throughout the country a surge of angry protest. The summary cashiering of a great soldier-statesman whose whole life had been spent in the service of his country evoked a bitter division of opinion—much of it with strong political motivation, it is true—which made it difficult for the public to distinguish the basic issue.

There were, and doubtless still are, extremists who have ascribed the darkest motives to both sides in this controversy—that there was, for instance, an almost traitorous "no win" clique (somehow connected with the two British Foreign Service members who had defected to the Soviet Union a short time before) in high places in the administration; or that MacArthur, on the other hand, was bent on embroiling us in all-out war on the continent of Asia. Both these charges were utterly groundless, as eventually became clear, I think, to the majority of our citizens.

The patriotism and loyalty of our highest government officials, civilian and military, were beyond the slightest question. The Truman administration was not seeking to appease our enemies but rather to avoid a universal holocaust. And MacArthur was always opposed to the use of United States ground forces on the Asian mainland. The real, basic issue was neither the wide divergence of views between Mr. Truman and General MacArthur on enlarging the Korean War nor the clash of two strong personalities. It was simply, as General Marshall pointed out in his testimony before the Senate Committee, the situation of a local Theater Commander publicly expressing his disagreement with a policy which superior authority had repeatedly communicated to him in the clearest terms.

My own feeling toward MacArthur was always one of profound respect, developed through a close association dating from the days when he was Superintendent at West Point and I was in charge of the athletic program, reporting directly to him. Because of his avid interest in sports, I was privileged to see a great deal of him in those years. And while my meetings with him in after years, until I went to Korea, were rather infrequent, I never lost my warm personal interest in his career. Accordingly I came to understand some traits of his complex character not generally recognized: the hunger for praise that led him on some occasions to claim or accept credit for deeds he had not performed, or to disclaim responsibility for mistakes that were clearly his own; the love of the limelight that continually prompted him to pose before the public as the actual commander on the spot at every landing and at the launching of every major attack in which his ground troops took part; his tendency to cultivate the isolation that genius seems to require, until it became a sort of insulation (there was no telephone in his personal office in Tokyo) that deprived him of the critical comment and objective appraisals a commander needs from his principal subordinates; the headstrong quality (derived from his success in forcing through many brilliant plans against solid opposition) that sometimes led him to persist in a course in defiance of all seeming logic; a faith in his own judgment that created an aura of infallibility and that finally led him close to insubordination.

A few of these traits were, I believe, derived from the extraordinary abilities that, from his early boyhood at Texas Military Academy, made him prominent in practically every activity he entered. His academic, athletic, and leadership achievements at West Point; his ability to cut through detail and lay bare the heart of a problem; his great personal gallantry; and his willingness to move swiftly and courageously toward a clearly envisioned goal—these eventually made men reluctant to overrule him or even face him with strong contradictions. His own persuasive powers, the dramatic manner in which he presented his arguments —these too tended to cause opposition to melt and doubters to doubt themselves. He was truly one of the great captains of warfare.

That he was bent on embroiling us in all-out war in Asia—that was the opposite of his aim. Indeed he always held that "no one in his right mind" would ever advocate sending ground forces into continental China. He spoke out again and again against the use of our ground forces beyond the confines of Korea. What he did argue for earnestly and continually was the use of our great sea and air power to isolate Communist China and to destroy "for a generation" her potential for armed aggression.

The leaders of the government, both civilian and military, were motivated by patriotism no less fervent than General MacArthur's. The real points of disagreement, however, were not generally understood until some of the heat had gone out of the Great Debate occasioned by the 1951 Senate Hearings, when MacArthur, after an absence of more than ten years, returned to his homeland to face critics and supporters in a seven-weeks' confrontation. With the differences between the General and the President finally elucidated, much of the public criticism of the President was stilled. There did remain, however, and probably always will remain, widespread disapproval of the summary manner in which MacArthur had been dismissed. (The General himself did not learn of his being relieved until word reached him through newspaper correspondents.)

While neither Truman nor MacArthur sought a land war in Asia, Truman and his advisers simply did not go along with MacArthur's plan for the isolation and devastation of China. What MacArthur sought was, plainly, a preventive war—the destruction of China's war-making potential, regardless of the danger that such an effort might bring the Soviet Union into the conflict and result in her overrunning Europe. Since we were already at war with Red China, MacArthur argued, there was every justification for such action. And in his view, Europe was already lost, no more than an industrial backyard for the Soviets. The future of the world, MacArthur believed, would be decided in Asia.

In presenting his arguments, however, MacArthur chose to picture the choice before the country as one between "victory" and "stalemate." When the choice was stated that simply, there seemed no doubt about which course a patriot should choose. This concept of "victory," set forth with all a master's consummate skill, proved difficult to oppose. It had long been MacArthur's watchword.

"Victory, immediate and complete!" That, said MacArthur in 1931, was the proper objective of any warring nation. Twenty years later the refrain had not altered as, in his classic address to the Congress of the United States, he proclaimed: "There is no substitute for victory!" And finally, in May 1962, as he addressed the graduating class at West Point, he repeated: "Your mission remains fixed, determined, inviolable. *It is to win our wars . . .* the will to win, the sure knowledge that in war *there is no substitute for victory.*" (Italics are mine.)

These words of course are the creed of the American fighting man, on the ground, on the sea, and in the air—and of those who breed and sustain him in spirit. Perhaps no rallying cry could have been found better calculated to stir the blood of Americans. It expresses the do-or-die spirit that inspired our armies through the eight years of the War for Independence, throughout the age-long conquest of the Western lands, through the travail of our Civil War, and through every other conflict in which our forces have engaged. Americans are not inclined by temperament to fight limited wars. As in the boxing ring, they want nothing less than a knockout. What red-blooded American could oppose so shining a concept as victory? It would be like standing up for sin against virtue.

Yet, as the foot soldier in Korea learned, one "victory" sometimes requires another. With one hill taken, there was always, it seemed, just one more to reach for, to secure the line or to prevent enemy observation. And what might have seemed like "victory" to most of our citizenry would have been just the winning of the opening battle of MacArthur's Grand Design.

When MacArthur spoke of victory, he did not mean merely victory in Korea—the destruction of all hostile forces on the peninsula and the unification of the country under a democratic government. What he envisaged was no less than the global defeat of Communism, dealing Communism "a blow from which it would never recover" and which would mark the historical turning back of the Red Tide. His "program" included not merely driving to the Yalu, but destroying the air bases and industrial complex in Manchuria; blockading Communist China's seacoast; demolishing its industrial centers; providing all necessary support to Chiang's invasion of the mainland; and the transportation of the Nationalist Chinese troops to Korea to beef up our ground forces there. He sincerely believed that these moves would break the Communist hold on the mainland. He was convinced that the Chinese masses were ready to welcome Chiang back, and he had persuaded himself that the Soviet Union would not intervene in a conflict of the sort he had in mind. But if, in the course of waging this preventive war on Red China, the threat of Soviet intervention had jeopardized its success, it is not illogical to assume that MacArthur would have urged the further step of an attack upon the USSR (whose growing strength, he thought, put time on its side). This would have been merely the logical extension of his ultimate aim, the destruction of Communism throughout the world by the use of armed force.

His plan therefore entailed the very considerable risk of igniting World War III and the consequent overrunning of Western Europe, with the loss of our oldest and staunchest allies sure to follow. It should be remembered too that we would have been running those risks when our own nation was lamentably unprepared, with our general reserve reduced to a single combat-ready army division.

This then was the "victory" MacArthur had in mind when he uttered his war cry. It was an ambitious and dangerous program that would demand a major national effort. Yet the program was not rejected out of hand by MacArthur's superiors. The highest echelons of the United States government—the President, the Secretaries of State and Defense, the National Security Council, the Armed Services Secretaries, and the Joint Chiefs of Staff, as well as leaders in Congress, pondered and discussed every question MacArthur raised. They examined it first against the background of the Far East Command, its responsibilities, and the local situation in Asia. They considered it further in the light of the world-wide situation, of current United States capabilities and limitations, of the state of West Europe's defenses, and of the extent to which the adoption of any or all of MacArthur's recommendations might be the precipitant of World War III. These officials gave the proposals sober, mature, and deliberate study.

They did not agree that our Air Force could bomb Red China into submission. I have mentioned General Hoyt Vandenberg's feeling that our "shoestring air force," should we try to knock out the Manchurian bases, would be so reduced by attrition and combat losses that it would be two years before we could rebuild it sufficiently to meet a test, if one should come, in another part of the globe. Beyond this, General Vandenberg had no taste for "pecking at the periphery" by bombing Manchuria—for paying a high price merely to nick the edges of the enemy's military power. Nor was the Pentagon at all convinced that China's source of industrial strength could be eliminated quite so swiftly as MacArthur seemed to believe. The bombing would surely involve the slaughter of thousands of innocents—millions, if A-bombs were used. And unless we bombed out the Trans-Siberian Railway—an action requiring sustained operations that might have been beyond our capacity and that would surely have brought on World War III—Communist China could still have received military supplies over that rail link while the USSR remained untouched.

Furthermore, the Truman administration and the Joint Chiefs of Staff were aware that any attack on the Manchurian bases or even on the Yalu bridges would put an end to the unspoken agreement that kept our South Korean and Japanese bases inviolate and had limited the war to the Korean peninsula.

As for blockading the Chinese coast, that would be an act of war. A blockade would be recognized by the neutral nations only if effective, and it could not be made effective unless Hong Kong, a British Crown Colony, as well as the ports of Dairen and Port Arthur were included. If we did extend the blockade to those ports, the reaction of Great Britain and the Soviet Union would not likely have been such as to lighten our difficulties.

An invasion of China by Chiang's forces would have no hope of success, in the Pentagon view, unless it received major United States naval, air, and logistical support—which of course Mac-Arthur meant it should receive. But we had little of this strength to spare, and what little we did have could be used more effectively in Korea. And even if an invasion should draw Chinese troops out of Korea and thus ease the pressure there, it was highly possible that a few reverses for Chiang's ground forces would bring wholesale defections, such as had occurred the last time Chiang's troops had met the Communists head-on.

The Pentagon had little faith in the fighting capacity of Chiang's soldiers, and MacArthur himself had only shortly before expressed his own lack of confidence in their battle-readiness. Their training levels were low. We would have to supply all heavy weapons, such as artillery and armor, and provide training in their use for an extended period before we could dare to rely on these troops in battle. But to divert badly needed material of this sort from the troops already in the field could not be justified. In addition, we had to reckon with Syngman Rhee's firm opposition to the introduction of Chinese troops into his country when, by his thinking, there was still Korean manpower not being properly utilized.

Nor did the administration share MacArthur's feelings about the relative unimportance of Western Europe. The industrial skills, the manpower, the technology, the mills and factories, the quickly exploitable raw materials, the badly needed air bases, and above all the close ties of blood and culture—all these persuaded Washington that Europe must come first and Asia second. The loss of Western Europe would promptly and decisively tip the scales in Russia's favor. NATO would be dissolved and the United States isolated. We would not be allowed time enough to make ready for a two-front war, if that should develop.

The Pentagon thought long and hard about the proposal to open a second front in the south to divert Chinese strength, and they rejected the plan. The use of Chiang's troops was wholly unacceptable to the British and other countries of the Commonwealth. The extension of hostilities to the Formosa area would greatly enlarge our tasks in the Pacific. And we would be faced with the certain disruption of the delicately balanced alliance we had put together for the Korea action.

And here was another point of disagreement between the General and the administration: whether to adhere to our policy of collective security within the United Nations or to go it alone. MacArthur quite clearly had decided that, if our allies would not stand by us in a confrontation with Communist China and the Soviet Union, we should shoulder the whole burden by ourselves. The United States, however, had long been committed to the course of collective security. While the actual manpower contributions of other member nations in the United Nations were not great, our ability to operate under the United Nations flag lent a moral flavor to our actions in Korea that was of inestimable value in our dealings with the rest of the free world.

In the course of the now historic Senate Hearings, these conclusions were restated and reconfirmed by most if not all of the principals who had earlier reached them: Acheson, Marshall, Bradley, Sherman, Vandenberg, Collins, and many others. These men were under oath. Their testimony was recorded. They were questioned and cross-questioned. Ultimately, that testimony, after deletions for security, was published, and the reasons for rejecting MacArthur's program were made a matter of public record. It would seem preposterous then for anyone to allege that these officials, and the President and Vice-President as well, had any less desire for "victory" than their critics; any narrower view of the world situation; any less determination to serve the best interests of their country. Yet such were the charges leveled against the administration, either in open, stinging criticism or by implication; while refusal to approve the MacArthur proposals was branded as appeasement.

It was not therefore a "no-win" policy insinuated into our high councils by faceless subversives that guided the administration in its rejection of MacArthur's recommended program. It was essentially adherence to a basically different policy: a different interpretation of the word "victory"; a different view of the facts based on a better knowledge of the world situation.

It is clear that the nation's top civilian and military leaders, using a wider-angle lens, with deeper sources of information on the atomic situation in the Soviet Union, and with more comprehensive estimates of the possible consequences of general war in Europe, had a much clearer view of the realities and responsibilities of the day. In their view, the kind of "victory" sought by the Theater Commander, even if it were attained in Korea, would have incurred overbalancing liabilities elsewhere. They thought their view was right. They believed MacArthur's view was wrong. Neither rightness nor wrongness could have been proved then, nor can it be demonstrated now. It was their duty to advise the President, which they did. It was his duty to decide, and he made the decision.

The administration's conclusions, together with the thinking behind them, were communicated promptly to the United Nations Commander. Moreover, that they might not lack emphasis and unmistakable clarity, the President himself explained them in a personal letter to MacArthur, dated January 13, 1951.

All disagreements finally came down to matters of opinion. MacArthur's beliefs, however keen his perceptions, were based in part on less information on the world situation (and of course on still less information on domestic political factors completely outside his purview) and in part on demonstrably erroneous evaluation of intelligence by the Theater Commander himself.

Debating the program as a whole in the course of the Senate Hearings, Senator Lyndon B. Johnson asked General MacArthur: " . . . assume we embrace your program, and suppose the Chinese were chased back across the Yalu River, and suppose they then refuse to sign a treaty, and to enter into an agreement on what their future course will be, what course would you recommend at that stage?"

MacArthur had nothing to recommend at all. He simply replied that he regarded that as an unreasonable and irrational hypothesis.

"They go back there," Senator Johnson persisted. "What course are we going to take?"

"I don't think they could remain in a state of belligerency," replied MacArthur.

The fact that MacArthur sometimes based his estimates not merely on wishful thinking but on faulty evaluation of the intelligence was, I believe, demonstrated during the Wake Island conference in early October 1950, when President Truman met with him for a private discussion of the situation in Korea. Notes taken at that meeting record that MacArthur estimated that, even if the Chinese did enter the conflict, the greatest number of troops they could hope to maintain in Korea was from 50,000 to 60,000. That would have meant a 2-to-1 superiority for the UN forces. In actual fact, Chinese strength, when they launched their offensive in late November, was estimated at 300,000. MacArthur's mistaken estimate was one of several that lay behind the "Home-by-Christmas" offensive that brought us close to disaster.

The conviction that we could drive the Chinese out of Korea was not always cherished by MacArthur. On January 10, 1951, long after the drive that resulted in our forced retirement back over the 38th parallel, and when our forces were still nursing the bruises dealt out by the Chinese New Year's offensive, MacArthur radioed the Joint Chiefs of Staff that, if the United States decisions stood as they were (that is, no reinforcements, no naval blockade of Red China, no bombing of Manchuria, and no operations by Chiang against the mainland), then, in his opinion, and "in the absence of overriding political consideration, the command should be withdrawn from the peninsula just as rapidly as it is tactically possible to do so." It was only after the resurgent United Nations Command, its confidence in itself and its fighting spirit restored, again approached the 38th parallel and particularly after the smashing of the two-pronged Chinese fifth-phase offensive in April and May of 1951, that the call for complete and decisive victory was heard again.

As for myself, I never did believe the Chinese could drive us out of Korea, without Russia's entry into the war. And I was sure, as was the Eighth Army, that we could have pushed right on to the Yalu in the spring of 1951, had we been ordered to do so. The price for such a drive would have been far too high for what we would have gained, however. We would have lost heavily in dead and wounded—my estimate at the time was 100,000—fighting against stern resistance across the rugged northern face of the country, and our prize would have been no more than many square miles of inhospitable real estate, much of it a-swarm with guerrillas for years to come. The enemy would have shortened his supply routes as we lengthened ours, and he would have faced us finally in great strength behind the broad Yalu and Tumen Rivers. Merely pressing the enemy back without destroying any appreciable part of his forces would, to my mind, have been a very poor bargain indeed.

At the end of the campaign, our battle line would have been stretched from 110 miles to 420 miles, and the major responsibility for holding it would have been ours, for it would have been far beyond the capability of the ROK army. The questions then would have been: Will the American people support an army of the size required to hold this line? Will they underwrite the bloody cost of a Manchurian campaign? Will they commit themselves to an endless war in the bottomless pit of the Asian mainland? I thought then and I think now that the answer to these questions was "No."

Another question that underlay the disagreement between the General and the President was that of all-out or limited war. In a sense this was merely a translation of the "victory or stalemate" issue into more specific terms: Should we bring all our strength to bear and try to roll back the Red Tide forever or should we endeavor to tailor our effort to keep the fighting within the confines of Korea? But it should be remarked that the partisan attacks on the Truman administration, particularly those led by the late Senator Robert A. Taft, did not endorse a full-scale land war either in Asia or in Europe. Instead they seemed merely to offer an updated version of the Fortress America concept of an earlier period: Don't reinforce our garrison in Germany. Halt further aid to Europe. Consider (this was the suggestion of former President Herbert Hoover) an alternative world policy based on withdrawal from the Eurasian continent. Defend the interests of the United States by sea and air power (and this was the strategy envisioned in the MacArthur program even for the Far East). In short, establish a Pax

Americana for the protection of Western civilization behind a shield of sea and air power, as had been done for two centuries under the Pax Britannica.

This program was pressed long after MacArthur's release. When the Eisenhower administration came to power, its basic tenet was control of the seas by naval power and the protection of existing borders through threats of "massive retaliation" by the A-bomb. We could never again transport large ground forces overseas, it was now argued, so the Army and the Marines could be downgraded. We could afford no more than the cost of fighting one kind of war—a big one—said the Secretary of the Treasury. And if war came, the Secretary of Defense assured us, it *would be* a big one.

Finally, the Truman-MacArthur controversy brought into relief an issue that was not widely recognized at the time—that is, the question of the supremacy of civilian authority over military authority in the determination of national policy.

As far as I can recall, only once, prior to Korea, had the authority of the President of the United States been in any way questioned by a military officer on active duty. That was during the Lincoln administration, when General George B. McClellan openly flouted the orders of his Commander in Chief. Mr. Truman himself notes this parallel in his *Memoirs,* where he writes: "Lincoln would issue direct orders to McClellan (then Commanding General of all the Union Armies) and the General would ignore them. Half the country knew that McClellan had political ambitions which men in opposition to Lincoln sought to use. Lincoln was patient—but at long last he was compelled to relieve the Union Army's principal commander."*

Nearly a century later, history repeated itself. Even before 1950, according to Mr. Truman, MacArthur treated the presidential authority with disrespect, insidiously at first, then with increasing boldness. Finally MacArthur clearly disregarded, if he did not deliberately ignore, the lawful orders of his superior. Mr. Truman characterized MacArthur's actions as "insubordination." Others used politer terms, ranging from "defiance" to "open revolt."

Like some other great figures on the world stage, past and pres-

* Some further comments on McClellan and MacArthur appear in Appendix 1.

ent, MacArthur seemed at times to have decided that his innate brilliance, so frequently illustrated by military successes, rendered his judgment supreme, above that of all his peers and even of his duly constituted superiors. But the crux of the matter was not whether the military or the political judgment was superior, but whether civil authority, in the person of the President, or military authority, in the person of the Theater Commander, was to determine which course the United States should take. It was Mac-Arthur's privilege, and his duty, to give his views as to the rightness of a contemplated course, and to offer his own recommendations, *before* the decision was rendered. It was neither his privilege nor his duty to take issue with the President's decision *after* it had been made known to him. In the heat of selfish political partisanship, and in the shame and frustration of the stinging reverses of late fall and early winter, 1950, a substantial segment of the American public seems to have lost sight of these elementary points.

These were the issues that underlay the confrontation of the two dominant figures on the American scene in the Korean War, and the issue of civilian authority vs. military authority was the most sensitive that the war produced. Logic would indicate that this issue never should have arisen. The principle involved is as long-standing and as firmly established as any in the life of our governmental structure. Had it stood alone, stripped of the false issues and trivia with which design and accident surrounded it, I believe the majority of the American people would have instantly supported the President. But the argument was too deeply intertwined with other vexing issues, none of which was perfectly understood. One such issue, of particularly long standing, was our China policy. Others were the proper uses of atomic power, the brand-new concept of limited war, and the necessary modifications of sovereignty consonant with the obligations laid down in the Charter of the United Nations.

Still, the essential issue remained: Was the President or the General to have the authority to decide major issues of foreign policy? As General Marshall expressed it in testifying on the matter before the Senate:

"It arises from the inherent difference between the position of a commander whose mission is limited to a particular area and a particular antagonist, and the position of the Joint Chiefs of Staff, the Secretary of Defense and the President, who are responsible for the total security of the United States . . . and must weigh the interests and objectives in one part of the world with those in others to attain balance.

"There is nothing new in this divergence, in our military history," he continued. "What is new and what brought about the necessity for General MacArthur's removal is the wholly unprecedented situation of a local Theater Commander publicly expressing his displeasure at, and his disagreement with, the foreign policy of the United States. [He] . . . had grown so far out of sympathy with the established policies of the United States that there is grave doubt as to whether he could any longer be permitted to exercise the authority in making decisions that normal command functions would assign to a Theater Commander."

Yet I think it can be argued that it was a boon to the country that the issue did arise and that it was decisively met by the elected head of the government, within the ample dimensions of his own high moral courage and without any pressure from political or military quarters. President Truman's decision should act as a powerful safeguard against the time, in some great future crisis, when perhaps others may be similarly tempted to challenge the right of the President and his advisers to exercise the powers the Constitution grants to them in the formulation of foreign policy.

On March 20, 1951, the Joint Chiefs of Staff informed MacArthur that the State Department was planning a presidential announcement to the effect that the UN was preparing to discuss conditions of a settlement in Korea. By March 24, the announcement was almost in final form. It would make clear our willingness to settle on the basis of a return to the general line of the pre-war boundary.

But on March 24, General MacArthur's own announcement cut the ground from under the President, enraged our allies, and put the Chinese in the position of suffering a severe loss of face if they so much as accepted a bid to negotiate. No one in possession of the facts could have been so naïve as to imagine that MacArthur was either unaware of what effect his announcement might have or innocent of any desire openly to oppose the President. A little more than three months earlier, on December 6, 1950, President Truman had issued a specific directive to all officials—including General MacArthur—to abstain from any declarations on foreign policy. But a specific directive was actually superfluous. It is never within the province of the soldier, under our Constitution, to make foreign policy. That is solely, specifically, and properly a function of elected officials, regardless of anyone's assessment of the "rightness" or "wrongness" of current policy. Only under a dictatorship does a military leader take council solely with himself in deciding what course the nation should pursue in its intercourse with other sovereign powers.

One sentence of MacArthur's wrecked the State Department plan to issue its announcement. For MacArthur said: "The enemy, therefore, must by now be painfully aware that a decision of the United Nations to depart from its tolerant effort to confine the war to the area of Korea, through an expansion of our military operations to his coastal areas and interior bases, would doom Red China to the risk of imminent military collapse." This statement so obviously suggested a radical shift in United Nations policy that it is hard to imagine anyone's pretending it was merely, as some said, an expression of a willingness to accept a military surrender. Even a call for surrender, which MacArthur's statement contained, implied a sudden hardening of the United Nations line and involved a humiliation that we simply had not the strength to impose at that moment upon China.

It was the setting of the stage for a showdown between the military authority and the civilian authority. And the showdown came at once. The outcome was inevitable, as it always should be in a democracy. The civilian authority is and must remain supreme. But it was also a showdown, long in the making, between the two schools of thought on Korea, those that argued for "complete victory" and those that argued, with equal sincerity and with patriotism no less fervent, for a truce that would give us time to build our strength and bolster our alliances.

This showdown brought no end to what became known as the Great Debate between the advocates of armistice and the cham-

155

pions of "military victory." The issue itself was settled with the removal of MacArthur. But the debate went on, largely because President Syngman Rhee of Korea was unalterably opposed to any negotiations at all and said so loudly and often. His bitter advocacy of reunification by force greatly increased the difficulties the administration met with during the protracted discussions between the truce teams. And they helped thin out the hair on my own head too. Yet I never could hold in my heart anything but admiration and sympathy for this gallant old man. Uncompromising as he was in his hatred of Communism, bitterly prejudiced as he was in favor of his own people, persistent as he was in asking the impossible, he was still moved by nothing more than a deep love for his own country, to whose cause he had devoted his long years of exile and all his waking hours since his return to his homeland.

Considering his own sacrifices and the fervor that burned within him, I do not see how he could have been expected to act differently. Yet we who had to deal with the military realities often found him a hair shirt. He continually insisted that there was a tremendous pool of Korean manpower that could be fighting for us if we would but give them arms. Yet we knew only too well how many hundreds of thousands of dollars worth of equipment had been abandoned in flight by certain units of the ROK army, during every Chinese offensive. Rhee insisted, too, that he had thrown his forces into the fight with the understanding that the United Nations forces were fully committed to "unifying Korea and punishing the Communist aggressors." He could never agree, he said, to truce terms that stopped short of unification, because they would mean "death for the Korean nation." While he finally conceded, in the face of United Nations determination to halt the fighting before it could grow into World War III, I do not doubt that the indomitable old patriot never really abandoned the goal of which he had dreamed. In the course of the negotiations, and before they began, his intransigence, and the lusty, sometimes self-serving cries of his supporters in the United States, put many thorns in our path, however, and prompted many of us privately to wish him far, far away. The United Nations had never committed itself to a forceful reunification of Korea. And only in the first great surge of optimism after the Inchon landing had any serious thought been given to operations above the 38th parallel, bent on destroying all hostile forces. Once the Chinese had entered the war, there were few moments indeed when the UN command seriously contemplated a new advance to the Yalu. Once the Eighth Army had been started forward again, we aimed for little more than the accomplishment of our assigned mission, "to repel the aggression and to restore international peace in the area," more or less a return to the status quo ante and an inevitable stalemate.

In the days immediately preceding the removal of MacArthur, a stalemate seemed to be what we would soon have on the battlefront. The offensive was still moving ahead, but the attacks we planned were all of the limited-objective type, toward carefully selected objectives, over terrain that had been thoroughly studied and with every care not to allow our aggressiveness to draw us into reckless pursuit with avoidable and perhaps heavy losses. Our strength had reached its peak and unless we were to be heavily reinforced or ordered to move on the Yalu-Tumen line, neither of which was a probability, we were planning on a continuation of current operations. This I reported to MacArthur, and in this he concurred.

While the enemy seemed to be maintaining his defensive mood, I warned the Corps Commanders that the positioning of his units fitted the offense as well as the defense, and that he had the capability of launching a general offensive almost any day. By this time, I had already received my new assignment to Tokyo, and Lieutenant General James A. Van Fleet was on his way to take over the Eighth Army.

The news of my sudden elevation to the position of Commander in Chief of the UN forces reached me, as dramatic news often does, in a most undramatic way. Actually, when the news did reach me, I did not realize what it meant, for it came in the form of a question by a war correspondent. I never could remember the name of the correspondent, but the question was, in effect, whether I was not due for congratulations. It was a question that would have made sense to me only if I had known that General MacArthur had been relieved and that I had been selected to replace him. I just stared back at the correspondent and told him quite honestly that I did not know what he was talking about. At the time, I was taking Secretary of the Army Frank Pace on a tour of the front, to show him, among other things, the 936th Field Artillery Battalion, formerly a National Guard unit, from his home state of Arkansas. And I was far more concerned with this visit than with the hidden meaning behind any cryptic questions.

The 936th Battalion, a 155-mm. gun unit that had just passed its final training tests and been cleared for commitment to action, had received a fire mission. The battalion and battery commanders invited Secretary Pace to pull the lanyard to fire the first projectile, on the casing of which some soldier had chalked a ribald greeting to the Chinese in the impact area. The Secretary eagerly accepted the invitation, fired the shot, and stood proudly back to await results. At this point, the accompanying officers, both old friends of mine, Lieutenant Generals Ed Hull and Ted Brooks, decided to apply the needle.

"Don't you realize," they asked him solemnly, "that as a civilian noncombatant you have no business firing that gun? If you fall into the hands of the Chinese now, you're a dead duck!"

For just half a second a look of dismay crossed the Secretary's usually good-natured face and we all burst out laughing. He joined in and we continued the tour. Several hours later it was my turn to be dismayed when I learned the true meaning of what had then seemed to me a nonsensical question the correspondent had asked me. I was ticketed for Tokyo, to take over from the man who had been my superior officer.

My last meeting with MacArthur came on April 12 in the Embassy library in Tokyo. It was one I did not relish. I have described this meeting in detail in a previous book.* Now I only want to emphasize one thing that particularly struck me at the time —MacArthur's apparent lack of rancor or resentment. He was as calm and courteous as ever, and seemed to have accepted the decision with better grace, I thought, than most men similarly situated might have done. Certainly his indomitable spirit seemed undiminished, as I recorded at the time.

* Quoted in Appendix 5.

I say my "last meeting" with MacArthur, for it was my last official conference with him. I did meet him again at the airport for a brief farewell. He shook my hand and without dramatics said: "I hope when you leave Tokyo you will be Chief of Staff. If I had been permitted to choose my own successor, I'd have selected you." This simple statement, which could hardly have been other than completely sincere, was a most generous act on the part of this great soldier-statesman. It meant a great deal to me, for it bore out the confidence he had expressed in me just before I left his office to take over the Eighth Army four months earlier, a confidence which he confirmed only a short time before as the United Nations Forces advanced once more to the 38th parallel. At that time he said to me: "You have done all that was humanly possible."*

* Thirteen years later, to the month, an enigmatic incident occurred with the publication of an interview which General MacArthur was reported to have given Pulitzer Prize winner Jim G. Lucas in January 1954. In the course of this interview, the record of which had been impounded until after General MacArthur's death, the latter, Mr. Lucas reported, rated me at the bottom of his list of field commanders. In the light of all that General MacArthur had said to me in Korea, and of his subsequent statement to Senator Harry P. Cain in Washington, which follows, this presents a puzzle for which I have no satisfactory answer.

Senator Cain: To my mind, it is proper to make mention of the extremely high regard in which General of the Army Douglas MacArthur holds General Ridgway. In response to a recent question of mine, General MacArthur said:

General Ridgway was my selection and recommendation as the commander of the Eighth Army after the death of that very magnificent soldier, General Walker. I have known General Ridgway for thirty years. I don't think you could have made a more admirable selection in the Far East than General Ridgway. I hold him in the highest esteem not only as a soldier but as a cultured gentleman and one of the most magnificent characters I have ever been acquainted with. I do not know how there could have been any more complete cooperation, devotion, and loyalty both ways than between General Ridgway and myself.

(Extract from *Congressional Record*—United States of America—Proceedings and Debates of the 82nd Congress First Session. Vol. 97, Washington, Thursday, May 10, 1951—No. 85.)

I wholeheartedly concur in the last sentence of General MacArthur's answer to Senator Cain, as given above.

I had come to Tokyo with Frank Pace in his Constellation, which he let me borrow for my return that same night to Korea, as it was much faster than my old B-17. This flight came very close to being my last. The pilot, a stranger to Korean fields, set us down at one o'clock in the morning on a light-plane landing strip, which he mistook for the K-2 field where he had been instructed to land. Through a miracle of good luck, or through God's own watchfulness, the pilot missed a mountain he never saw, a peak that rose sheer from one side of the strip, only yards from our wingtip. Then finding himself suddenly careening down a runway intended for nothing more ambitious than an occasional C-47 landing, he had to slam on full brakes to keep from winding up tail-high in a rice paddy. We stopped right-side up. But we did smash up all the crew chief's best chinaware and we blew four tires. That meant that Frank Pace had to do without his private plane until new tires could be obtained from hundreds of miles away and flown to Korea.

Just before I had taken off on this flight, Frank Pace had paid me a gracious compliment, which this incident helped to imprint on my mind. "Matt," he had said, "you have worked not only a military miracle, but a spiritual one with this army." And now, I thought, a few minutes after this blind circling of the mountain and the hair-raising stop on the tiny runway, our pilot has pulled off a mechanical miracle to get us all down here in single pieces.

Our next move on the battle front was Operation Dauntless, a continuing advance through phase line Utah to the Wyoming Line. We were well aware of the enemy buildup in the rear areas, especially in the Iron Triangle, and among the alternative developments to be discussed we included a possible withdrawal to the Kansas Line. A few days of bad weather would make many of the roads useless and cut down our air support, perhaps making it necessary to stop the attack or even, if opposition were very strong, to pull back in places. A withdrawal would be initiated, I told the Corps Commanders, only on my direction and then to successive phase lines already designated. There would be no passive defense, but a mobile active one designed to inflict maximum damage on the enemy.

Before these operations began, however, I had turned over command of the Eighth Army to General Van Fleet and had flown to Tokyo to take over my new duties. I made a point, however, out of courtesy to my old Commander in Chief, to stay away from his headquarters. Until he had left Tokyo for good, I quartered myself at the Imperial Hotel. Eight days after I had settled in there, the Chinese Communist Forces opened their two-punch fifth-phase offensive, destined to be their final all-out effort to cast us into the sea. It was an advance in great strength, and had the Chinese earlier been able to trap any considerable number of our forces by luring them into unphased pursuit, they might have done us great damage. As it was, however, except for the sudden disintegration of some ROK units with the loss of large amounts of equipment and much ground, our defenses proved equal to the job—as I had been confident they would. The collapse of one ROK division, dangerously exposing the flanks of other UN troops, forced them to give ground too. It also impelled me on April 26 to send a trusted officer of my staff, Lieutenant Colonel (now Major General) Paul M. Smith, to convey a suggestion to General Van Fleet, i.e., that he send a general officer to Ambassador Muccio to urge him to carry to President Rhee, in the presence of our Liaison Officer, General Coulter, and no other, a message to the effect that Rhee's primary problem was to secure competent leadership in his army. This he simply did not have, and I wanted him to be told so flatly and specifically—that from his Minister of Defense on down there was a serious weakness in command, as had been too often evidenced by repeated battle failures of major ROK units. Until he developed proper leadership, I felt he should be told that there would be no further talk of our equipping additional ROK forces. Too many major items of badly needed equipment had already been abandoned without justification.

I believe the message was brought to Rhee, but nothing came of it. Instead he continued to subject us to pressure, some of it inspired in the United States press through Rhee's agents and supporters, for the arming of the "huge reservoir of unarmed, experienced Korean personnel," which he insisted was always available and was not being used.

This, however, was one of my smallest problems at the moment, and as I have remarked, I could never find the heart to resent this old warrior's efforts to build an image of a high-spirited and dedicated army of freedom fighters awaiting merely his command to drive the invaders off the last inch of Korean soil.

Much in my mind as I took over Supreme Command of the UN forces was the proper relationship between myself and General Van Fleet, and the Corps Commanders in the field. I had no desire to try to hold all the reins in my own hand, as MacArthur had done prior to my assuming command of the Eighth Army. Nor had I ever thought it proper for a distant commander to try to keep tactical control when he had able and trusted commanders on the spot. I was determined, instead, to follow what I had seen habitually practiced in combat in Europe. That is, I would accord the Army Commander, General Van Fleet, the latitude his reputation and my high respect for his ability merited, while still retaining the right of approval or disapproval of his principal tactical plans. And in appraising these plans I intended on each occasion to consult personally and separately not only with the Army Commander himself, but with the Corps and Division Commanders of the Eighth Army, all of whom I knew intimately. I wanted in every instance to get for myself the feel of the situation as these officers responsible for execution of the plans might sense it. With this firsthand knowledge of their views added to all other relevant information, I would be in a position to make sound decisions—for which I as Theater Commander would accept full and sole responsibility.

In reaching my decisions I wanted to keep always in mind the clear policy decisions communicated to me by President Truman and the Joint Chiefs of Staff, the most immediate of which was to avoid any action that might result in an extension of hostilities and thus lead to a worldwide conflagration. General Van Fleet; Vice-Admiral Joy, Commander Naval Forces, Far East; and General Stratemeyer, Commander Far East Air Forces, were all apprised of this basic guideline and each commander had expressed his full understanding and agreement.

Pending receipt of a summarization of up-to-date missions and policies from Washington, and in keeping with the broad policy directive just mentioned, I undertook to place reasonable restrictions on the advances of the Eighth and ROK Armies. Specifically I charged General Van Fleet to conduct no operations in force beyond the Wyoming Line without prior approval from GHQ. And I wished to be informed ahead of time of whatever advances beyond the Utah Line the Eighth Army Commander felt were warranted.

In all this I was studiously trying to avoid those practices on the part of my predecessor that I regarded as faulty. In any event, one of my cardinal rules of battle leadership—or leadership in any field—is to be yourself, to strive to apply the basic principles of the art of war, and to seek to accomplish your assigned missions by your own methods and in your own way. General MacArthur's ways were not mine. MacArthur, besides being a dominating personality, had military experience vastly greater than that of any officer under his command. He had overridden strongly voiced and almost unanimous opposition from subordinate commanders as well as from principal staff officers and had achieved a brilliant success. It was only natural that he would have far more confidence in his own judgment than in that of any of his commanders. But beyond that he actually lacked confidence in one of his two ground commanders during the first six months of the Korean War. Consequently he had undoubtedly felt justified in holding a tight rein on his field commanders and in making all major tactical decisions himself, leaving only details of execution to the discretion of his field subordinates.

By contrast, I had full confidence in General Van Fleet, a courageous and competent field commander. Moreover, I had always felt that the views of subordinate field commanders were entitled to the most thoughtful consideration. Even so, I had to walk that tightrope familiar to all top commanders in any profession, civilian as well as military: To maintain the proper balance between according sufficient latitude to the subordinate commander in carrying out broadly stated directives, and in exercising adequate supervision, as befitted the man who would bear the ultimate responsibility for the success or failure of the entire effort. I sought during all my time in Tokyo to maintain that balance.

There were two top-priority tasks, practically of equal importance, as I now saw them. One was to grasp the dimensions of the primary mission assigned me by my superiors in Washington, namely, the defense of Japan. This meant that I must immediately review existing plans and satisfy myself of their adequacy to meet the possible though unlikely contingency of a Soviet attack. The other was to take all proper feasible actions within my authority for carrying out the policy firmly and clearly stated by President Truman of preventing enlargement of the conflict into a general war.

In connection with the top-priority tasks, the first action I considered necessary was to request a summarized clarification of the many directives issued by the JCS during the preceding months or deriving from policies enunciated by the President and the Secretary of Defense. In addition to the mission of defending Japan in case of attack, a mission assigned unilaterally by my government, I had other missions as the United Nations Commander in Korea. These were to maintain the integrity of UN forces; to continue to fight in Korea as long as, in my judgment, such action offered a reasonable chance of success; to maintain a blockade of the entire Korean coast; and to stabilize the situation in Korea or evacuate to Japan if forced out of Korea. There were others, still on the books, which ceased to have any meaning since the forced retrograde movement of the UN ground forces in late 1950.

At the same time it was highly important that I make my wishes unmistakably clear to General Van Fleet with respect to the tactical latitude within which he was to operate. These two tasks, in turn, called for action along parallel lines.

The first was to place reasonable restrictions on the Eighth and ROK Armies' advance, pending the drafting of carefully phrased letters of instruction which would go not only to General Van Fleet but also to Admiral Joy and General Stratemeyer. These letters would define objectives and policies in broad but clear outline. I quickly initiated this action by confirming oral instructions I had issued on the day of Van Fleet's arrival and adding this prescription: "I desire that there be no operations conducted in force beyond the WYOMING LINE (Junction of IMJIN and HAN Rivers—CHORWON—HWACHON RESERVOIR—TAEPO-RI) without prior approval of this headquarters. To the extent you feel the situation warrants, please inform me prior to advance beyond the UTAH LINE [a line considerably short of WYOMING]."

The second of the two tasks, drafting letters of instructions, I put in train at once, even though these letters might not be put in final form until a summary of up-to-date missions and policies had been received from Washington. Meanwhile, however, I freely consulted with the three commanders, and by the time the letters were issued, on April 25, 1951, each commander had stated his full agreement with the contents.

The letters of instruction were accompanied by a memorandum, the purpose of which, I said, was to present certain concepts intimately related to the letters and constituting, in themselves, instructions of basic and equal importance. Extracts from the memorandum of transmittal and the letter of instructions to General Van Fleet follow. The letters to Admiral Joy and General Stratemeyer, containing differing instructions, are given in extract form in Appendices 6 and 7.

EXTRACT FROM THE MEMORANDUM

"The grave and ever-present danger that the conduct of our current operations may result in an extension of hostilities, and so lead into a world-wide conflagration, places a heavy responsibility upon all elements of this Command, but particularly upon those capable of offensive action.

"In accomplishing our assigned missions, this responsibility is everpresent. It is a responsibility not only to superior authority in the direct command chain, but inescapably to the American people. It can be discharged only if every commander is fully alive to the possible consequences of his acts; if every commander has imbued his command with a like sense of responsibility for its acts; has set up, and by frequent tests has satisfied himself of the effectiveness of his machinery for insuring his control of the offensive actions of his command and of its reactions to enemy action; and, in the final analysis, is himself determined that no act of his command shall bring about an extension of the present conflict, except when such act is taken in full accordance with the spirit of the accompanying Letter of Instructions.

"In the day to day, in fact hour to hour, performance of his duties, I therefore desire that every responsible commander, regardless of rank, bear constantly in mind that the discharge of his responsibilities in this respect is a sacred duty."

While the foregoing had less application to the ground forces than to the naval and air components of my command, where the action of a single Navy ship or Air Force plane could bring on the most serious consequences, they nevertheless served to focus attention on this vital point, as I explained orally to General Van Fleet during my next visit to his headquarters.

EXTRACT FROM THE LETTER OF INSTRUCTIONS TO THE COMMANDING GENERAL, EIGHTH ARMY

1. a. Until our Intelligence justifies different concepts, you will base your operations on the assumptions:

(1) That forces opposed to you are fixed in their determination either to drive you from the Peninsula, or to destroy you there, and

(2) That the U.S.S.R. may at any time elect to exercise present capabilities by the direct military intervention of its armed forces, ground, sea, and air, against United Nations forces in this Theater, and that such intervention, if made, will be coordinated with the exercise of their offensive capabilities by Chinese Communist and North Korean Peoples Army military forces, all so timed as to take maximum advantage of weather and of its effect on terrain.

b. You will further base your operations on the assumptions:

(1) That your own forces will be brought to and maintained at approximately Tables of Organization and Equipment strength, but that you will receive no major reinforcements in combat organizations or service support units.

(2) That the duration of your operations cannot now be predicted.

(3) That you may, at any time, be directed by competent au-

thority to initiate a withdrawal to a defensive position and there be directed to defend indefinitely.

(4) That you may at any time be directed by competent authority to initiate a retirement designed to culminate in an early evacuation of the Korean Peninsula.

2. a. Your mission is to repel aggression against so much of the territory (and the people therein) of the Republic of Korea, as you now occupy and, in collaboration with the Government of the Republic of Korea, to establish and maintain order in that territory. In carrying out this mission you are authorized to conduct military operations, including amphibious and airborne landings, as well as ground operations in Korea north of the 38th parallel, subject to the limitations imposed in b(1) below, and subject to the further limitation, that under no circumstances will any of your forces of whatever strength cross the Manchurian or U.S.S.R. borders of Korea, or will any of your non-Korean forces even operate in North Korean territory contiguous to those borders.

b. In the execution of this mission you will be guided by the following prescriptions:

(1) Advance of major elements of your forces beyond the general line: Junction of IMJIN and HAN Rivers—CHORWON—HWACHON RESERVOIR—TAEPO-RI, will be on my orders only. [This was the WYOMING LINE.]

(2) You will direct the efforts of your forces toward inflicting maximum personnel casualties and matériel losses on hostile forces in Korea, consistent with the maintenance intact of all your major units and the safety of your troops. The continued piecemeal destruction of the offensive potential of the Chinese Communist and North Korean Armies contributes materially to this objective, while concurrently destroying China's military prestige.

(3) You will maintain the offensive spirit of your Army and retain the initiative, through maximum maneuver of firepower, within the limitations imposed by logistics and terrain, and without undue sacrifice of men or equipment.

(4) You will exploit the enemy's every weakness and take advantage of every opportunity to show the world the true measure of the combat effectiveness of the forces opposing you.

(5) * * *

(6) Acquisition of terrain in itself is of little or no value.

(7) You will support the Commander, Naval Forces Far East,

and the Commanding General, Far East Air Forces, in the discharge of their assigned missions.

3. a. Copies of these instructions, which provide the basis for your planning, should be furnished only to United States officers under your command who "need to know." However, the restrictive provisions of these instructions, designed to prevent expansion of the Korean conflict, will be disseminated to the extent necessary to guarantee understanding and compliance by all members of your command.

b. * * *

c. You are invited to discuss these instructions with me at any time for the purpose either of clarifying any feature of them, or of proposing changes therein.

M. B. RIDGWAY
Lieutenant General, U. S. Army

The responsibility of my new job reached far beyond the sphere of action in Korea, however, and I sometimes wondered whether I might be slighting one in favor of the other. Secretary of State John Foster Dulles, visiting me in Tokyo, expressed his feeling toward my newly enlarged duties. "I hope," he said, "that you will not consider your responsibilities toward Treaty problems as secondary among your other responsibilities." (The Japanese Treaty, of which Dulles was the chief architect, was then in an advanced state of negotiation.) I assured him that I would not, adding that I would get into this problem area as quickly and as fully as possible. I pointed out that during this first week I had deliberately given precedence to the problems relating to the defense of Japan, since the Soviets, so the Defense Department had informed me, had the capability of launching their Far Eastern military forces against our forces in this theater with little or no warning, and the possibility of their doing so could not be overlooked. The problems that this capability presented, therefore, had urgency that no other problem confronting me had.

If I was to have the job of defending this land, I knew I must develop an intimate knowledge of its terrain, as well as the current state of our troops and installations in Japan. So I soon began a series of reconnaissance flights and ground visits to key areas. This filled all the spare corners of my days for some time to come. Concurrently, it was my resolve to do all I could to prevent the rebirth of the garrison attitude that still prevailed in some quarters in Japan. I also wanted to know where our forces stood, what their strength was, how competent were their commanders, and how best we could maneuver to meet a Soviet thrust if it should develop. Within a few days of my arrival in Tokyo I made a reconnaissance flight around the whole periphery of Hokkaido, which I felt would most likely be the first Russian objective. On this flight I came as close as I thought prudent to Soviet territory— only a few miles distant across La Perouse Strait. I scouted the other areas, too, in my B-17, sometimes directing the pilot to fly just over the treetops, so I could make a close-up study of the terrain over which our forces might some day be fighting. (Once I took Mrs. Ridgway with me, inviting her down into the bombardier's bay for an unobstructed view of the hills and forests that reeled by just beneath our feet. She quickly decided that skimming the treetops in a Plexiglas bubble was not nearly so much fun as riding topside where the ground seemed farther away.)

While I recognized the unlikelihood of a Soviet attack and while I was determined to carry out President Truman's directive to avoid any action that might tend to embroil our nation in a world war, I was also set upon keeping all the forces under my command in a state of combat-readiness, prepared to deal with what the enemy *could* do rather than with what we thought he *would* do.

The defense of Japan was a responsibility assigned to me unilaterally by my own nation. As United Nations Commander in Korea, I had other new missions: To continue the fighting in Korea as long as I felt such action offered reasonable hope of success; to maintain the blockade of the entire Korean coast; to stabilize the situation in Korea or to evacuate UN forces to Japan if forced out of Korea. There were manifold administrative jobs, too, that went with my new authority. One in which I took much personal pleasure was the rectification of what I regarded as an unintentional though marked slight to a splendid officer, Major General Doyle Hickey. When Major General Almond, in September

169

1950, left Tokyo to command the X Corps in the Inchon Operation, General Hickey had been designated "Acting Chief of Staff, GHQ." From that time on, apparently to satisfy some personal idiosyncrasy, General MacArthur continued Almond on paper as "Chief of Staff, GHQ" as well as "Commanding General, X Corps." His admiration for Almond's abilities, which I knew to be well deserved and in which I fully concurred, actually made it appear that Hickey, upon whom devolved all the heavy responsibilities of the Chief of Staff of a major headquarters, was no more than a temporary filler-in. I am sure the arrangement was as little to Almond's taste as it was to Hickey's, but bold indeed was the subordinate who questioned such matters. At any rate, soon after General MacArthur's departure from Tokyo, I had orders issued appointing Hickey Chief of Staff, GHQ, vice Almond, relieved, who continued as Commanding General, X Corps.

There were petty drawbacks as well as small satisfactions of this sort in my new position. One matter that used to both amuse and annoy me was the splendor of my new accommodations at the Dai-Ichi Building. The steps of this building were not constructed for an American soldier, being too low for a full-sized stride and too deep to be taken two at a time. Going up them was like trying to walk railroad ties. To take one at a time was to mince up like a child, and so, like the ties, they were "too short for one, too long for two." Just how to ascend these steps without turning myself into what P. G. Wodehouse once described as a "dignified procession of one," was a problem that annoyed me on my first day on the job. I solved it by going up the steps in a series of jumps. And of course a news photographer managed to catch me in mid-flight one day so that it looked as if I were leaping upstairs like an eager bridegroom, or a tardy schoolboy. This exercise did not quite compensate for the lack of Korean mountains to climb. Visiting an advanced unit high on a ridge had been all the keep-fit exercise I required while commanding the Eighth Army, and I had visions of growing broad and bulgy here in Tokyo. Fortunately the Embassy provided a fine swimming pool and I quickly had a badminton court laid out on the grounds. With two former first-string West Point football players on my staff, I had no trouble finding partners to work out with and I managed to keep from outgrowing my uniform.

But, of course, while such things might clutter the corners of my mind, the major preoccupation of all of us remained the tactical maneuvers and the fortunes of the United Nations in Korea. I knew we had tough days ahead, particularly as the worsening weather diminished our advantage in firepower. My confidence in the army's ability to meet any Chinese threat remained complete, however, and even after the fifth-phase offensive began I never knew a moment of doubt.

Only the behavior of the ROK units caused me distress. Once more, the advancing Chinese drove unit after unit of the South Korean troops into headlong flight, in which they abandoned again quantities of costly equipment difficult to replace. The Chinese began their offensive, as they so often did, by moonlight, after light-to-heavy artillery and mortar fire. The offensive opened in the mountains of central Korea and spread, by daybreak, across the whole peninsula. We had expected extensive use of enemy tanks this time, but I don't recall that any appeared. Instead, the enemy resorted to the familiar tactics to which the ROKs found it so difficult to adjust: night attacks by great numbers of foot soldiers, moving in almost at arm's length behind the artillery barrage and hurling grenades without regard to losses. And again the wild bugles and barbaric screams sounded up and down the lines, while enemy infantry, padding silently up dark hillsides in rubber shoes, infiltrated our positions.

Our lines held firm everywhere against the first assaults except in the central sector, where the ROK 6th Division occupied the center with the U.S. 24th Division on the left and the 1st Marine Division on the right. The Chinese struck the ROKs hard and sent them reeling back in confusion, south of the Utah Line. Then the enemy moved into the gap, in an effort to envelop the U.S. troops on either side. The 24th and the 1st Marines held, but General Van Fleet immediately ordered the I and IX Corps, in the face of this danger, to pull back step by step to the Kansas

Line, yielding up all the ground recently taken, but gaining valuable time in exchange and severely punishing the enemy. Other forces quickly plugged the gap left by the retreating ROK 6th Division and kept the enemy from exploiting his sudden advantage.

Fighting was fierce all along the front and the toll of Chinese was heavy. Our careful preparations for this very sort of attack had begun to pay off. Without such preparation, our easy advance of the previous weeks might have left us in a trap, for the Chinese poured into, through, and around our positions in the central sector in great numbers. By 10 P.M. of the first day, there were Chinese 1000 yards behind the IX Corps positions and firing on artillery units that had been moved forward that very afternoon. But well-manned perimeter defenses charged the enemy a heavy price. As an instance, the fighting around the position of the 92nd Armored Field Artillery Battalion was especially bitter, with Chinese swarming all over the position in the hours before dawn. But Lieutenant Colonel Leon F. LaVoie had seen to his defenses and they could not be panicked. Before the enemy was beaten off, the Chinese had lost 179 dead, as against fifteen lost by the 92nd. The IX Corps alone, in three days of fighting, fired 15,000 artillery rounds.

On April 26 the enemy cut the wide highway that connected Seoul with Chunchon in central Korea and Kansong on the east coast. Van Fleet immediately pulled the IX Corps back to the Hongchon River. The Chinese had already waded the shallow Imjin River in a midnight crossing, to establish small bridgeheads on the south bank, while other Chinese forces moved south along the road between Chorwon and Seoul. The I Corps retired in good order, inflicting severe punishment, as far as the Kansas Line, where it meant to hold. But the enemy drove the ROK 1st Division south of the Kansas Line in a sudden surge, leaving exposed the left flank of the British 29th Brigade. The 1st Battalion of the Gloucestershire Regiment was cut off and overrun by the enemy in spite of repeated I Corps efforts to relieve it. Lieutenant Colonel J. P. Carnes (who had been with that regiment for twenty-six years) and his men courageously and grimly held on to their position for several days, until their ammunition was exhausted.

172

43. Enlisted men using Korean A-frames to carry mats, stovepipes, and other equipment during the withdrawal from the Pyongyang area to the 38th parallel. On December 16 Hamhung was abandoned. *U.S. Army photograph.*

44. The USS *Begor* lies at anchor ready to load the last UN landing craft as a great explosion rips harbor installations at Hungnam, denying their use to Chinese forces. *Official U.S. Navy photo.*

45. South Korean civilians plodding through heavy snow south of Kangnung, near the east coast, January 8, 1951. *U.S. Army photograph.*

46 and 47. This rail bridge was built by the 62nd Engineer Battalion, U.S. Eighth Army, across the Han River at Seoul. It was demolished by another Engineer unit during the evacuation of Seoul. *U.S. Army photographs.*

48. A C-119 Flying Boxcar flies over jagged mountains to a drop zone, January 1951. *U.S. Air Force photo.*

49. Near the front lines on January 28, 1951. General Douglas MacArthur is at the right, accompanied by Major General Courtney Whitney, his military secretary, second from left; General Ridgway, and, behind General MacArthur, Major General William B. Kean, Commanding General, 25th Division. *U.S. Army photograph.*

50. A corporal of the 4th Signal Battalion fastens a jumper as the power lines are rehabilitated from Tanyang to Chechon. Railroad is part of main rail system from Pusan to Seoul. January 31, 1951. *U.S. Army photograph*.

51. American infantrymen take refuge from Chinese mortar fire as they fight their way to the Han River, February 13, 1951. *U.S. Army photograph.*

52. Near Wonju on February 20, 1951, left to right: Lieutenant General Frank W. Milburn, Commanding General, U.S. I Corps, General MacArthur, and General Ridgway. *U.S. Army photograph.*

53. White-phosphorus shells falling on Chinese positions north of the Han River, March 5, 1951. *U.S. Army photograph.*

54. Infantrymen of the 5th Regimental Combat Team, 24th Division, trudge up another enemy-held hill in the central sector, March 19, 1951. *U.S. Army photograph.*

55. Infantrymen of the 3rd Division climbing up the trail to their objective near Uijongbu, March 23, 1951. By the end of March, the enemy had pulled back to a line north of the 38th parallel. *U.S. Army photograph.*

56. Marshaling yard on the main rail line leading south from Wonsan on the east coast undergoes a fiery napalm-bomb attack by B-26's of the Fifth Air Force. *U.S. Air Force photo.*

Only a few of the battalion's soldiers made their way back to UN lines.

Once they had cut the main east-west highway from Seoul, the Chinese gathered their strength for a full-scale assault on the capital city, which they had boasted would soon be back in their hands. Uijongbu, just north of the city, had to be abandoned when the Chinese threatened to envelop it. Van Fleet undertook then to establish a new defense line to hang on to Seoul and halt the enemy north of the Han. The U.S. 3rd Division held fast just four miles from the city limits.

The most dangerous Chinese thrust toward Seoul came on April 29 when 6000 Chinese attempted to cross the Han in small boats, west of Seoul, where they could move down the Kimpo peninsula and outflank the city's defenses. It was here that our command of the air worked most tellingly. Our pilots swooped down upon the attackers while they were still waterborne and decimated them. The shattered remnants that succeeded in reaching the south bank were no match at all for the ROK 5th Marine Battalion, then defending the peninsula. Another effort to outflank the city by slugging a way across the Han, at the junction of the Han and the Pukhan, was checked by the U.S. 24th and 25th Divisions.

With the enemy's effort to cross the Han finally halted, a new defense line was established (called No Name Line because it was never given a name) that extended clear across the peninsula from just north of Seoul through Sabangu, in central Korea, and thence to Taepo-ri, a coastal town just north of the 38th parallel on the shores of the Sea of Japan. Artillery and air bombardment had aided the ground forces tremendously in bringing this desperate offensive to a halt so far short of its objective. From April 21 to 29, UN fliers had flown 7420 missions and the incessant pounding of our big guns had pockmarked the whole face of the countryside.

It was Van Fleet's aim to expend fire and steel rather than flesh and blood to as great an extent as possible, and his forces made full use of our now overpowering advantage in air and in artillery of every caliber. Once it became clear that the enemy had

173

temporarily run out of steam, the Eighth Army returned at once to the offensive, allowing no time for the enemy to regroup and rearm. We knew that supplies were still pouring down from Manchuria, into the Iron Triangle—that flat plain completely closed in by jagged ranges of granite mountains, with Pyonggang at its apex and its base running from Chorwon to Kumhwa. The plan was to push back to the Kansas Line if we could, to menace the Triangle and even to seize it if practicable, and at any rate to take full advantage of more defensible terrain. Our tank patrols, in early May, thrust deep into enemy territory, as far as twelve miles north of No Name Line, where they harassed the withdrawing Chinese. The Kimpo peninsula was quickly cleared of the small enemy forces that had managed to penetrate there and the ROK 1st Division fought its way toward the Imjin. The 1st Cavalry took Uijongbu back again, closing off that approach to Seoul while other forces drove the enemy away from the city on the north and east. There was fierce fighting on the road to Chunchon, where the enemy had dug himself in deeply and fought tenaciously. The U. S. Marines had to clear this area in close-quarter fighting before Chunchon was retaken. The far right flank moved forward too and it seemed for a time that we might be able to mount an offensive that would put us back on the Kansas Line. But in the second week of May the enemy resistance, heretofore sporadic, began to stiffen everywhere. Our observers brought news of new airfields a-building with enemy air strength estimated at a thousand planes. Supply columns moved steadily down from the far north, despite our air attacks, and heavy enemy troop movements were noted every day. General Van Fleet decided then to postpone the offensive and to strengthen his defenses to meet this fresh assault. Over five hundred miles of barbed wire were strung out along No Name Line. Mines were laid and drums of gasoline and napalm, which could be triggered by an electric contact, were added to the minefields. Fields of fire were carefully plotted and we were prepared to feed the enemy a dose of concentrated firepower such as had not been employed in Korea before.

The Chinese resumed their efforts just after dark on May 15, using an estimated twenty-one divisions, with nine North Korean divisions on the flanks. The drive was aimed at the center of our defense line and specifically at the U.S. X Corps and the ROK III Corps. Late on the second day of the drive, the ROK 5th and 7th Divisions, which held high ground to the right of Chunchon, crumpled under heavy Chinese pressure and retreated in disorder. It was a scramble then to plug the gap in the line. Van Fleet moved the U.S. 2nd Division and the 1st Marine Division over to the right to hold against the western edge of the enemy penetration, with the IX Corps extending its own front to the right to take up the slack left by the 2nd Division and the Marines. He directed two infantry regiments into position to block the enemy drive at its southernmost point, while a regimental combat team and the U.S. 2nd Division moved up rapidly to set their own shoulders against the western face of the bulge. It was a tense twenty-four hours, as the Chinese swarmed into the bulge and set out to envelop our positions. For a time the men of the 2nd Division were fighting Chinese and North Koreans on front, flank and rear, with their main supply route severed. The U.S. 9th Infantry Regiment drove northward, however, while the French and Dutch Battalions of the U.S. 2nd Division, plus the U.S. 23rd and 38th Infantry Regiments, drove southward to regain control of the main supply route and then the 2nd Division held fast. One of the mightiest artillery bombardments in the war, with the 38th Field Artillery Battalion firing more than ten thousand 105-mm. rounds in twenty-four hours, helped stand off the enemy and cost him heavily in wounded and dead. On May 18, the third day of the new Chinese attack, General Almond ordered the 2nd Division to a new line some five miles to the south. General Clark L. Ruffner, the division commander, successfully executed this withdrawal, counting 900 men killed, wounded, and missing in the three-day battle, while Chinese and North Korean losses were estimated at 35,000.

Heavy pressure against other ROK units in the east central sector and along the coast drove them far back of No Name Line, with the ROK I Corps, on the shores of the Sea of Japan, pulling back some thirty-five miles, to the village of Kangnung. In the western sector, the enemy attempted to drive down the

Pukhan River to outflank Seoul, but the U.S. 25th Division and the ROK 6th Division, in three days of hard fighting, halted the Chinese in their tracks just south of Masogu-ri, a village about 20 miles east of the South Korean capital. There were some feeble efforts to launch a direct attack on the city but these were quickly beaten off and the Chinese once more had to stop for breath, still far short of the goal they had boasted of. In the eastern and central sectors, they had pushed south and bought a great deal of real estate, for which they paid an exorbitant price. But the Chinese had not succeeded in trapping any of our forces. Except for the quantity of equipment they had been able to seize from the ROK, they had nothing to show for the blood they had spent except much rugged terrain that looked like a landscape from Dante's Inferno, and some villages that had been so blasted by heavy bombardment that hardly a roof remained. The equipment abandoned by the retreating ROK forces was nothing to be shrugged off, however. It was enough to have equipped several complete divisions. Still the stories appeared in the Washington press and elsewhere at home bemoaning the friction between my headquarters and the ROK government—friction resulting from the repeated stories, emanating from Rhee's office, of the existence of a great reservoir of trained ROK manpower which, if only properly armed and equipped by the United States, would permit the reduction of UN forces in Korea. Such a prospect naturally proved alluring to readers at home. But it was based on pure illusion. Until Rhee could secure better battlefield performance from the ROK forces already under arms, or until there was a cessation of heavy fighting, there were neither personnel nor resources to spare to supervise and to provide training for an expansion program of the kind envisioned.

On May 9, in company of Ambassador Muccio and General Van Fleet, and with no one else present but Rhee himself, I had visited the ROK President and bluntly laid before him the need to develop better leadership in the ROK army. General Chung, the ROK Army Chief of Staff, had always had our full confidence. But the demands of combat—and political interference by the very civilian authorities who owed him ungrudging support—had made it nearly impossible for him to develop field commanders of the quality the ROK army needed and deserved. I do not think there was room for a trace of ambiguity in the straight-from-the-shoulder talk we delivered to the old warrior that afternoon. I may even have revealed more to him about our military situation than discretion called for. Yet his headquarters persistently fathered these fairy tales about untapped sources of soldiery that we refused to make use of. This was becoming a political rather than a military matter and I consequently urged Van Fleet to see that he and his senior officers—his Chief of Staff and his three U. S. Corps Commanders—should avoid all public statements about any matters that lay outside the purely military field. There would be time eventually to withdraw whole ROK Divisions from the line and put them through a training program that would make them into first-rate fighting forces. Until then we would have to do all we could to keep from exacerbating this sore spot on our political flank.

And now that the Chinese offensive had once more sputtered out, it was time to take up the offensive again. Two new UN battalions were about to finish their final pre-combat training and join the Eighth Army, and the temporary "shortage"* of ammunition, caused by Van Fleet's artillery-saturation tactics, was no longer a factor. But meanwhile the logistical situation had to be kept in mind—both ours and the enemy's. Offensive operations carried too far meant lengthening our supply lines unduly and shortening the enemy's, as well as incurring heavy casualties. South Korea still had only one first-class port fit for unloading military supplies—that was Pusan, far to the south now, and the only one where deep-draft vessels could dock. Inchon, the port of Seoul, was subject to the great tide differentials of the Yellow Sea, which made it necessary to bring cargo to shore on landing craft from ships standing far off the mudflats.

But it was good sense to threaten and even to seize, if we

---

* There was never any shortage at the firing batteries. What had happened was that the level of stockages in the depots in Korea had fallen below the level authorized, because of the sudden and drastic increases in the expenditure of ammunition.

177

could, the Iron Triangle, terminus of the formerly one good railroad from Manchuria and center for many good roads that kept the enemy's front fed and supplied. It may be recalled that the Wyoming Line, a bulge of the Kansas Line, had been aimed at the base of the Iron Triangle. It was also vital to us to control the Hwachon Reservoir, previously the source of water and electricity for Seoul and the heart of the enemy supply route. Consequently the new offensive was meant to roll on over the 38th parallel again, without our giving that line any further thought, and to destroy as much as we could of the enemy's potential.

On May 19 I flew to Korea to meet at the X Corps CP near Saemal with Van Fleet, Almond, and Hoge, the IX Corps commander. After being briefed by these commanders, I summarized my understanding of the conference as follows:

1. Eighth Army will attack on May 20, Corps missions as follows:

a. X Corps will check and stop the penetration on its east flank and will attack in coordination with east flank of IX Corps and will protect IX Corps flank.

b. IX Corps will attack and seize high ground west of the Chunchon basin.

c. I Corps will attack on the axis Seoul-Chorwon and protect the left (west) flank of IX Corps. The progress of this attack must be closely watched by CG, Eighth Army.

That afternoon and next morning I visited all the other U. S. Corps and Division CPs and some of those of the ROK army. My swing along the front concluded with a visit to General Chung, to stress once more the necessity of his insuring that every echelon of his command should realize the seriousness of the situation and make particular effort to see that ROK units behaved like soldiers on the battlefield.

At the end of the day, as I was visiting with Pat Partridge at his Fifth Air Force CP, I learned the distressing news that George Stratemeyer, Commander of the Far East Air Forces, had suffered a heart attack that afternoon. The attack proved serious enough to compel his relief and hospitalization for some weeks, following which he had to be sent back to the States and later retired. He was a most gallant, experienced, and resourceful officer. But sudden changes are the rule in war, and much as I deplored this turn of fate, I was highly gratified to receive Lieutenant General Otto P. (Opie) Weyland, whom the Air Force promptly assigned as Stratemeyer's replacement. I had long known Weyland, having served with him on the Inter-American Defense Board and during the negotiations of the Rio Treaty, and I could not have had a more willing or able teammate for the remainder of my Far Eastern Service.

The shift in forces decided upon before the offensive allotted a good share of the Hwachon Reservoir to the IX Corps, which heretofore had its zone boundary placed at the reservoir's edge. The X Corps, once it had reached its initial objectives, could now seep to the northeast and block enemy forces withdrawing up the coast. The ROK I Corps would push along up the coast, attacking in a northwesterly direction to crush the enemy between itself and the X Corps. The ROK III Corps, badly mauled in the Chinese advance, had been deactivated and its units divided between the X Corps and the ROK I Corps.

The UN forces started forward on May 20 and pushed ahead against melting resistance, with the U. S. Air Force giving constant close support. This would be no drive to the Yalu, even though we had current forces probably capable of going there. But Van Fleet moved his army forward, through the first phase line, Topeka, extending from Munsan-ni, on the west by the tidal plain of the Yellow Sea, through Inje and on to Hwangpo-ri, about ten miles below Kansong on the Sea of Japan. Then the army went on toward the Kansas Line and north to the Wyoming Line, which breasted the base of the Iron Triangle. Enemy resistance was strong, as usual, in those places where the terrain favored him, where roads were narrow or nonexistent and where our supplies had to be hand-hauled up the ridges. In the last week of May, the weather came to the enemy's rescue too, slowing our armor, almost wiping out many of the roads, and grounding our aircraft. As a result, the enemy was again able to trade space for time and make off with much of his force and supplies intact. By the end of the month, however, South Korea was once more practically free of hostile forces. The enemy had lost an estimated 17,000 dead and we had taken an equal number of prisoners. South Korean casualties in this advance had been unusually heavy—about 11,000 killed, wounded, missing, or stricken down by sickness.

With our forces back on or beyond the Kansas Line, it was our turn again to go on the defensive and Van Fleet once more undertook to make his line as nearly impregnable as possible, with barbed wire strung thickly all along the front and mines and barrels of inflammables strewn in fields before our positions. Wherever possible, shelters were dug with overhead cover. Again road blocks were set up and artillery concentrations plotted. Offensive operations continued toward the base of the triangle into June, despite heavy rain and strong enemy resistance. The U.S. 3rd and 25th Divisions plugged ahead, using flame throwers to drive the Chinese from their log-lined bunkers. Chorwon, the western foot of the triangle, was taken on June 11, and Kumhwa, the eastern foot, was abandoned by the enemy without further struggle. Two tank-infantry task forces then sped across the triangle to Pyong-gang, which was also bare of defenders. But the enemy was discovered in possession of commanding ground north of the town, so the task forces withdrew. From that time forth neither side endeavored to occupy the flat plains of the triangle in force.

Another area the enemy held dear was an ancient volcanic crater we named the Punchbowl, about twenty-five miles north of Inje and the same distance from the east coast, near the zone boundary of the U.S. X and ROK I Corps. Its rim was nearly knife sharp all around the edges, rising abruptly several hundred feet above the crater floor, and thickly wooded on every side. The enemy was solidly entrenched on the rim here and well-armed with mortars and artillery. Much blood was to be spilled in the coming months to win control of this area. In the Eighth Army's possession, it would shorten the line, provide better observation, and lessen the chance of strong enemy surprise attacks in that quarter. Once we had seized it, we never gave it up.

Now the first year's fighting was over and the United Nations Forces had accomplished the original objective—to free South

Korea of the enemy and to re-establish and hold the boundary. All across the peninsula, except at the extreme west, where the southward-flowing Imjin provided the most easily defensible line, our forces were established north of the 38th parallel, strong enough to withstand any assault by the enemy, unless he should receive massive reinforcement.

But efforts to seize and hold commanding ground near the vital areas were meeting bitter and bloody resistance. The enemy, like our own forces, had established a strong defensive line, with screening positions out front—a line he meant to hold. So the message I received on June 25 from the Joint Chiefs of Staff that cease-fire negotiations with the Communists might soon be initiated was not unwelcome. I immediately sent Lieutenant Colonel A. D. Surles, Jr., of my staff to confer with Van Fleet, taking with him a map prepared by our planners that showed our present front-line positions; the Kansas Line; a theoretical outpost line for Kansas; and a theoretical cease-fire line that would support the Kansas positions. I asked that Van Fleet tell me if he felt it practicable and desirable for the Eighth Army to seize the high ground between his present front-line positions and the theoretical cease-fire line.

In the light of later statements by Van Fleet to the effect that I had prevented him from driving on to total victory, it is interesting to recall his reply to this query. His views then were that he did not favor an advance by the Eighth Army to seize the ground at this time. An advance on the eastern front, he felt, would be costly in American lives and would gain real estate only. And, while an advance on the western portion of the front would be relatively easy, Van Fleet's view was that it would expose him unduly to offensive action by the enemy. He concluded that the cost in lives and the resulting relative vulnerability of the Eighth Army was too much to wager on the chance that there might be a cease-fire. He also urged that the negotiations on the cease-fire, should any ensue, should take into account that portion of Korea west of the Yesong River and south of the 38th parallel, which we had no desire to occupy, yet which might be traded at the bargaining table to gain the ground we desired in the eastern zone. He also remarked that the enemy in front of the 1st Marine Division—two North Korean Corps—were well dug in in strong defensive positions, were fighting hard, were up to strength, and seemed even more effective than the Chinese Communist Forces. I concurred in all these views and we decided to hold tight to see what the negotiations might bring.

The call for an armistice, first delivered on Sunday, June 23, by Jacob Malik, Deputy Foreign Commissar of the Soviet Union and Soviet Delegate to the United Nations, brought increased activity on the political and propaganda fronts, and brought me an influx of VIPs. The Chinese Communists soon seconded Malik's suggestion and many voices in our own country began to call for peace. On June 29, I was delighted to welcome to GHQ in Tokyo Admiral Forrest Sherman. After him came Arch Alexander, with whom I had had many pleasant dealings when I was in the Pentagon and he was Under Secretary of the Army. Soon afterward Governor Thomas E. Dewey of New York flew in to share with us his vigorous views on foreign affairs.

On June 30, at the direction of my superiors in Washington, I made a broadcast to the Chinese High Command stating that if, as was reported, it was ready for a cease-fire, the United Nations command would be willing to send representatives to discuss an armistice. It took but a few days to make contact and agree upon a meeting place—the west coast town of Kaesong, just south of the 38th parallel. I named Vice-Admiral C. Turner Joy to head the United Nations delegation. The chief Communist negotiator was Lieutenant General Nam Il, Chief of Staff of the North Korean Peoples Army. But the real power on the Red side was clearly General Hsieh Fang, Chief of Staff of the Chinese Peoples "Volunteer Army."

I was not unfamiliar with the Communist tactic of trying to wear down an opponent through endless and pointless argument, for in two and a half years with the United Nations I had experienced plenty of it, but I could not begin to foresee the wearying months of fruitless discussion that lay ahead. While both sides had immediately agreed that hostilities should continue during negotiations, it seemed to me, with a cease-fire faintly visible on the horizon, that I should do all I could to keep our losses at a justifiable minimum. I notified our commanders therefore that we would conduct no major offensives but would seek to retain the initiative through the use of strong patrols and local attacks designed to seize key terrain which would extend our observation and curtail the enemy's. When the first anniversary of the opening of hostilities arrived, I thought peace might be just around the next corner. Yet there were still two years and many lives and much blood between us and this constant dream of every soldier.

CHAPTER SEVEN

TRUCE TALKS AND STALEMATE –
BITTER FIGHTING ON THE RIDGES –
THE NATURE OF THE ENEMY

IN THE WAR'S second summer, while the negotiators droned on at Kaesong, in a rococo "teahouse" building not at all unlike a nineteenth-century New England high school, the foot soldiers fought over trackless hilltops and climbed painfully up granite ridges to take or retake positions the enemy would not let go. Most of the extensive fighting took place in the vicinity of the Punchbowl or the Iron Triangle, with perhaps the most blood spilled in trying to seize and hold the hills that dominated the deep valley of the Punchbowl.

On the west of this wide and fertile hollow, the folded hills lay almost one against the other, all thick with tough brush and hardwood trees and high grass. Tallest of them all was a peak we called Hill 1179, which the Koreans had named Taeu-san. This had a rounded summit, like a child's drawing of a mountain, and steep slopes and ridges that were almost knife sharp along the top. Standing 3900 feet above sea level, Hill 1179 was held by North Koreans in regimental strength. General Van Fleet knew that he must get the enemy off this hill to keep him from observing the Kansas Line and to force the Chinese artillery back where they could not menace our positions. After a vain effort by ROK Marines to dislodge the enemy from this prize, Van Fleet ordered

185

units of the 2nd Division, with close air and artillery support, to take the hill. It was a bloody and wearying assault. Men had to zigzag up the wooded slopes and finally climb hand-over-hand up rocky steeps to close with the enemy. Sweating Korean laborers, carrying on their ancient A-frames loads heavy enough to founder a pony, provided the only transportation for ammunition, armament, and food. Infantrymen carried full loads themselves, to set up the recoilless rifles, the communications lines, and the aid stations on the slopes. After four days of inch-by-inch advance the enemy was finally shaken loose and Hill 1179 was ours.

Another range of hills west of the Punchbowl became known as Bloody Ridge, from the price paid to win and hold it from the enemy. First taken in August, Bloody Ridge was held by a unit of the ROK 5th Division. One night the Chinese counterattacked in force and the ROKs were driven off. The 9th Infantry of the U.S. 2nd Division stormed the ridge then and fought bitterly there, inching forward and edging back, against an enemy dug in and well-supported by artillery. This position the enemy would not yield for five days, and only after the U.S. 1st Marine Division and the 2nd Division attacked simultaneously northward along the Punchbowl rim.

Enemy defensive strength obviously improved during the summer. Despite our constant and consistently successful effort to knock out railroads and bridges, to demolish marshaling yards and deny the highways to enemy traffic, supplies continued to flow down from Manchuria. Chinese artillery activity greatly increased, helping to slow all our ground operations. More and more enemy antiaircraft fire appeared and we began to lose some bombers. Whatever may be said for the value of air power—and there is no question that without it many of our advances would not have been possible—it simply could not keep the enemy from bringing in the armament he needed. It could slow him down and keep him working nights; but it could not isolate the battleground.

The fighting on Bloody Ridge, and on adjacent Heartbreak Ridge, was perhaps the bloodiest to date and the most strenuous, demanding the utmost in physical strength, endurance and raw courage. Infantrymen fought like Indians, crawling up hillsides, lugging mortar rounds as well as their own rifles and ammunition and sometimes having to blast the enemy out of dug-in positions at point-blank range.

The enemy worked with Oriental doggedness to fortify himself in the hills, sometimes tunneling, with hand labor, from the reverse slope to the forward slope of a hill, so that he could pull out of his forward positions under air and artillery attack and find shelter on the reverse slope of the hill, where it was difficult to zero in on him with airstrikes or heavy howitzers. He might build tunnels as much as a thousand yards long to enable him to take quick shelter from bombardment, yet move forward to meet an attack on the ground. The forward ends of these tunnels were usually camouflaged with great skill and care, and it took sharp observation to spot them. Once spotted, however, they could be knocked out by direct hits from our howitzers sighting directly at their targets. Our artillerymen demonstrated some pinpoint accuracy in blasting out these strong points with 8-inch howitzers that had been hauled into position by bull-dozers—a novel and effective use for these invaluable weapons.

By July 1, the enemy buildup had brought his total troop strength to an estimated 460,000, with a corresponding increase in offensive capabilities. At this time I asked Van Fleet to submit a plan for advancing to the waist of the peninsula—the Pyongyang-Wonsan line that we had once considered in the weeks just after we crossed the 38th parallel for the first time. This was Operation Overwhelming, a plan that might be ordered executed in the event of an enemy withdrawal, a change in mission ordered by Washington, or a major augmentation of combat strength. I withheld approval of this plan, however, for I felt it best to wait and see how armistice negotiations turned out. Battle casualties among the ground forces had dropped in a heartening manner during July and August, as ground commanders of all ranks hesitated to fight for ground that an early armistice might require them to relinquish.

Van Fleet meanwhile decided to move to a more active defense, particularly in the vicinity of the Punchbowl, where much high ground still remained in enemy hands. In Korea, as in so many other ground campaigns, there was always just one more hill to seize to keep the current positions secure. And around the Punchbowl, the hills seemed to be elbowing each other in their effort to look down into the hollow of the ancient crater. The hills just west of the Punchbowl, to be known as Bloody Ridge, were well organized for defense and stubbornly held by North Korean divisions. The infantry units of the U.S. 2nd Division of the X Corps here met the fiercest opposition of the campaign, often finding themselves shoved off a ridge they had just secured and having to fight their way back to it in a matter of hours. In one 24-hour stretch, the 2nd Division threw as many as eleven separate assaults against a single ridge and still could not clear it of the enemy. But by the end of September Bloody Ridge and the Punchbowl itself were in our hands to stay.

During the fighting for the ridges, I received from Van Fleet a plan for a much more ambitious advance in the same general sector, designed to shorten our lines still further. This was Operation Talons, a plan to which I gave immediate approval. Van Fleet, however, had apparently been persuaded by the size of recent casualty lists (from smaller-scale operations) that the prize would not be worth the cost. Instead he planned to have the Eighth Army shift the weight of its effort to the west, the zone belonging to the U.S. I Corps. Then, if all went well, and armistice negotiations made no progress, he would seek approval for an amphibious operation on the east coast about halfway between his right flank and Wonsan. While I withheld approval of the amphibious landing (a plan Van Fleet's Corps commanders did not endorse) I did authorize limited-objective attacks for important terrain features. As a result of this, Van Fleet initiated a plan to seize and hold ground some four miles west of the Punchbowl, the range of hills later to be known as Heartbreak Ridge.

The U.S. 2nd Division was given the job of dislodging from this ridge the North Korean troops who had dug themselves in securely, with well-camouflaged bunkers and weapon emplacements. The heavy foliage of late summer made it doubly difficult to spot these strong points and the North Korean troops fought with great tenacity. The attack on the ridge was begun in piece-meal fashion and despite great gallantry the troops of the 2nd Division soon found themselves stalled, short of their objectives, after having sustained heavy losses.

Losses by this division had long been of special concern to me. Quite aside from the heavy losses sustained by the division at Kunu-ri in late November and early December and again in Feb-ruary and May, during the final Chinese offensives, losses that were incident to the accidents of combat, this division, day in and day out, week in and week out, had a higher casualty rate, particularly in KIA (killed in action) than any other division in the Eighth Army. I had taken occasion to discuss this matter with General Ruffner when he had commanded the division, as well as with Van Fleet. In mid-September, when Major General Robert N. Young took over command of the 2nd, I told him I wanted him to give this matter his personal attention.

Soon thereafter, Colonel James Y. Adams, who had led his own unit as it battered itself bloody against Heartbreak Ridge, bluntly reported to General Young that to continue the operation on its current scale would be suicide. For a field commander to arrive at such a decision, and to express it to his superior, takes high moral courage, the sort of courage I have always felt is more important in a commander even than physical courage. Physical courage is never in short supply in a fighting army. Moral courage sometimes is.

General Young then reviewed the situation and decided that piecemeal attacks would not do. Instead he substituted a fully coordinated attack by the entire division, with thorough artillery preparation and powerful close air support. As a result, the 2nd Division secured Heartbreak Ridge on October 15 and never gave it up again.

In all this action, close air support and air-drops of food, am-munition, and medical supplies were of inestimable value and I know the foot soldiers often gave open and fervent thanks for the intrepid actions of their brothers in the air, who seemed to ask only a little clear sky and a bit of daylight to work in.

Weather, as always in a Korean summer, was as treacherous

in battle as the enemy. Sudden cloudbursts would wash out the whole shoulder of a narrow road along a cliff-edge and leave a truck-train stranded. Or a flash flood would sweep a pontoon bridge downstream and send soldiers stripped to their undershorts and clinging breathlessly to a lifeline, out into the roaring waters to try to salvage some precious equipment.

During these operations, Van Fleet had submitted to GHQ plans calling for major offensive operations by the U.S. I and IX Corps, to be followed by an amphibious assault on the east coast. These operations, if approved and successfully executed, would have placed the advance elements of the Eighth Army on a line extending from Pyongyang to Kojo, a town on the east coast about twenty-five miles below Wonsan. Van Fleet had asked me for quick decisions on both plans, named Operation Cudgel and Operation Wrangler. But a few days later he decided to discard both plans in favor of one far less ambitious and less hazardous in the U.S. IX Corps zone. This advance, named Operation Commando, approved and launched on October 3, encountered a defense just as tenacious and counterattacks just as persistent as the 2nd Division had had to deal with in the east. But it reached and secured its objective on October 19, establishing the Jamestown Line, a new bulge out of the Kansas Line, and removing the enemy threat to the Chorwon-Seoul railroad.

These efforts, by the U.S. 2nd Division and the IX Corps, brought us new losses and resulted in a strong adverse reaction at home, and particularly in Congress, where it was felt there had not been sufficient improvement in the over-all situation to warrant such expenditure of blood. Secretary of War Frank Pace was moved to write me to report this home-front feeling. The fact, was, however, that these actions had greatly improved our defensive positions, and had also impressed the Communists, who had suspended the armistice talks meanwhile, that they had best get back to the negotiation table. The front grew relatively quiet again after that, with battle deaths in November 1951 down about one-half from the October total and those during December down two-thirds from the total in November.

With the resumption of truce negotiations, I instructed Van

Fleet to assume an active defense, giving him authority to seize suitable terrain along the general trace of his present lines, but limiting offensive operations to the taking of outpost positions requiring commitment of no more than one division. With rumors (always unreliable) circulating to the effect that the Communists now wanted an early cease-fire, combat became a series of small-scale operations and patrol actions. Both sides now occupied ground that had been strongly organized in depth. Neither side had any appetite for a general offensive. So it seemed a good time to undertake the elimination of a persistent annoyance—the existence of large bands of guerrillas in South Korea, particularly in the mountainous areas northwest of Chinju, where they had taken refuge after the Communist retreat. Van Fleet assigned Lieutenant General Paik Sun Yup, with two ROK divisions, to Operation Ratkiller, designed to rid us of this potentially dangerous threat. By the end of January 1952, nearly 20,000 freebooters—bandits and organized guerrillas—had been killed or captured and the irritation was ended for good.

Plans for limited-objective attacks, submitted by Van Fleet during this period, I ordered held in abeyance. Indications of progress in the truce talks inclined me to withhold approval of plans (most of which lacked the concurrence of Van Fleet's subordinate commanders whom I had consulted) that would have caused a sharp rise in battle casualties with nothing like commensurate results.

But all this time a major air effort, called Operation Strangle, had been in progress. The aim of this effort was obviously to throttle enemy supply efforts along the railroads and highways reaching north, but it became evident that our Air Force simply could not maintain the sustained effort required to knock out the railroads and keep them out of operation. Despite extraordinarily fine work by the Air Force, Navy, and Marine Corps aviation, the enemy continued his buildup, until it became quite clear to General Weyland and to me that, short of a major change in the battle situation that would force the enemy to increase sharply his expenditure of supplies and ammunition, he would be in a position to launch a major offensive by spring.

191

The air operations, supplemented in the coastal areas by naval gunfire from battleships and destroyers, did at least keep the enemy from attaining superiority in firepower and so held down, if it did not diminish, his capabilities. Enemy artillery strength had been growing dangerously and the importance of limiting that growth may be indicated by the fact that the number of artillery and mortar rounds falling within our lines increased, between April and June of 1952, from 2388 to something over 6800.

But for the most part, as the truce talks droned on in this last winter of my command, a stalemate obtained all across the peninsula and I found time to accomplish some of the tasks that had been assigned a lower priority when the situation was acute.

There is, however, one high-priority job that I have not mentioned. While I was still in command of the Eighth Army I had received from Major General William B. Kean, then commander of the U.S. 25th Division, an earnest and thoughtful recommendation for the integration of white and Negro troops. Kean had had full opportunity to observe Negro troops both in peacetime, at Fort Benning, and in Korea, where the all-Negro 24th Infantry Regiment was part of his command, and he felt that, both from a human and a military point of view, it was wholly inefficient, not to say improper, to segregate soldiers this way. This coincided precisely with my own views and I had planned in mid-March to seek authorization from General MacArthur, who would in turn sound out Washington, to commence integration at once. In both the U.S. 9th and 15th Infantry Regiments under my command, there was a battalion of Negro troops and we had numerous other combat and support units with all-Negro personnel, except for officers. Because we were in the middle of a major offensive then, no action was initiated until I had taken command at GHQ. At that time, I had a chance to discuss this matter with General Maxwell D. Taylor, then the Army's Assistant Chief of Staff, G-3, who had come to Tokyo on an official visit representing both the Secretary and the Chief of Staff of the Army. I told him that, if I could secure the approval of higher authority, I planned to effect full integration beginning with the largest all-Negro combat units, the 24th Infantry Regiment and the two

192

infantry battalions, one in the 9th and the other in the 15th Infantry Regiments. After that we could break up the smaller all-Negro combat units of artillery and armor and finally do the same with the numerous small service of supply units both in Korea and Japan. It was my conviction, as it was General Kean's, that only in this way could we assure the sort of *esprit* a fighting army needs, where each soldier stands proudly on his own feet, knowing himself to be as good as the next fellow and better than the enemy. Besides it had always seemed to me both un-American and un-Christian for free citizens to be taught to downgrade themselves this way, as if they were unfit to associate with their fellows or to accept leadership themselves.

General Taylor heartily approved this move and commented that this was a most auspicious time to make it, inasmuch as it was bound to have a profound effect upon the whole Regular Army from this time forth. In early June, when Secretary Marshall visited Korea and Tokyo I discussed my plan with him and he carried it back to Washington. The plan was ultimately approved and I promptly executed it in my theater. After that, the entire United States Army adopted this long-overdue reform, with all the beneficial results we had foreseen—in morale as well as in civilian acceptance.

The relative stability of the fighting front enabled Van Fleet and me to turn our attention to some other problems that had been nagging at us for months, but which had been necessarily pushed aside by the succeeding military crises. Number one perhaps was the tragic lack of leadership in the Republic of Korea Army, leadership that barriers of language and protocol prevented us from fully supplying. Now that the pressure had diminished, we could undertake a thorough training program that would provide the indigenous leadership that could make the Korean soldier the equal of any. So much of the best qualities of the Korean fighting man had been dissipated through political favoritism and complex political fence-mending that the cost to us in both men and matériel could not be measured. Korean units had been shifted here and there at the whim of various politicos, had been used to crush "banditry" or to bolster some local big wig's ego, and youthful officers had found it impossible to criticize, dissent from, or even differ with their unschooled superiors. Leaders whose "training" had been one hundred percent political were the first to break under enemy pressure and invariably their own panic was promptly transmitted to the troops, too many of whom had themselves received none of the drill required to teach them to respond instinctively and aggressively in a crisis.

What had been particularly lacking was training in the uses of artillery, a major feature of this war, where we had to make up in firepower what we lacked in manpower. The Far East Command had long frowned on any increase in ROK artillery. They felt that the terrain, the extreme difficulty of ammunition resupply over very poor roads and precipitate ridges, combined with the lack of trained ROK artillerymen and the shortage of pieces, provided reason enough for opposing expansion. But as the fighting slowed down and the flow of armament increased, we had both the time and the equipment to strengthen the ROKA in this respect. And I felt strongly that the ROK units must have long-range artillery to be capable of mutual support, division to division, along our thinly manned line.

In September 1951, I authorized the activation of four ROK 155-mm. howitzer battalions by the year's end. As each unit was activated, it was attached to a U. S. Corps and received eight weeks' intensive training. Soon afterward, I authorized three Headquarters Batteries of 105-mm. howitzers and six more battalions of the same caliber, these too to be activated by the end of 1951. It was my aim to produce eventually sufficient batteries of 105-mm. and 155-mm. howitzers to provide for each of the ten ROK divisions a full complement of four artillery battalions, three 105-mm. and one 155-mm. Early in 1952, I received approval from Washington to go ahead with this plan. By this date, ROK officers were returning from artillery school in the United States to add incentive to the expansion.

On the fighting front the careful retraining of ROK officers was making itself felt. Many of our offensive operations now in the eastern and east central sector were carried out almost entirely by ROK troops. On both sides of the Punchbowl, while our forces in the west sent out combat patrols to divert the enemy reserves and our naval forces lent the support of their heavy guns, the X Corps and the ROK I Corps advanced into more defensible terrain. These actions involved ROK forces almost exclusively. In the western sector, too, later in the year, the ROK 1st Division fought with great gallantry as the IX Corps moved the front forward three to four miles.

The South Korean Service Corps, too, offered its own priceless contribution. I authorized Van Fleet to increase this force to 60,000 laborers and porters. Their valiant willingness to clamber up the steep slopes with A-frames loaded with supplies, to construct bunkers, fill sandbags, shore up trenches and tunnels, and generally to perform the sweaty tasks of feeding, supplying, and fortifying a fighting army under constant fire earned a large share of the credit for our ability to regain and hold tight to the Kansas Line.

While the long long months during which the negotiations continued are usually referred to as a time of stalemate, it must not be thought the fighting was any less grim. Every day saw its own list of casualties, far fewer, thank God, than the major offensives had brought us, but still a reminder that we were paying a dear price for whatever we would win at the truce table. We were strung out now in a shorter line across the peninsula but the forces, numbering somewhat less than 600,000, of which 230,000 were Americans, were still too scanty to man the line more than thinly. The enemy of course heavily outnumbered us and but for our massive firepower, our constant close air support, and our tight control of the seas, the Chinese might have overwhelmed us. It was our guns—our ability to concentrate untold amounts of hot steel at any point along the battle line—that gave us our superiority. Of course our lately developed skills at using the terrain to our own advantage, at getting off the narrow twisting roads up into the wild hillsides and along the rocky ridges, had helped tip the scales in our favor too. But now Van Fleet's aim, once he had established control of the dominating heights, was to get the enemy out into the open where our big guns could destroy him.

The Chinese, of course, delighted to attack at night, when our air power was grounded and our observers blind. Our defenses were not really "in depth" for they were scattered and thinly manned, but we did have screening forces to outpost a line about a rifle shot from the main line of resistance and these were the men whose task it was to bring out the enemy in force to a place where we could blast him with our heavy artillery. Often the men in a lonely redoubt, sandbagged and wired all around for defense from every side, would blink at the sight of a silent enemy standing inside their position in the dark, or would discover that four or five Chinese, padding noiselessly on rubber soles, already stood between them and the outpost line of resistance. The signal flares would go up over the enemy lines, frantic calls would go out to bring the outguards in, and the battle would be joined almost before a challenge could be issued.

I can recall that I made constant efforts to secure more battle-field illumination to enable us to zero in on enemy forces even at night. More and more flares were used and we tried all sorts of devices, including powerful searchlights that bounced their glare off low-hanging clouds, as we had done with good effect in Europe in World War II. This helped, both literally and figuratively, to lighten the tasks for the men in the lonely outpost line, who spent tense hours peering into the dark at unknown shapes, and who sometimes had little more protection on a granite ridge than a few loose scraps of rock piled up to break the silhouette. The night attacks were as weird and dreamlike as ever, preceded by the unworldly wailing of taps on the Chinese bugles, or English profanity screamed by half a hundred Chinese throats, or threats of death and other noises designed to chill a Westerner's blood. Our battle-seasoned troops by this time, however, had grown used to the musical accompaniment and sometimes set out to capture a Chinese bugle and throw the enemy signal system into confusion.

Meanwhile the negotiations went on, with one long interruption when the enemy insisted we accept the blame for fake "incidents" that we retorted had never occurred, and the truce that had seemed right at hand at the end of the first year's fighting kept

57. A Korean woman, aided by her family, makes the trek south as UN troops withdraw from above the 38th parallel in the face of heavy Chinese attacks. April 23, 1951. *U.S. Army photograph.*

58. The Hwachon Dam is torpedoed by Navy AD Skyraiders on May 3, 1951, using aerial torpedoes for the first time during the Korean War. The dam was damaged in an attempt to break up a mounting Communist grouping preparing for the spring offensive. *Official U.S. Navy photo.*

59. Marine patrol closes in on a Korean hut in search of a Communist sniper offering stubborn resistance in front-line action, September 24, 1951. The feet of an enemy casualty are visible in the doorway. *Defense Department photo, Marine Corps.*

60. General Matthew B. Ridgway, Commander in Chief, UN Command, visits a forward command post of the 24th U.S. Infantry Division on May 19, 1951. Left to right: Lieutenant General William M. Hoge, Commanding General, IX Corps; Major General Blackshear M. Bryan, Commanding General, 24th Division; Lieutenant General James A. Van Fleet, Commanding General, U.S. Eighth Army, and General Ridgway. *U.S. Army photograph.*

61. Crouching low and moving fast, U.S. airborne troops cross a field under fire near Umyong-ni as they attempt to cut off retreating Communists. *U.S. Army photograph.*

62. U.S. cavalry troops moving across rice paddies before starting the climb up Hill 513, north of Tokchong, June 1, 1951. *U.S. Army photograph.*

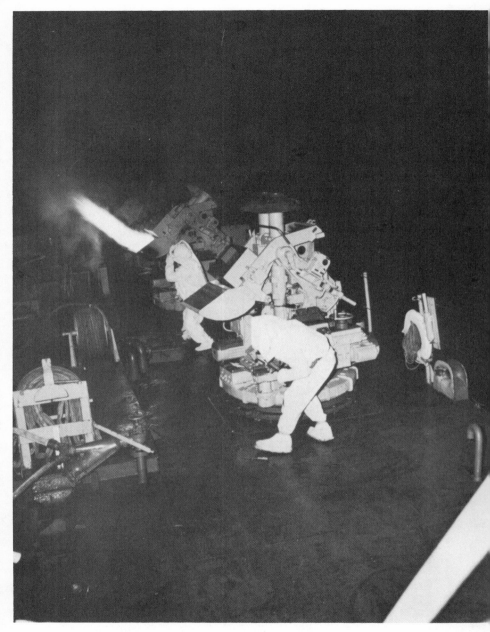

63. Plastic-clad American Navy gunners firing rockets at enemy-held Wonsan. The white blur at upper left is the trail of flame left when a rocket is launched. The men are wearing one-piece suits, with hood and gloves, made of plastic-coated glass fabric designed to give head-to-toe protection against back blasts of fuming acids. *Official U.S. Navy photo*.

64. UN truce delegation at Kaesong, July 17, 1951. Left to right: Major General Laurence C. Craigie, U.S. Air Force; Major General Paik Sun Yup, Commanding General, ROK I Corps; Vice Admiral C. Turner Joy, Far East Naval Commander, chief delegate; Major General Henry I. Hodes, Deputy Chief of Staff, U.S. Eighth Army, and Rear Admiral Arleigh A. Burke, U.S. Navy. *U.S. Army photograph.*

65. Communist truce delegation at Kaesong. Left to right: Major General Hsieh Fang and Lieutenant General Teng Hua, Chinese Army; Lieutenant General Nam Il, chief delegate, and Major General Lee Sang Cho and Major General Chang Pyong San, North Korean Army. *U.S. Army photograph.*

66. Conference site in Kaesong, July 10, 1951, the day the negotiations opened. *U.S. Army photograph.*

67. Enemy soldiers captured in the Punchbowl area are searched by South Koreans, August 18, 1951. *U.S. Army photograph.*

68. Men of the U.S. 2nd Infantry Division work desperately, August 11, 1951, to save equipment in the Soyang River, swollen by heavy rains. *U.S. Army photograph.*

69. Heartbreak Ridge from the northwest. The Punchbowl area is at the upper left. *Photograph taken by the U.S. Army on October 25, 1951.*

slipping away like a foxfire, for month after wearying month. I know that many citizens at home began to feel that lives and blood were being wasted on the battlefield while stubborn men kept trying to score debating points at the truce table. But the negotiations were just an extension of the battlefield. Whatever was eventually agreed on would necessarily reflect the military realities, and it was the bitter task of the soldier to impress the enemy with our ability to resist all his efforts to move the battle line farther south.

The negotiations were trying indeed. Sometimes the repetition of points already made, the oratorical flourishes, the tiresome vituperation were nearly enough to make men welcome a return to battle. But I was determined to prove the sincerity as well as the tenacity of the United Nations Command and I made up my mind I would not give way to impatience or intemperance any more than I would yield to bullying or threats to break the parley off. The story of the negotiations themselves has been well told many times and in full detail. But there are some aspects that are relevant to this narrative or that bear telling again.

That the United Nations made serious mistakes in the negotiations cannot be denied. And I think all the mistakes derived from two major misconceptions, both of which were rooted partly in naïveté and partly in the failure to appreciate fully a fact that Admiral Joy, Chief of our Delegation, stated a year or more later, in hindsight:

Communists neither blunder into conferences nor rush pell-mell to engage in negotiations. First they carefully set the stage. Their concern for maintaining "face," as well as their regard for practical advantages arising from favorable negotiating conditions, causes the Communists to consider carefully the physical circumstances in which a parley is to occur.*

The propaganda gain they wrung from our missteps was no doubt of substantial value to them, particularly among Asian peoples.

* *How Communists Negotiate,* C. T. Joy, The Macmillan Company, 1955.

By now, I assume, our officials both civil and military, certainly those who might have to endure the almost intolerable tirades of lies and vituperation at conference tables, are forewarned and mentally prepared.

Early in the negotiations I wrote to Admiral Joy:

To Communists the use of courtesy on your part is synonymous with concessions and concessions with a sure indication of weakness. I suggest you govern your utterances accordingly, employing such language and methods as these treacherous Communists cannot fail to understand, and understanding, respect.*

For Westerners who have never been exposed to Communist negotiating tactics, I would say it is virtually impossible to conceive in advance the extent to which the truth is perverted and facts distorted. A tax is placed on patience that even Job would have found all but unendurable.

At the very start we made a concession that we early had cause to regret. When I first offered to open the discussion, the suggested meeting place was the *Jutlandia,* a hospital ship under the Danish flag, to be anchored in Wonsan harbor. It seemed then that "neutral ground" of this sort, yet under the enemy's guns as well as our own, would invoke the spirit of compromise at once. The Communists did not even acknowledge this suggestion. In accepting the bid, they named the city of Kaesong— theoretically in "No Man's Land" south of the 38th parallel—as the meeting place. Washington directed me to accept this suggestion at once, in a further effort to expedite the end of the fighting and to prove our sincerity.

But when the talks opened, there was no atmosphere of neutrality at all. The city of Kaesong was in Communist hands. Their armed guards infested the area of the truce talks, and Red soldiers with Tommy guns gruffly ordered our envoys about. The appearance of our delegates, in jeeps carrying the white flags of truce, was photographed for the Asian press as a scene of sur-

* *Fighting Front and Truce Tent,* W. G. Hermes, Department of the Army, Office of the Chief of Military History, 1966.

render. Our press was excluded from the scene, as were our photographers. I immediately straightened out this imbalance by informing the Chinese that our delegation would not return unless the area of the conference was truly neutral and correspondents from our side of the line could be present. In true Communist style, the enemy negotiators sparred for time on this, asking that we await a decision from higher-up. But when they learned that I was not going to let the delegation return at all until the press from our side was represented, they gave in promptly.

Even so, the atmosphere of that negotiation site was never satisfactory. At one point, we had to make a serious protest at the sudden appearance of an armed Chinese unit, complete with machine guns and 60-mm. mortars, that marched directly across the path of our jeeps. I had previously suspended the talks until the Reds had promised to demilitarize the zone around the meeting place and this was a flagrant violation of our understanding. Admiral Joy protested at once and was told that the offending unit was merely a company of Military Police. To ask us to believe that Military Police had to go about armed with machine guns and 60-mm. mortars was rather too extreme and I immediately broadcast an announcement that the talks had been suspended until we could have a satisfactory agreement concerning demilitarization. The Communists held out for five days, then finally asked us to resume the talks under proper safeguards. But I was quickly advised that, where the English language broadcast had spoken of their "request" for us to return, the broadcast in Japanese had reported a "demand." I announced that I found their reply evasive and would not authorize resumption of the talks. This brought a more courteous request and a specific agreement.

Soon afterward, however, the fat fell into the fire again. On August 17 a Chinese security patrol near the neutral zone was fired on from ambush and the leader killed. The Reds demanded satisfaction and apology. Our investigation indicated that there had indeed been an ambush, but the troops that did the firing had been haphazardly dressed, without steel helmets, quite clearly partisan irregulars over which the United Nations Command had no control. We rejected the Red request and the talks went on.

Just five days later, long after dark, in a drenching rain, the Chinese asked our liaison officers to come at once to verify a bombing attack by a United Nations plane upon the neutral zone. Colonel Andrew J. Kinney, USAF, our chief liaison officer, and his aides accompanied the enemy liaison officers to the scene of the supposed attack and examined the evidence by flashlight. Kinney found some small holes in the ground such as might have been caused by buried explosives of grenade size, some bits of metal that appeared to be part of an airplane fuselage, a crumpled bit of metal that could have been an external gas tank from a plane. But there was no crater underneath and no scorching, as there would have been if napalm had been used. There was also the tail-fin of a rocket found on the ground northwest of the residence of the Red delegates. There were no injuries, no damage, no scorching, just a story of a plane, with its landing lights focused on the ground below, that had "attacked" the area. No United Nations plane had been in the area and the evidence available was far too flimsy to give the protest any substance. Yet the Communist delegate refused to wait for daylight, when a more painstaking investigation might have been made. He wanted a "confession" and an apology at once, to make clear to the world the "guilt" of the United Nations Command. This was refused and the talks were abruptly suspended. When they were eventually resumed I refused to return to Kaesong but insisted that future meetings be held at Panmunjom, a tiny village in truly neutral territory closer to our lines.

There had been a number of minor obstacles along the way that the good humor and common sense of our negotiators had managed to overcome. In the very beginning we had hit an obstacle that, petty as it was, could have aborted the whole conference before it began: The chief Communist liaison officer just would not discuss a date for the talks to start. This, said he, had been set by the superior officers, could not be discussed at his level, and that was an end of it. Kinney, who was opening the parley between the liaison forces, knew that no date had been set at all, by anybody, but he could not establish this point. The date, said Colonel Chang of the North Korean army, chief Communist liaison officer, was not subject to discussion. Well, no date, no conference, and Kinney was up a tree. Then one of his associates whispered to him that he should just name a date on his own, as if it had been agreed on. He did this, Chang accepted it, and the negotiations proceeded.

Actually, at this lower level, the negotiations seemed far more realistic. Obviously the Communist colonels felt no need to speak "for the record" at all times, or to indulge in vituperative oratory for the home-town press, so talk was always more down to earth and practical. It is too bad some of this spirit could not have been transmitted upward.

The personalities of the Communist negotiators were immediately fascinating to our side, most of whom had never dealt face to face with Communist leaders before. Most noticeable was the almost complete lack of humor. There were no smiles, except the cold smiles of contempt that sometimes accompanied the scoring of verbal points. And apparently no Communist dared laugh aloud, even when, as once happened, an American officer had his chair fold up under him so that he landed on the floor. That is, there was no laughter among the leaders, and particularly among the North Koreans, who were clearly determined to be more Communist than the Kremlin. Colonel Tsai, the Chinese liaison officer, often had difficulty choking his laughter down, however, and did let go with a loud yawp when the American officer sat suddenly on the air. The man who exhibited the most iron control was undoubtedly North Korean General Li Sang Jo, whose stoniness of feature kept our junior officers entranced. One day flies lit on Li's face, one walking across his brows and down his nose. Not a muscle in Li's face twitched. His eyes and mouth remained utterly impassive. "What the hell," our officers asked each other, "is he trying to prove?" Like the Indians our grandfathers fought with, Li may have been trying to show the white man that he was rock-hard and not to be diverted from his aim. But the West in this age was too sophisticated to be impressed.

On October 10, the enemy finally responded to my invitation to resume our talks. I do not question that our success meanwhile in taking and holding all the high ground in the strategic areas along the front had helped persuade the enemy that he was not going to push us back and had better prepare to settle. But he was as uncompromising as ever at the truce table and clearly hoped to gain by talk what he had been unable to earn in the field.

Almost as soon as the talks had resumed they were disrupted by a UN air attack on Panmunjom—not a faked one this time but a real instance of misdirected bombing, for which we accepted responsibility and for which we offered apologies. It caused a two-week break in the talks, however, that added still further to our frustrations. The agreement we sought was a fairly simple one—a cease-fire; a buffer zone that ran across the peninsula in rough approximation of the current battle line; an agreement for each side to stay on its side of the zone and three miles off the opponent's shores; a halt in the bringing in of troops and matériel, and no increase in the number of troops; and an International Commission, not necessarily under the United Nations, to supervise the truce.

But the Reds were not interested in compromise or in negotiation. They had propaganda points to make and we did not perhaps appreciate that what looked like obvious fakery and deception to us could be made to look wholly different to the Asian peoples. The Reds were also convinced, I believe, that they could accomplish their aims to some extent by exhausting our patience and by conducting agitation, particularly among the prisoners of war, that would provide propaganda fuel for the truce table.

Quite early in the negotiations, as I have mentioned before, I cautioned Admiral Joy, whose patience had been tried most severely, that the use of courteous language was accepted by the Reds as a concession, a yielding to their bullying tactics, and I urged him to deal with them in terms just as tough as those the Reds used themselves. Thereafter, he was more than a match at the truce table for the tough-talking Communists and he refused to grant them a single point that they could turn into propaganda.

The major sticking point at the start was, as might have been expected, the placing of the cease-fire line. The Communists insisted on the 38th parallel, while we, with Washington's full backing, insisted that the line must be more in keeping with the military realities. We were ready to give up the ground north of the Imjin and west of the Yesong—an area that could not have been defended and that was south of the 38th parallel. But elsewhere, we wanted the buffer zone to be established right where the general line of battle stood. To have withdrawn our troops to the 38th parallel, placing them along a line that could not have been held, would have been indeed a surrender. To follow the current battle line seemed only realistic. We felt too that some weight should be placed on the superiority of our naval and air forces—an advantage we would give up in the event of truce and troop withdrawal.

The Red forces made some effort, as the talks dragged on, to push us back toward the 38th parallel and thus to bring their own suggested truce line a little closer to the military realities. But our defenses by this time were too strong for them to pierce. While some of the bloodiest engagements of the war were to come, with the negotiators still meeting, there was no major change in the battle line during the remainder of my service in Tokyo.

There still were, of course, voices that urged that we drive on to the Yalu again to clear the aggressor out of Korea altogether but Van Fleet's was not one of them. No one who was conscious of the military facts could have believed that with the limited forces at our disposal, we could have won anything resembling a total victory. General Mark W. Clark, who was to succeed me as Supreme Commander of the United Nations Forces, put it this way, in an article published more than a year after the truce was signed: "We never had enough men, whereas the enemy had sufficient manpower not only to block our offensives, but to make and hold small gains of his own. To have pushed it to a successful conclusion would have required more trained divisions and more supporting air and naval forces, would have incurred heavy casualties, and would have necessitated lifting our self-imposed ban on attacks on the enemy sanctuary north of the Yalu." It may be added that lifting that ban would have laid Japan open to attack and, if that had happened, would have greatly and immediately widened the war. No responsible leader in the United States at that time could have sold such a course to the American public.

The negotiations with the Communists were my major concern throughout most of my remaining tenure in the Far East Command. They were tedious, exasperating, dreary, repetitious, and frustrating, and I very soon lost hope of an early end to the killing. The Base Camp set up in an apple orchard on the outskirts of Munsan, a small village on the Imjin just fourteen miles from Panmunjom, developed into a permanent installation. There was a volleyball court, a baseball diamond, horseshoe pits, even a skeet range. There was a tent where movies were shown; there was a social club; and there were separate messes for enlisted personnel, for junior officers and for senior officers. A helicopter strip and a conference tent were added; and the newsmen were housed in a "Press Train" on a railroad siding a mile away. It seemed sometimes as if this installation might stand for years.

The Prisoner of War disturbances, which were to grow into one of the most vexing nontactical problems of the entire war, were closely connected with the truce negotiations. For a time they threatened to disrupt the negotiations altogether, and there is proof positive that they were part of a deliberately drawn long-range plan by the Communists to present the United States to the people of Asia as brutal oppressors whom only Chinese power could withstand. Because they developed just as my tenure in Tokyo was drawing to a close, I felt some urgency to solve them quickly, so as not to leave them in the lap of my successor, General Clark. But they did not lend themselves to ready solutions. They were not spontaneous nor spasmodic. They were but the ugly excrescences of a devious and callous plan on the part of the Communist High Command, both Chinese and North Korean, to make use of the prisoners of war to exert pressure upon our negotiators, and to score major propaganda points.

CHAPTER EIGHT

THE FINAL MONTHS–THE POW
RIOTS–CLARK SUCCEEDS ME–
THE TRUCE IS SIGNED

As EARLY AS January 6, 1951, I became sufficiently concerned with the problems of what to do about the prisoners of war in our custody to include the subject in my letter to General MacArthur. What we were faced with and what had me worried, was the presence close to the fighting zone of some 140,000 prisoners of war whom we had to feed, water, guard, and care for. It took a substantial fraction (which we could ill spare) of our armed forces just to guard the compounds and it took much of our scanty transportation to carry supplies to feed and clothe and house them. If we had to withdraw from the peninsula, there was their removal to fret about. If we held on, a substantial part of our own logistic effort would have to go into their subsistence, medical care, clothing, even their drinking water.

MacArthur's reply was to inform me he had already recommended the removal of the prisoners to the United States. They could not be brought to Japan, not only because their presence was likely to enrage the populace but because their establishment there might provoke a charge of Japanese belligerency. No immediate decision on removal was forthcoming from Washington and eventually plans were made to house the prisoners in compounds on large islands off the southern coast of Korea. The first

205

island selected was Cheju-do. But there was a resident population there of a quarter million. To transfer there, as was originally planned, the POWs and various categories of Korean military and civilian personnel, along with the forces we would require to guard and maintain the compounds, would more than double the population. Without a staggering expenditure of both time and money, the island simply could not support such an influx. I therefore urged against the move.

Thereafter a decision was made to transfer the prisoners to Koje-do, a much smaller island just a few miles southwest of Pusan. This was merely a choice between evils, for Koje-do was itself hardly the ground a sane man would have chosen to erect camp sites. It was rocky and mountainous, with almost no flat ground for construction and proper dispersal of the compounds. As a result, Koje-do was very soon crammed full with far more humans than nature had ever planned for it to support. Besides the increasing thousands of prisoners there were the hundreds of guards and other custodial personnel, with many more prisoners in the compound than was desirable for proper oversight or discipline. In consequence the Communists found it relatively easy to execute the plans of which we were then wholly unaware—the fomenting of mass demonstrations, riots, mutinies, and breakouts, and the subjugation of the non-Communist prisoners. The personnel we could spare to take charge of the camps was not of a quality to insure the alertness needed to detect these plots or to identify and isolate the ringleaders.

Four barbed-wire enclosures were built on Koje-do, each cut up into eight compounds, with each compound planned to hold 6000 prisoners. But by 1952, the POW population had outgrown this island and had to be housed on still another southern island, Pongam-do, as well as on the site first contemplated and rejected: Cheju-do. Yet, despite the dangerously close quarters in which the prisoners were contained and the inadequate guard detail, no real trouble was experienced at any of these camps until after the truce talks began. Then, without our having any inkling of the plot, the Communist High Command, in the person of Nam Il, contrived to stage a whole series of incidents that were intended to damage the United Nations in the eyes of the people of Asia.

To stage these incidents properly and to time them correctly, it was necessary to create a whole network of well-disciplined "troops" who would carry out orders promptly and without question. This called for a tight system of intercommunication—made easy of course by the narrowness of the confines and their unusually close juxtaposition. The Communist leaders in the camp —many of whom had deliberately surrendered in order to bring down the orders from on high—sent messages from compound to compound and from camp to camp in every manner conceivable. Orders brought in from the High Command by newly surrendered prisoners might be tied to stones and flung from compound to compound. Or they could be conveyed over greater distances by chants and songs, smuggled among supplies, or conveyed by signal. Altogether the communications system was elaborate enough to overcome almost any obstacle.

The hospital wards provided an excellent area for the holding of high-echelon conferences among Communist leaders, who would feign illness in order to meet with their subordinates or counterparts and work out details of new disorders. To secure the needed obedience in their "troops" a regular disciplinary system was created, with kangaroo courts and sentences—even including the death sentence—for all derelictions from the party line. In this way the non-Communist personnel were kept thoroughly cowed and the more influential or intractable ones eliminated.

As the talks stumbled along in the truce tent, the POW camps began to stir, in response to Nam Il's direction, and to coincide with the almost daily charges of villainy on the part of the "Western Imperialists" that wearied the ears of our negotiators (but were eagerly seized upon by Communist correspondents and dutifully reported in the Red press).

The camps under the Eighth Army supervision were run in strict accordance with the 1949 Geneva Convention, with the clear implication that captives merited humane treatment because they were no longer waging war. By the same convention, it was accepted that captives had voluntarily or involuntarily rendered themselves subject to the "laws, regulations, and orders in force

207

in the armed forces of the Detaining Power" which shall be "justified in taking judicial or disciplinary measures in respect of any offense committed by a prisoner of war against such laws, regulations, or orders." Neither North Korea nor Communist China had ever declared their adherence to this convention nor would they permit, as we did, inspection by representatives of the International Red Cross. We had already observed the attitude of the North Koreans toward prisoners, whom they would shoot in the back of the head after wiring their arms together behind their backs. The Chinese, as I have noted, were rather more humane (for purposes of propaganda) but we had little understanding of their attitude toward the prisoners in our custody. Perhaps we should have foreseen that, in Communist style, they would consider these people thoroughly expendable, and of value only to the extent that they might contribute to the final triumph of Communism. The fact is, we did not foresee this. The Geneva Convention had concerned itself chiefly with the rights of the prisoners. We had not envisioned a need for any special concern with the right of the Detaining Power to take strong steps to deal with hard-core rebels in the POW camps.

The first signs of real trouble came in January 1952 with the attempt to sort out the prisoners into those who would accept repatriation and those who would resist it. There had been a previous screening, the year before, to separate the Korean civilians who had been pressed into service, either as soldiers or laborers, by the Communists. At that time no resistance was met and 38,000 captives had been classified as civilians and set free.

There had been random disorders in the camps from time to time, but nothing that could not be handled by the guards. As 1952 began, however, the negotiators were discussing the repatriation of prisoners. Washington had taken the stand that we would never agree to the sending into Communist China of any prisoners who did not want to go. The Communists held that, in order to discuss this point productively, they needed to know how many prisoners would be returned and how many would be granted asylum of some sort. To this end, we set out to conduct another screening. This time, there was violent resistance, on direct orders from Panmunjom, as we later learned, where the Communist leaders needed a strong showing in favor of repatriation in order to strengthen their hands at the bargaining table.

The inmates of one compound, armed with every type of makeshift weapon ingenuity could devise—pick handles, barbed-wire flails, knives and axes put together and sharpened in secret out of odd bits of metal, even tent-pole spears—set upon a battalion of the U.S. 27th Infantry Regiment, which had been sent in to keep order while the ROK screening committee counted noses. Conscious of the importance of avoiding any killing—which could be magnified by the Communists into a massacre—the GIs used concussion grenades to hold back the rioters. Finally, the commander had to order the troops to fire into the mob—and only then did the prisoners pull back. One American was killed in the fracas. Several inmates were killed and more than a hundred wounded.

It was after this riot that it was decided to disperse the POW camps to Cheju-do and Pongam-do and to increase the number of guards. But we still had not really grasped the intricacies and the depths of the plot.

Throughout the spring, the disorders in the camps multiplied, with mass-meetings, display of banners carrying anti-U.S. slogans, raising of the North Korean flag, and organized defiance of every sort.

By the end of April, seven of the seventeen compounds on Koje-do remained unscreened. In these, defiance was at a peak and it was clear that only forcible entry and restraint, with certain loss of life on both sides, could permit a proper counting of those both for and against repatriation. Van Fleet moved in an additional battalion of U.S. troops to assist in the pacification of these compounds and ordered several other combat units to Pusan to be ready for immediate transfer to Koje-do, if serious rioting erupted. He then warned me of the outlook, pointing out that the compounds already screened would undoubtedly join in the resistance if force were used in the recalcitrant compounds.

Looking back in the light of later knowledge, one might say that it would have been better to use force at that moment and get the dirty job over with. There is no question that the job could have been accomplished, although not without the spilling of much blood. Perhaps if our intelligence had discovered then, as they did soon afterward, the existence of the intricate and far-ranging plot to organize and exploit the spirit of defiance in these camps, I might have taken a different stand. But I did not know then, nor do I know now, how far the Communist command might have gone in its readiness to sacrifice the lives of its own people in order to achieve a propaganda victory.

But what did happen is that, with the armistice negotiations seeming to have taken a favorable turn, I asked the Joint Chiefs of Staff for permission to suspend screening and merely to count all the men in the defiant compounds as having declared in favor of repatriation. The JCS concurred promptly, expressing the belief that any prisoners in those compounds who strongly opposed repatriation would be able to make their feelings known before the actual exchange took place, or even while it was being effected.

I was pleased that the Communists had lost this opportunity for loading unfavorable publicity upon the United Nations Command and that lives were not to be spent in this fashion when peace seemed so near. It was not my intent, however, that there should be a relaxation of discipline or control at the compounds. The Prisoners of War were ultimately my concern, although the authority to deal with them had been delegated to the Army Commander. His was the primary responsibility and I soon had to remind him of the need to meet it.

In early May, the Provost Marshal of my command made a tour of inspection of the camps on Koje-do and brought me a disturbing report concerning a dangerous lack of control there. There had been several incidents of United Nations officers being seized and held hostage for short periods by prisoners; and in some of the hard-core compounds the prisoners had refused even to bring in their own food and supplies. I immediately sent Van Fleet a sharp reminder of the need to maintain proper control, no matter that the screening program had been abandoned. His reaction to this was seemingly to express concern at the fact that the Provost Marshal had reported to GHQ before informing him, Van Fleet, of his observations in the compounds.

In the light of this report, I found it hard to understand why the dismaying events that followed immediately might not have been foreseen and prepared for. On May 7, the Communist prisoners seized the UN camp commander, Brigadier General Frank T. Dodd, and sent out word that he would be killed unless their demands were met. The General, without proper safeguards, had met with Communist prisoners ostensibly to discuss grievances. Once they had him in their hands, they announced his life would be forfeit if there was any shooting. Dodd himself sent out a message asking that no troops be sent to effect his release until after five o'clock that evening (it was then late afternoon); and Van Fleet directed that no force be used to free Dodd unless the Eighth Army commander himself had approved such action. It was not simply that Dodd's life was in danger; but a full-scale breakout attempt appeared imminent and the use of force seemed certain to result in a pitched battle, with severe loss of life among the prisoners and consequent disastrous publicity.

This crisis developed almost on the eve of my scheduled departure for Europe, where I had been ordered to replace General Eisenhower, who was then preparing to campaign for the Republican nomination for the Presidency. My successor, General Mark Clark, was already in Tokyo when news reached me of the seizure of General Dodd. I immediately asked Doyle Hickey, my Chief of Staff, to summon an early-morning (May 8) conference of key members of my staff to discuss the matter. I planned to leave for Korea immediately after the conference. Because General Clark would have this whole problem laid in his own lap within four days (I had received orders from JCS calling for my departure on May 12), I asked him to come with me. But I was determined to work out a solution to this prickly matter myself, along with Van Fleet, and not toss it, on such short notice, onto General Clark's dinner plate.

Before we arrived in Tokyo, Van Fleet had ordered reinforcing troops from Pusan to Koje-do and had sent Brigadier General Charles F. Colson, Chief of Staff of the U.S. I Corps, to take over command of the POW camps from Dodd, whom Van Fleet formally relieved. Colson arrived at Koje-do on May 8, immediately informed the Communists that Dodd was no longer camp commander, and warned them that if Dodd were not released unharmed before a designated deadline, UN troops would enter the compound and free him by force.

The Communists meanwhile had submitted their demands, with Dodd having consented to act as intermediary. Initially, they asked for recognition of a POW association, and for telephone and motor vehicle communications between the several compounds. Van Fleet informed me, when General Clark and I reached Korea, that he planned to negotiate with the POWs for Dodd's release. This would mean a forty-eight-hour delay at least and to me such a delay, with its implication of defeat, was wholly unacceptable. But I knew that every move we made would have its effect upon the truce negotiations, so I felt I should consult with Admiral Joy, our chief negotiator, before issuing any orders. Together, we flew to Seoul, where Admiral Joy wholeheartedly agreed with me that any temporizing would be accepted by the Communists as a sign of surrender. He, too, felt that we should demand immediate release of Dodd and back that demand by use of force.

I thereupon directed General Van Fleet in writing to establish order in the prison camps immediately and to maintain it thereafter, using whatever force was required, even tanks. Van Fleet at once ordered a battalion of tanks of the U.S. 3rd Division to move the two hundred miles by road from their positions in the north and to be transshipped by LST to Koje-do. If the Reds resisted or delayed in carrying out our demands I was determined to shoot and to shoot with maximum effect. Naturally I understood that my order might mean that the Communists would carry out their threat against Dodd. That was a possible consequence for which I was prepared to take full responsibility.

While I could sympathize with the desire of Van Fleet and others to save a friend's life, I felt that Dodd, like every other professional soldier, had accepted the risk of violent death when he chose his profession. A great many men had already given their lives to back up our government's refusal to confess un-committed offenses to the Communists or to compromise our stand on repatriation. In wartime a general's life is no more precious than the life of a common soldier. Each is asked to risk his life every day to protect the safety, the freedom, and the honor of his country. If, in order to save an officer's life, we abandoned the cause for which enlisted men had died, we would be guilty of betraying the men whose lives had been placed in our care.

This was no mere security problem. These Communists, defying all lawful orders in the POW camp, obviously considered themselves still combatants and were ready to attack and attempt to overwhelm our troops. This was another battle, like those in which men for the past two years had risked death every hour rather than compromise the cause for which they were fighting. These were my feelings as I issued the order that might have meant death to General Dodd.

Van Fleet, however, postponed carrying out my order, in part because of the delay in arrival of the tank battalion and in part for other reasons not clear to me. Dodd, fulfilling his role of intermediary, had received from the Communists a long set of charges of the killing and injuring of prisoners by camp authorities, and they had obtained from him (according to the Reds) ad-missions that, in some instances at least, the camp authorities were guilty. Colson had directed his troops to prepare for forcible entry into the camp if Dodd had not been released by 10 o'clock on the morning of May 10. With troops and tanks finally ready for action, a new set of Communist demands was sent out, far more sweeping than any heretofore offered and requiring almost complete humiliation of the UN authorities, who were asked to confess to crimes more barbarous than those committed by the Nazis in World War II. Here are some extracts, just as they were presented—hasty translation and all:

1. Immediate ceasing the barbarous behavior, insults, torture, forci-ble protest with blood writing, threatening, confinement, mass murder-ing, gun and machine-gun shooting, using poison gas, germ weapons, experiment object of A-bomb, by your command.

2. Immediate stopping the so-called illegal and unreasonable volunteer repatriation of NKPA and CPVA PWs.

3. Immediate ceasing the forcible investigation (screening) which thousands of PWs of NKPA and CPVA be armed and falled in slavery.

In short, the United Nations Command was asked to plead guilty to every wild and utterly baseless charge the Red radio had ever laid against us and the repatriation policy upon which the UN negotiators at Panmunjom had taken an immovable stand would have been shot right out from under them. This would have been as humiliating and damaging a defeat as any that might have been imposed in bloody battle. Colson consulted with his immediate superior, General Paul F. Yount, then drafted a reply which except for one relatively unimportant exception, denied all the Red charges, but did agree to cease further screening. The exchange of messages, the preparation of replies, and the tedious translations consumed still more time, and the first deadline passed without action.

By this time the language of the new demands had reached my headquarters and I radioed Van Fleet at once, asking that Colson's reply be held up, lest serious damage be done to the UN cause. At the same time I pointed out to Van Fleet that I was still unable to get an accurate and prompt accounting of what action the camp commander had taken in response to my orders, and I told Van Fleet that I was unable to understand why he had not carried out my instructions of May 8 to use whatever force was needed to establish and maintain order.

At 8 P.M. on May 10, ten hours after the "deadline," Colson and Dodd had worked out a draft reply that proved quite acceptable to the Reds—as indeed it might have, for in the first paragraph the former camp commander pleaded guilty to one of the worst charges trumped up by the leaders of the POWs. Here is what the first paragraph of the reply said:

"1. With reference to your item 1 of that message I do admit that there have been instances of bloodshed where many PWs have been killed and wounded by UN Forces. I can assure in the future that PWs can expect humane treatment in this camp ac-

214

cording to the principles of International Law. I will do all in my power to eliminate further violence and bloodshed. If such incidents happen in the future, I will be responsible."

The Communists tried to extract even further specific confessions, postponing the showdown until late that night. Then they apparently decided that, having won their main point, they had no need to provoke the use of armed force. Dodd was released at 9:30 P.M. on May 11. My departure from Haneda Airport was scheduled for midafternoon the next day. It was clear that further action would be needed to pacify the POW camps completely, but these would require decisions by General Clark, to whom the responsibility would pass in a few hours. I thereupon suggested and General Clark agreed that the command should pass to him at 8 o'clock the next morning.

General Clark acted decisively within the next few days to recover control of the camps on Koje-do. He ordered Brigadier General (later Major General) Haydon L. Boatner to take what steps were needed and Boatner moved swiftly and effectively. He immediately ordered all civilian residents off the island and reorganized the staff. He set the engineers to rebuilding the compounds so that no more than five hundred men would be retained in each. Guards were ordered to enter any compound where anti-UN banners were displayed or where the North Korean flag was shown, and to remove the emblems, using all the force necessary.

The Communist leaders were determined to resist this attempt to dilute their strength. They secretly built crude weapons of all sorts, including Molotov cocktails made with gasoline used for cooking. In one camp they even dug a trench before the main gate, where they meant to make a stand. Van Fleet ordered the 187th Airborne Combat Team to Koje-do to reinforce Boatner's troops and on June 10, they entered the compounds, where leaders had refused to form their men into small groups for reassignment. Using tear gas, which set fire to the hidden gasoline stores, and rifles, the United Nations troops methodically cleaned out the resisting compounds. After an hour and a half, resistance had ended. More than 150 prisoners had been killed or injured. One American had lost his life and thirteen had been wounded and the barracks had been destroyed by fire. But thereafter despite spasmodic violence and acts of defiance, the POW camp was under control. The non-Communist prisoners were screened out and placed in separate compounds. The Communists were split into groups of five hundred or less, and subsequent riots were quickly quelled by tear gas.

There were other dangerous incidents at all the camps while the truce negotiations continued, but the only major disorder occurred at Pongam-do in December 1952, when a mass break-out attempt by hard-core Communist prisoners resulted in the killing of eighty-five and the wounding of more than a hundred. Soon after this attempt, a handwritten summary of the riot prepared by the Communists came into our hands and in this the cold-blooded willingness of the Communists to sacrifice these lives for their propaganda value was clearly illustrated.

"Our fighting comrades," the summary set forth, "were determined to die a glorious death. . . . They lost nothing but their shameful lives in the fight, and these were for liberation and glorious victory. . . . The sons of Korea, the fatherland, and honorable fighters of the Great Stalin, exposed nakedly the inhumanitarian, brutal, cannibalistic, slaughtering violence of the American imperialists, causing the peaceable peoples of the world, the fatherland, the party and all democratic nations to shout for revenge."

Whether earlier forceful action could have robbed the Reds of this opportunity to make propaganda is questionable. Certainly there is no reason to believe they would have balked at spilling even more blood in struggles still more hopeless—just as long as they were able to make headlines in the Asian press that would indict the Americans as murderers. I do believe, however, that a swift and prompt crushing of the defiance at Koje-do, in accordance with my instructions, would have deprived the Reds of a telling argument and might even have brought the truce more quickly.

The fighting in Korea, however, was now no longer my immediate responsibility, as I relinquished command and left the Far East on May 12. Admiral Joy, after one final effort to present a proposal the Communists would agree to, had asked to be relieved of the job of negotiating, an assignment he had carried on for more than ten months with extraordinary skill and patience, and on May 22, Lieutenant General William K. Harrison, Jr., whom I had earlier appointed to the delegation, replaced him. Harrison, a direct descendant of the 9th President of the United States, William Henry Harrison of Tippecanoe fame, stayed on the job until the signing.

Conditions on the battle front now grew to resemble the fighting in World War I, with deep-dug emplacements, trenches, barbed-wire defenses and an extensive outpost line where most of the action took place. As the enemy built up his artillery strength, increasing it in efficiency as well as in number, the possession of dominating heights, for observation, became more and more important, and so the fights along the outpost line were often bloody and persistent. In July and August there were long periods of lull because of the heavy rains, but whenever weather allowed it, the enemy made fierce efforts to capture and cling to our outpost positions, particularly in the vicinity of Chorwon and Kumhwa, the left and right legs, respectively, of the Iron Triangle.

The UN forces, now more than half South Korean, were able in almost every instance to hang on to our important outposts or to retake them by counterattack and in several places drove deep into the Chinese defenses to take dominant heights and hold them. In these outpost battles, the enemy losses were heavy. Often several hundred dead were found on the field when the Chinese withdrew. In the Eastern Sector in late fall, the enemy made a major attempt to penetrate our Main Line of Resistance, but after an initial penetration, he was thrown back and the line was restored. Again the cost in enemy dead was heavy, as he relied once more on his customary tactics, which sent troops against our positions without regard to losses and left the dead strewn thick before our guns.

The extent of the enemy artillery buildup, in the face of continued heavy and accurate bombardment by Air Force and Navy, could be measured in the steady increase in the number of artillery rounds of all calibers that dropped into our front-line positions. On one day in September 1952, more than 45,000 rounds fell on the Eighth Army's front. In October, a record 93,000 rounds fell in one day on UN lines. The enemy had increased his accuracy too and had improved his tactics. He now could concentrate his fires on a single target and then move his guns frequently to prevent our pinpointing their positions.

As the ROKs, under Van Fleet's new intensive training program, of which he could well be proud, developed into a capable and self-sufficient fighting force, Van Fleet was able to use them in every sector until, by the end of 1952, they constituted nearly three-fourths of the front-line troops. Of the sixteen divisions manning the front in December 1952, eleven were South Korean, three were United States Army, one was United States Marine Corps, and one was the British Commonwealth Division. Other South Korean units reinforced some of the United States Divisions, with a South Korean Marine Regiment adding strength to the 1st Marine Division. In reserve Van Fleet could count on one South Korean Division and three United States Divisions.

Further shifts in January 1953 put twelve South Korean Divisions and eight UN Divisions on the front, with most of the added strength going into the IX Corps Zone, at the base of the Iron Triangle, where the enemy had made a desperate effort to penetrate the Main Line of Resistance and to seize our outposts on the commanding heights. Altogether now the Eighth and ROK Armies had a total strength of 768,000 men, counting the service and security troops. Facing them along the broken battle line were nearly a million Chinese and North Koreans—seven Chinese Armies and two North Korean Corps, numbering 270,000, on the front line, with eleven Chinese Armies and a North Korean Corps—531,000 men—held in reserve.

The air fighting in 1952 attained a scale heretofore unreached in Korea. A Fifth Air Force attack on Pyongyang on August 29 involved hundreds of aircraft: Marine, Air Force, Navy, as well as planes from Australia and the United Kingdom. The North Korean capital, a supply center and the home of repair shops, rail yards, and troop concentrations, as well as military headquarters, was nearly devastated in the massive strike. The enemy responded to this stepped-up bombing by a sharp increase in the number of MIG interceptors sent out to tackle our Sabrejets. But the superior training of our pilots maintained our sky mastery. During the month of September 1952 Fifth Air Force pilots shot down sixty-four MIG 15s, while losing only seven Sabrejets.

In the winter months, activity along the fighting front was reduced to patrol activity and harassing attacks on a small scale. The enemy at this stage in the war seemed to make a specialty of ambush and our patrols often found enemy forces lying in wait among the ravines and along the wooded hillsides. Despite the apparent stalemate there were continuing losses all along the front. It simply is not possible to sit tight and do nothing in a defensive war. While the enemy was far too strong for us to drive him northward, with the limited increase we possessed, we still had to conduct an active defense, to keep him at a proper distance from our main lines, and to limit his own defensive build-up. It is necessary, too, in fighting of this sort, to maintain an aggressive attitude in the fighting forces, for laxity can lead to total lack of alertness and subject the forces to quick demoralization under sudden attack. Consequently there was always sharp fighting, day and night, somewhere along the line. We defended our outposts fiercely and made the enemy pay a dear price for whatever he gained. A number of key hills along the front during the summer changed hands several times, as determined counterattacks, supported by the heaviest artillery concentrations of the whole war and smashing airstrikes, won back positions from which the enemy had temporarily dislodged us. A few outposts were deemed not worth the price we would have to pay to win them back; but generally along the line from the lush coastal plain on the Yellow Sea to the rugged coast of the Sea of Japan, our lines held firm or bulged slightly forward. Little by little we were impressing the Chinese that the truce line was not to be shoved southward by any force they could apply.

In the final winter of the war, the fighting dwindled again to clashes between frozen-footed patrols along the outpost line, except when the Eighth Army, to prevent the enemy from digging in too deep, conducted smashing raids against Chinese and North Korean positions. Hitting all at once with concentrated artillery fire and closely coordinated airstrikes, small UN forces in every zone would move out to capture, kill, and dislodge the enemy, then demolish his emplacements. The enemy began to strike back when the smell of spring—not always one of new blossoms and fresh grass in Korea—returned to the land. By this time the Eighth Army had a new commander, Lieutenant General Maxwell D. Taylor, replacing Van Fleet, who was retiring from active duty.

The war reawakened first in the western zone, where the Chinese endeavored to break through the Main Line of Resistance by attacking hilltops that were in the hands of the U.S. 2nd and 7th Divisions. They achieved near breakthroughs here, at tremendous cost in lives, surging through minefields and barbed wire and shoving the defenders off the top, only to pull back in the face of our counterattacks, and suffering further heavy losses as our massed artillery pounded the routes of their retreat. In the 7th Division sector, northwest of Chorwon, the Chinese, at an estimated cost of 750 killed, seized and held one of the main line positions on a hilltop. They made an effort farther west to drive the 1st Marine Regiment back from its outpost line, but after several days of surging back and forth, with the fighting continuing all night, and fierce artillery bombardment isolating the battleground, the Marines re-established and held fast to the outpost line. Meanwhile the enemy continued to ambush our patrols and raiding parties, inflicting many casualties upon us in these engagements. General Eisenhower, newly elected President, had visited Korea in December with a promise to seek an early peace. But along the battlefront peace still seemed as distant as a dream.

Full spring, with its melting snows and fresh fruity odors of unpent night soil in the paddies, brought another lull in the fighting, with roads made impassable by mud, and streams swollen too deep and swift for crossing. It was clear too that the negotiators at Panmunjom were at last getting down to straight give-and-take, particularly on the matter of repatriation, so that even the front-line fighters, always skeptical of rumors of truce, began to believe it might really be at hand. By April 11, agreement had actually been reached on an exchange of 605 UN prisoners for ten

70. Hill 983, Bloody Ridge, September 6, 1951. *U.S. Army photograph.*

71. A Korean village in the foreground borders the barbed-wire enclosures of the UN POW camp on Koje-do (Koje Island), where as many as 170,000 military and civilian Communist prisoners were held in thirty compounds. *U.S. Army photograph taken March 5, 1952.*

72. An American infantryman receives medical attention after he and a South Korean soldier, being helped up the bank, are wounded while scouting near Kumhwa, February 14, 1952. *U.S. Army photograph.*

73. UN troops enjoying a USO performance on New Year's Day, 1952, at a forward command post south of Kumsong. *U.S. Army photograph.*

74. President Syngman Rhee of the Republic of Korea reads a citation to General Ridgway, May 9, 1952, during General Ridgway's final visit to Korea before leaving for his new assignment in Europe as commander of SHAPE. General Mark W. Clark, right, was appointed Commander in Chief, UN Command, succeeding General Ridgway. Next to President Rhee is General James A. Van Fleet, Commanding General, Eighth Army. *U.S. Army photograph.*

75. An F-80 Shooting Star fighter-bomber releases a tank of napalm during the largest single strike of the Korean War, May 8, 1952. *U.S. Air Force photo.*

76. T66 multiple rocket launchers fire a salvo of rockets at Communist positions, November 26, 1952. *U.S. Army photograph.*

77. General Mark W. Clark, Commander in Chief, UN Command, at right, with Lieutenant General Reuben E. Jenkins, Commanding General, IX Corps, left; Lieutenant General Maxwell D. Taylor, Commanding General, Eighth Army, succeeding General Van Fleet, and Colonel Coumanakous, commanding the Greek Battalion. *U.S. Army photograph.*

79. A Communist woman prisoner, repatriated under terms of the POW exchange, is turned over to Communist medical personnel at Panmunjom, May 3, 1953. *U.S. Army photograph.*

OPPOSITE
78. Operation Little Switch. United States military personnel, former prisoners of the Communists in Korea and repatriated under terms of the POW exchange, board a C-92 plane bound for the United States, April 28, 1953. *U.S. Army photograph.*

80. Signing the Armistice agreement at ten A.M., July 27, 1953, ending the three-year conflict. Lieutenant General William K. Harrison, Jr., at left, signs for the United Nations, and General Nam Il, at right, for the Communists. *Official U.S. Navy photo.*

81. Shoulder patches of the U.S. Eighth
Army, I Corps, IX Corps, and X Corps.
U.S. Army photographs.

times that number of the enemy. Morale was high, thanks to many factors: Our ability to contain the enemy attacks; the growing power of our air force and its increased flexibility in supplying close support of our ground forces; and largely too to the rotation system that allowed many a veteran who had served his share of time to make it home to see his family. The UN forces at this time counted troops from many nations—from the Netherlands, from Turkey, from Greece, from the Philippines, from Norway, from Sweden, from Colombia, from France, from India, even from Thailand, in addition to the many we had long had with us from Australia and other areas of the British Commonwealth. Catering to all the peculiar preferences, in food, in clothing, in religious observances—gave our service and supply forces a thousand petty headaches. The Dutch wanted milk where the French wanted wine. The Moslems wanted no pork and the Hindus, no beef. The Orientals wanted more rice and the Europeans wanted more bread. Shoes had to be extra wide to fit the Turks. They had to be extra narrow and short to fit the men from Thailand and the Philippines. American clothing was far too big for the small men from the East. Only the Canadians and the Scandinavians adjusted easily to United States rations and clothes. Yet our 2nd Logistical Command solved all problems and met all demands.

While the great brunt of the war was borne largely by the men on the ground, the Navy and Air Force continued their gallant and often unsung contributions. There were islands along the North Korean coast where guerrillas friendly to the South Korean regime required supplies and support from our guns, that only the Navy could supply. The enemy port of Wonsan was kept almost continually under bombardment of our warships, and our ships, both large and small, closely patrolled the Korean coastline to keep the noose of our blockade pulled tight, and to prevent enemy forces from side-slipping along our flanks on either coast.

Air Force, Marine, and Navy planes provided constant surveillance of enemy lines, smashed troop and supply convoys, damaged or destroyed great segments of the North Korean industrial complex, and performed hair-raising rescue missions on land and sea. While the use of helicopters had not yet attained the level of efficiency or number it has since reached in Southeast Asia, we were already lifting lost men from the sea by cables from our choppers and carrying them to safety. We were transporting severely wounded soldiers from isolated hilltops to our surgical hospitals in one to two hours, against the many hours that would have been required otherwise. Low-level bombing flights by our planes now were as common as artillery missions and sometimes even more effective, coordinated as they were with troop movements by direct order from the ground commanders.

General Taylor was no more eager than Van Fleet and I had been to see lives spent to buy Korean real estate, when peace seemed so close. But when the enemy, in April 1953, decided he needed to conclude the war with a "victory," Taylor was more than ready for him. Toward the end of April, the Eighth Army observers reported significant changes in enemy movement. Troops were being brought down from the north to take positions close to the battle line. Artillery and tanks were moved into positions to provide close support, and our patrols met enemy forces far more frequently on the prowl in the area between the outpost lines.

Near the end of May 1953, the Chinese began a series of attacks that constituted their final offensive and continued almost to the signing of the armistice. They first struck in the IX Corps area at the base of the Iron Triangle, and as they had so often done before, they aimed their first blows at the South Korean positions. Fire from howitzers and mortars was exceptionally heavy and the Chinese attacked in regimental strength. But this time the South Koreans held fast and the Chinese, withdrawing, were severely hurt by zeroed in fire from corps and division artillery. Our forces in this area had been greatly strengthened in the past year, and the buildup had made the line nearly impregnable.

The Chinese tried again in an attack against five outposts in the I Corps area, held by the 25th Division's Turkish Brigade. The fighting here reached a desperate pitch, with the Chinese apparently determined to seize these outposts at any cost. The Turks fought the Chinese hand to hand, while the enemy attacked right through his own mortar and artillery barrage. The

Turks counterattacked fiercely after the first assault had moved them back and they succeeded in regaining two of the outposts, to which they clung. The Chinese could not be moved from the others. For the three outposts they had gained in a two-day battle, the enemy paid a forbidding price: an estimated 2200 killed and 1075 wounded. The Turks lost 471, including 104 killed in action.

These attacks proved but diversionary efforts. The major offensive to which the enemy had been building was obviously due to fall in some other sector. Finally, on June 10, just six weeks before the war was destined to end, the major Chinese effort to shove back the battle lines began. It was the mightiest blow to fall upon our forces since the spring offensive in 1951 and it began, as that one had, in the early evening with intense artillery preparation fires. The fighting started in the zone controlled by the ROK II Corps, near Kumsong, about half way between the Iron Triangle and the Punchbowl, where the UN lines bulged northward on both sides of the Pukhan River. Employing coordinated attacks in battalion and regimental strength, the Chinese first attacked the positions held by the ROK 5th Division, along the east banks of the river. They quickly drove the South Koreans back half a mile south of their main line of resistance. Counterattacks failed to restore the line and the Chinese next day resumed the offensive, forcing the ROKs back steadily for the next five days until they were about three miles south of their original positions. On the other bank of the river meanwhile another Chinese division broke through the lines of the ROK 8th Division and within two days had enveloped the regiment on the right flank, forcing a deep retirement. Still another Chinese force made a holding attack in moderate strength on the left of the zone controlled by the X Corps. This attack might easily have been contained, but the retreat of the ROK 8th Division, following the withdrawal of the ROK 5th, put the left flank of the X Corps in danger and forced a slight withdrawal in that area. Eventually the whole line was stabilized, with the ROK 5th Division holding a new line at a point where the Pukhan River swung sharply eastward to place a barrier between the ROKs and the enemy, and the ROK 8th Division establishing its main line of resistance some four miles south of where they had been when the Chinese offensive opened.

The Chinese made further small gains in the west, against the I Corps, and in the east they forced a minor withdrawal by the X Corps. But within ten days the offensive had been brought to a standstill. General Taylor about this time received major reinforcements from Japan, in the form of the 187th Airborne Regimental Combat Team and the 34th Regimental Combat Team, minus one rifle battalion, followed by the other two infantry regiments of the 24th Division. This new strength enabled him to hold fast against the final phase of the Chinese offensive which began in July. The June offensive had gained the Chinese several commanding hills and much ground along an eight-mile front. But it had cost them an estimated 6600 men. The ROK II Corps had lost heavily too in the engagements, casualties, including dead, wounded and missing, amounting to more than 7300.

The July assault by the Chinese was aimed at the ROK Capital Division, which was holding the sector on the right flank of the IX Corps, near Kumhwa, the right leg of the Iron Triangle. The Capital Division, nearly overwhelmed by three Chinese Divisions which broke through their lines and threatened complete envelopment, fell back in confusion. Farther east, on the left flank of the ROK II Corps, which was dangerously exposed by the withdrawal of the Capital Division, a Chinese division attacked the ROK 6th and drove it slowly back. The ROK 3rd and 8th Divisions, endangered by this retreat, pulled back in good order to a new main line of resistance on the south bank of the Kumsong River. The ROK 7th Division, newly added to the ROK II Corps, helped establish this line by driving the Chinese off the high ground along the river. There was strength enough along the front now to have re-established the old line. But the negotiators at Panmunjom had already reached substantial agreement and it seemed an extreme folly to spend lives to gain ground that would add nothing to the security of the Eighth Army.

On July 19, just one day before the ROK II Corps had established its new line, a final agreement was reached at Panmunjom. It took a week then—a week of relative quiet all along the front—for liaison and staff officers to draw up the boundaries of the de-militarized zone. On July 27 at 10 A.M. General Harrison, for the United Nations, and General Nam Il, for the Chinese and North Koreans, signed the agreement. The shooting stopped at 10 P.M. that same day. There was no wild celebrating or fraternizing such as had marked the end of other wars. Men just grinned at each other or flopped wearily on the ground, or gathered about a jug of whiskey to share their joy. Along the ridges, raked bare by artillery, it was almost joy enough just to be able to climb up out of a hole in the ground and look out over the countryside without getting shot at.

It was three years, one month, and two days since the war began and just about an even three years since Task Force Smith, that outnumbered, outgunned, ill-prepared but gallant band of run-of-the-mill GIs, staged the most brilliant delaying action, and the least celebrated, in our recent military history.

CHAPTER NINE

ISSUES AND ANSWERS – MEANING OF
THE MACARTHUR CONTROVERSY –
MILITARY AND POLITICAL IMPLICATIONS

AFTER SO MANY lives had been lost to purchase an uneasy peace which, as General Eisenhower warned the nation, was "just an armistice on a single battlefield" in a worldwide struggle, it was to be hoped that whatever lessons had been so dearly bought would be well-learned and well-applied. Yet voices still persist that sound the old discredited slogans. And those great national objectives so clearly outlined in the Great Debate of May and June 1951, when American Far East policy was subjected to critical analysis in the Senate—even these seem to have been forgotten by many of our citizens.

At that time Senator Richard B. Russell made this statement:

"We may differ on the proper policy to be applied in the Far East. We may separate on questions of strategy. We may divide on personalities. But we shall remain united in our devotion to liberty and justice; be single-minded in our will to preserve our institutions. We hope that they may be preserved in peace. But preserve them we shall—the objectives of the people of the United States are unchanged by anything that has transpired during this ordeal of controversy."

The objectives, of course were, and remain, the security of the nation and the preservation of its independence, its moral principles, and its fundamental institutions. All our dealings with the rest of the world must be directed ultimately to the attainment of these objectives, and our leadership of the free world imposes on us the need for a strong foreign policy. Korea, if it taught us nothing else, taught us the folly of trying to implement such a policy with inadequate armed force to back it up if it should be challenged. Or rather Korea repeated the lesson to us after we had first learned it at the time of World War I.

After World War II, perhaps no statesman or politician alive could have persuaded our war-weary people to keep their sons under arms. As I have said in Chapter One, the press, the radio, the voices of office-seekers and of plain citizens everywhere quickly drowned out the few who warned against tearing down our great military machine with such improvident haste. Once demobilization had begun, nothing could stem the tide. Our ships, like our swords, were allowed to rust, our planes to deteriorate, and our mighty wartime industries to convert to peacetime uses or be scrapped. Safe behind our mental Maginot lines—our faith in the United Nations and in the deterrent power of our atomic bomb—we turned our thoughts to making money, to ball games, to new cars and homes, to new machines to make life easy, to vacations, and to the purchase of a thousand small necessities we had too long gone without.

The hundreds of thousands of skilled and seasoned noncommissioned officers and ratings, the backbone of our armed services, laid their uniforms away in the happy conviction that they had paid in full their debt of duty to their country. Could they have looked ahead a few seasons, to see themselves hustled back into service, hurriedly outfitted, and transported, often by air, with breathless haste back to a new war, they too might have asked the nation to stay its unilateral disarming. But in that day it seemed the height of illogic to imagine we would ever again fight anything short of another world war, the danger of which seemed remote indeed. The concept of limited war was yet to be recognized. And our people found it easy to persuade themselves that they might fight and win any war without ever setting their feet on hostile ground, doing it all through air and naval power and the nuclear bomb.

Our tragic misreading of the future could not be laid to any lack of strategic or tactical intelligence. No, we simply failed properly to evaluate the intelligence at hand. We neglected to plan for contingencies both foreseeable and probable. We forgot that our diplomacy could be no stronger than the military muscle we maintained to support it. We had hardly any Army left in the Far East and what troops we did have there were, in MacArthur's words, tailored for occupation rather than combat. The situation in Europe was little different.

I have pointed out earlier that it was cruelly unfair to put back on the firing line the men who had but recently caught their breath after years of war. But I must emphasize again that we could not take green, newly drafted youngsters and fly them to combat with the dispatch necessary to keep the enemy from driving our pitifully weak forces in Korea into the sea.

But could we have avoided the conflict altogether? Could we have written off Korea, as our country had so often done before, and let the infant Republic expire?

The question went straight to the White House, the only place where it could have been answered. Never before had the issue of peace or war faced a President of the United States with such explosive suddenness, and attended with such limitless potential for disaster. Other foreign wars had always evolved from a long train of events that had shaped and solidified public opinion sufficiently to enable the Chief Executive to muster public support. The long history of cruelty against Cuba that led to our war with Spain; the three years of hostile acts and violations of neutrality that helped to ready our people's minds for the first war with Germany; the treachery at Pearl Harbor that rocketed us into World War II—all these facilitated, for Presidents McKinley, Wilson and Roosevelt, the making of the fateful decisions.

But in June of 1950, war burst upon us without prelude. While the jolting surprise of the event was comparable to that of Pearl Harbor, there was no such clear-cut choice of alternatives. In 1941, there was but a single honorable course to take. In 1950,

President Truman might have chosen to dodge the issue and the public protest would have been minimal. But the President met the challenge with decisive dispatch. To his everlasting credit he decided we must fight.

It did not take long for our people, once they had time to assess the situation, to concur in his decision. The United States could not in honor have allowed Korea to be overrun. The real challenge was militant Communism, unmasking its intent to use naked armed force to extend its grasp. It was a direct challenge to our security which, if permitted to go unanswered, would have led step by step to World War III.

Yet the answer, while given promptly, was not given without deliberation or without consultation within the executive and legislative branches of our government and within the United Nations. For the immediate question implied a further question that was fraught with dangers we could scarcely measure. Should we move in concert with other nations or should we go it alone? This question would bedevil us again during the war as we considered expanding our blockade or our air attacks. But at the start President Truman determined that the morality of our decision to use force in Korea would be upheld before the peoples of the world if we fought under the aegis of the United Nations, to whose principles we subscribed. Such a course committed us to consultation with our allies in matters of strategy, or at least to consideration of their interests and possible reactions. It may be said that this requirement hampered our operations, and to a certain extent it did. But it also laid a restraining hand on military adventures that might have drawn us into deeper and deeper involvement in Asia.

It is true, of course, that our original objective—to repel aggression, to expel the invaders from South Korea, and to restore peace in the area—underwent drastic change once the Inchon success had put us in a position to push north across the 38th parallel. We then tacitly altered our mission to encompass the occupation and unification of all Korea—the goal that had long been the dream of Syngman Rhee and the prize that beckoned to MacArthur.

The entry of the Chinese into the war forced another modification, until finally we were ready to settle once more for keeping South Korea independent of Communist control. But at no time, except briefly after the first success and again after the pull-back from the Yalu, did we operate in a mission vacuum or without specific political or military objectives. Our objectives were always within our capabilities, or what we judged our capabilities to be. At no time did our top authorities feel free to escalate the conflict without restraint, or without clearly defined political, military, and geographical objectives. There was no pursuit of a vaguely envisioned "victory" without definition or dimensions. The willingness to settle for a stalemate, provided the status quo ante, or a facsimile of it, was restored, was all that brought peace to Korea. We knew we did not then have unlimited forces to call upon, and our civilian authorities well understood that our people would not sanction a war that might spread over much of continental Asia and require the expenditure of hundreds of thousands of lives. We had finally come to realize that military victory was not what it had been in the past—that it might even elude us forever if the means we used to achieve it brought wholesale devastation to the world or led us down the road of international immorality past the point of no return.

As we saw in an earlier chapter, the issue of civilian vs. military control of our foreign policy—or more properly the place of the military in determining foreign policy—seemed to have been settled in the clash between President Truman and General MacArthur. After tempers had cooled and the facts had become known and time had been allowed for sober reflection, there was reason to hope that the clear provisions in our constitution for civilian supremacy in setting foreign policy would be honored in every heart. Yet General Eisenhower, on leaving the Presidency, felt the need to warn the nation against the possible growth of a military-industrial combine that might take over from an unperceiving people the formation as well as the implementation of our foreign policy. And in the 1964 presidential campaign there was actually a suggestion that the military leaders be freed from interference by civilian authorities. I am sure this extreme view is

231

shared by relatively few Americans. But the military, in monarchies, in oligarchies, and in other democracies has many times won dominance. The persistent contention by some of our own private citizens as well as military men that wars, once started, should be shaped and conducted solely by the military indicates that, improbable as it now may seem, and incompatible as it is with our whole way of life, military dominance over our affairs "could happen here."

To forestall such a tragedy, we must insist rigidly on civilian control of the shaping of our foreign policy in war as well as in peace. Yet, under today's conditions, when men have control of machines capable of laying a world to waste, there must be a close interweaving of political and military goals, lest some misstep set us suddenly beyond the hope of salvaging more than a few scraps of our civilization. Civilian authorities, therefore, need to work closely with military authorities in setting attainable goals and in selecting means to attain them. A war without goals would be most dangerous of all, and nearly as dangerous would be a war with only some vaguely stated aim, such as "victory" or "freedom from aggression" or "the right of the people to choose their own government." Generalities like these make admirable slogans, but authorities today must be hardheaded and specific in naming exactly what goal we are trying to reach and exactly what price we are willing to pay for reaching it. Otherwise, we may find that, in spite of ourselves, the whole conduct of the war will be left in the hands of men who see only victory as the proper objective and who have never had to define that word in terms plain enough to be understood by all the world's people.

In the past, the military man has too often aimed only at the complete destruction of the enemy in the field. He should not be the one to set the political objectives our military effort seeks to attain. But in the complex warfare of today he must be more than ever free to speak up frankly and boldly in the highest councils of our country concerning the policies our civilian leaders are considering. Once a policy is set, however, it is the military man, in keeping with the oath he takes and with the very phrasing of his commission, who should either execute that policy or resign from the service.

General MacArthur would have introduced a wholly different doctrine from this. In an address to the Massachusetts General Court (state legislature) in July 1951, he tried to draw a distinction between the loyalty and obedience owed by a soldier to his Commander in Chief and the loyalty owed "to country and Constitution."

"I find in existence," he said, "a new and heretofore unknown and dangerous concept that the members of the Armed Forces owe their primary allegiance and loyalty to those who temporarily exercise the authority of the executive branch of the government, rather than to the country and its Constitution they are sworn to defend. No proposition could be more dangerous. None could cast greater doubt on the integrity of the Armed Forces."

This statement may be contrasted with the assurance he offered to President Truman on the occasion of his appointment as United Nations Commander. At that time, July 11, 1950, he sent the following radio message to the President:

I have received your announcement of your appointment of me as United Nations Commander—I can only repeat the pledge of *my complete personal loyalty to you* [italics are mine] as well as an absolute devotion to your monumental struggle for peace and goodwill throughout the world. I hope I will not fail you.

It strikes me that in this instance it is the General who is introducing a "heretofore unknown concept," and one that seems at odds with the most basic traditions not only of our civilian government but of our armed forces. The Constitution an Army officer is sworn to defend says nothing about loyalty to an individual. It does clearly express the determination of our people, from the very beginning, to make the civilian authorities supreme. It designates the President as commander in chief of the armed forces. It provides that he shall appoint, with the advice and consent of the Senate, all officers in these services. The commission each officer receives directs that he shall obey the orders of the

233

President or of his successor in office and in no way demands loyalty to him as a person. Nor does the Constitution even faintly suggest, as General MacArthur and his supporters seem to have done, that there is some agency or individual, apart from "those who temporarily exercise the authority of the executive branch of the government," that can assume the authority and the responsibility vested in the President.

This tradition of civilian supremacy has been so long and so deeply imbedded in our political structure as to cause one to wonder how even the most adroit casuists could call it into question. A vast and unique authority such as is vested by the Constitution in the President of the United States carries with it a corresponding responsibility. In these times, when we hold in our hands an instrument that could, in a brief span, destroy hundreds of millions of people and render homeless and destitute hundreds of millions of others, the responsibility is awesome. Yet responsibility, unlike authority, cannot be delegated to another individual, whether he wears a uniform or not. Decisions as to the composition, maintenance, dispositions, and missions of our armed forces may, any one of them, affect the whole future of mankind. Surely it is a wholly new and unheard-of doctrine that would allow any but our highest elected officials to make such decisions, and it is a doctrine rife with great and unpredictable danger.

The code to which our officer corps demands that its members conform permits no such misplacing of allegiance as MacArthur enunciated in the capitol at Boston, no matter how leniently some segments of the public may view the General's behavior. The concept of duty, in military service, has been elevated to extreme importance, and obedience to properly constituted authority is primal. No man in uniform, be he private or five-star general, may decide for himself whether an order is consonant with his personal views. While the loyalty he owes his superiors is reciprocated with equal force in the loyalty owed him from above, the authority of his superiors is not open to question.

Moreover, I would categorically reject the hypothesis advanced by one writer, that MacArthur faced "the most painful question which the soldier can ever confront: How could he be true to his oath to the Constitution and serve the best interests of the United States as he understood them and yet remain faithful to the Administration in power—he could not serve the Constitution and the Government without betraying his duty to one or the other."*

That MacArthur himself eventually came to understand this truth might be inferred from the ringing statement he made in his memorable talk to the Corps of Cadets at West Point when he accepted the Sylvanus Thayer award in May 1962: "Let civilian voices argue the merits of our processes of government . . . These great national problems are not for your participation."

Yet this was the man who, a decade earlier, had promised to "raise my voice as loud and as often as I believe it to be in the interests of the American people." This was the voice that had entered public debate on such matters as "our economic frontier"; the possible reduction of our standard of living "to a level of universal mediocrity"; and the "dwindling value of both the national currency and private income." Surely subjects such as these were at the very heart of the "controversial issues, both national and international," from which he urged his young listeners to stay aloof.

Had he meant to exempt himself from this description of the role of a military officer? Had the intervening years, with their opportunity for sober reflection, wrought a change in his thinking? Or was he, indeed, as James Reston put it in 1950, "a sovereign power in his own right with stubborn confidence in his own judgment?"

We lesser ones of today, and the myriads of others tomorrow, standing outside the halls of fame that Douglas MacArthur long ago entered, must continue patiently to search history's records for both the sound and the faulty judgments of the great. Only so can we look to improve humanity's lot and avert or mitigate disaster. The MacArthur record is full of rewarding research ma-

---

* *The Truman-MacArthur Controversy and the Korean War,* John W. Spanier, Belknap Press, Harvard University, 1959, p. 234.

terial. But certainly we must conclude that one of the most important lessons to be learned from it is this new elucidation of the proper relationship of civilian to military authority.

If the President had failed—after MacArthur's repeated neglect to comply with directives and after the General's public airing of displeasure with approved government policies—to relieve MacArthur from duty, he would have been derelict in his own duty. Even MacArthur had written, in an earlier day, that for the President to delegate his own responsibility to any subordinate authority (MacArthur himself, for example) would have been "not delegation but abdication." We can be grateful the President did not abdicate.

There are many other questions raised even today about the conduct of the Korean War and the means chosen to bring about a cease-fire, questions that have a distinct relevance to our current difficulties in Asia. Was it really a choice between an armistice and a third world war? Was it sound strategy to limit our troop commitment? Were we prompted by groundless fears when we failed to respond to Chinese intervention with the full use of our power, incluing the atomic bomb? Was this a tragic backing down for which future generations will have to pay? Were the truce talks but a Communist trick that robbed us of the victory that lay within our grasp? Some of these questions must remain unanswered until the judgment of history is rendered. And we cannot divine, no matter how earnestly we seek parallels in the past or in the present, exactly what the outcome might have been had we made other choices than we did.

It can be shown, however, that some of today's misconceptions are based on inadequate information and that some of the supposed "lessons" of Korea have been improperly drawn. While I have full respect for the motives and the patriotism of many who believe with deep sincerity that the Korean War was a shameful military, political, and psychological defeat, involving outright appeasement and accompanied by loss of national self-respect, I disagree with them utterly.

As I explained in a previous chapter, I knew to a certainty that there was no doubt in the collective mind of the Eighth

Army of its ability to push on at least to the western stretches of the Yalu in the summer of 1951 and to administer, with the support of the naval and air arms of the United Nations Command, a tactical defeat on whatever Chinese Communist or North Korean ground troops might have sought to contest its advance. But, as I said, this would have been only the opening of a whole new page of our military history. For we would still have had facing us the prospect of endless guerrilla warfare and our certain knowledge of the inability of the ROK ground forces to hold the region unaided. Perhaps the American people would eventually have resigned themselves to the retention of large forces on the Asian mainland on a pacification mission that had no clear end. Undoubtedly there are some who feel we should have blockaded the Chinese coast, bombed the Manchurian bases, and even dropped the A-bomb. But I was not the only one who saw in such actions no promise of military victory. The President, the Secretary of Defense, and the Joint Chiefs of Staff are on official record that they did not think the probable short-range gain would be at all commensurate with the long-range loss.

When Communist China launched her secretly massed armies against our forces in North Korea in the surprise offensive of November–December 1950, there would have been much justification for an open declaration of war, even for the dropping of the A-bomb on her troops south of the Yalu and her military bases north of that river. Such action was maturely debated and finally rejected by the United States authorities responsible for such decisions. It was concluded that our objectives in Korea— except for a brief period following Inchon should remain what they had been from the beginning—namely, the defeat of the aggression, the expulsion of the invaders, the restoration of peace in that area, and the prevention of an expansion of the conflict into a third world war. In those decisions the great majority of the non-Communist members of the United Nations strongly concurred.

As for the armistice itself, I firmly believed (as the magazine *Newsweek* noted in its issue of December 31, 1951), and the Pentagon agreed, that the Communist leaders actually desired a truce. The ground war had been in a condition of stalemate since June and both sides were maintaining large armies along a static battle line at a cost far exceeding the military value. Both sides had a simple choice: either broaden the war to reach a decision, or arrange a truce. I have already related my own estimate of the probable cost in killed and wounded that a drive to the Yalu would have incurred; and the paucity of the military advantages to be gained thereby. The Chinese had no desire to extend the war to other areas or to invite air or naval bombardment of their own soil. A truce would obviously be mutually advantageous.

The truce negotiations were to prove fantastically difficult, but there was never any doubt in my mind that there was no justifiable alternative to undertaking them. The armed aggression had been stopped. The invader had been expelled. A far better defensive zone had been seized and held, much more of it on the North Korean side of the 38th parallel than on the South Korean side. It is true that, when the truce was about to be signed after months of negotiations, the Chinese opened a strong offensive. But it was not, as some have charged, the largest of the war, not by any means. And it succeeded in winning no more than a few outposts and territory of no great strategic value, all well above the 38th parallel. It was merely a final and vain attempt to push us into a less easily defensible truce line and to end the war with some sort of "victory." We held on to our strong defenses and we turned aside the proposed policy of striking directly at China. In view of all this, and of the fact that the Chinese also wanted to bring the fighting to a halt, was it not time to start talking in order to stop shooting?

It is a fact that, whether or not we should have entered into any negotiations at all, directives emanating from Washington made the negotiations more difficult and may well have helped delay the final agreement. On more than one occasion such directives cut the ground out from under our negotiators and deprived them of the sort of forceful support that alone commands Communist respect. As a most striking example, after our negotiators had insisted on including in the armistice terms a prohibition against the construction of new airfields and the rehabilitation of old ones, Washington directed the negotiators to concede on this issue. There was at that time not a single combat-effective airfield left in all North Korea, thanks to our bombings, and without such a prohibition, the Communists could—as they promptly did, once the armistice became effective—move their fighter planes down from Manchuria into North Korea, where they could strike deep into South Korea. This order from Washington was bitter medicine.

So too was the order that we alter our stand against including the Soviet Union (on the ground that it had not taken part in the war) as a member of the Neutral Nations Supervisory Commission, along with Poland, Czechoslovakia, and others. The war had been instigated by the Soviet Union and had been fought with tanks, planes, and guns supplied by that country. To count that country neutral was fantastic and we argued against its inclusion with the utmost vigor. But Washington ordered that we base our opposition solely on the fact that the Soviet Union had a common border with Korea, a shift in stance that was bound to look to the Communists like an admission of weakness.

Still, I do not believe that our people lost any self-respect as a consequence of holding the truce talks. I do not believe that we suffered any abridgment of our national independence or diluted our deep-rooted beliefs in moral values, our faith in God, or our dedication to the ultimate triumph of right.

There was a time, five decades ago—and the record is still fresh in many minds—when men refused to consider negotiation even after the bankruptcy of force as a national policy had been clearly demonstrated. In World War I, the Nivelle offensive of April 1917 and Field Marshal Sir Douglas Haig's Flanders offensive the following October blew into bleeding corpses hundreds of thousands of the strong and vibrant sons and strapping husbands of England, France, and Germany. Yet history will surely question whether any gain to any cause was purchased by this shattering sacrifice. The ghastly toll did awaken some statesmen to sanity, but with a chance to negotiate beckoning to them in that year, they lacked the vision and the courage to do more than press

239

on to "victory." A military stalemate existed and both sides were nearly drained of blood; it would have been an act of simple wisdom to stop the fighting at that point.

Lloyd George, after he had visited the front, said: "If people really knew, the war would be stopped tomorrow, but of course they don't and can't know. The correspondents don't write and the censorship wouldn't pass the truth. The thing is horrible and beyond human nature to bear, and I feel I can't go on any longer with the bloody business."*

Yet, almost at this very time, the British government made a formal demand upon the United States for half a million of our young men "in their shirt-tails" to be given "seven weeks' training in trench warfare—then seven days' orientation in France before being sent into battle as riflemen." Fortunately our leaders refused to consign our young manhood to this fate, balking at having them fed into battle as replacements for foreign casualties. They insisted instead upon building our own army, which would not be subject to the whims of Allied leadership.

In Flanders, meanwhile, the lure of "total victory" still exercised an irresistible attraction, and the slaughter went on until the folly of trading a thousand yards of bottomless morass for a hundred thousand lives appalled generals and politicians alike and the winter floodings put a merciful end to the madness.

In Korea, however, when an opportunity offered to stop the killing, our government welcomed it. The attempt to break up the United Nations' collective effort and leave the United States to go it alone failed. The conclusion of the armistice found the sixteen allies with combat forces in Korea solemnly reaffirming their resolve to respond promptly if the aggression should be renewed and, in that event, not necessarily to limit themselves to operations on the Korean peninsula.

So, regardless of our having missed "total victory" in Korea (if any such consummation could ever have been found there), we did deliver to international Communism its first resounding defeat. We proved that collective security was indeed workable. Nor did the United Nations crumble into impotence as it might

* Quoted from *In Flanders Fields*, Leon Wolff.

have done if it had not, under United States leadership, picked up the iron gauntlet thrown down by the Communists. In April 1951, after taking over the Supreme Command in Tokyo, I made this statement: "I believe military history offers no parallel of so many allies serving side by side in battle so harmoniously—with such complete mutual confidence, respect, and cooperation. I have no hesitancy in saying that the presence of these troops (UN) has greatly enhanced the effectiveness of the United Nations Command."

Finally, on the purely military side, in less than *three months*—July 5 to September 30—the Communist thrust into South Korea had been met and brought to a stop, and the invading forces all but destroyed. In less than *two weeks* the Communist offensive, begun on New Year's Day, was halted. And in exactly *three weeks* from the second evacuation of the South Korean capital on January 4, 1951, the United Nations Command passed over to the offensive. This offensive, with only temporary checks, was maintained until the aggressor was expelled from all but a small fragment of relatively indefensible ROK territory and with a far larger segment of North Korea under ROK control, where it remains today.

In May 1951, while Commander in Chief of the United Nations and United States Far Eastern Commands, I reported my estimate that the enemy "will not again have the capability of making as strong offensive efforts as those launched on April 22 and May 15." At about the same time I sent the following message to the Eighth Army and its Commander, then General Van Fleet:

I believe it is quite possible that history may some day record that . . . this Army challenged, met, and hurled back the most vicious forces which have yet threatened mankind in its age-old struggle for individual dignity and freedom. It is, I believe, quite possible . . . that the crest of the Communist wave was broken against your arms and your will to fight, and that the flood of this menace . . . thereafter began its recession.

I hope that this may be the judgment of history.

241

CHAPTER TEN

LESSONS LEARNED AND UNLEARNED –
THEIR SIGNIFICANCE IN OUR
SEARCH FOR PEACE

THERE WOULD BE little purpose in dwelling at length on the lessons taught us by wars of the past if we did not endeavor seriously to apply those lessons to the military problems of today. Above all, I believe we need to read the lessons closely lest we repeat, at inestimable cost, the mistakes for which we paid so dear a price.

One of the major mistakes of Korea was our tendency to try to base our strategy on a reading of enemy intentions, while failing to give proper weight to what we knew of enemy capabilities. MacArthur and those who supported him belittled the Chinese threat to intervene in Korea, even though they knew that Red China was perfectly capable of carrying out that threat promptly. But we based our moves on the theory that "no commander in his right mind" would commit his forces south of the Yalu at that time.

Today, as we grapple with our mounting difficulties in Southeast Asia, it is satisfying to note that we seem to concern ourselves more with what we *know* the enemy is capable of and less with what we *think* he is planning. President Johnson has said that he takes Red China at her word—something we failed to do in Korea. I have no doubt, therefore, that our planners are well aware that the Red Chinese are capable, if their leaders so

243

decide, of provoking us into a war with them. Their public statements have already made it clear that their regard for human lives, even of their own citizens, bears little resemblance to ours. While I am not privy to current plans, I feel confident that we are preparing to meet the exercise of Red China's most dangerous capability. I am uneasy only when I hear influential voices assuring us that China "would not dare" make this move or that, and I trust that our military planners will never again be lulled by faulty reading of the Communist Chinese mind.

Still, even though we may have learned that one lesson well, there are other mistakes that at least a portion of our citizenry seems bent on repeating. There were those who felt, at the time of the Korean War, that air power might accomplish miracles of interdiction, by cutting all the flow of reinforcement and supply to the embattled enemy. The fact that it could not accomplish these miracles has not yet been accepted as widely as it should have been. No one who fought on the ground in Korea would ever be tempted to belittle the accomplishments of our air force there. Not only did air power save us from disaster, but without it the mission of the United Nations Forces could not have been accomplished. In Vietnam too it has made all the difference between success on the ground and frustration. But air power does have its definite limitations, and even some in high position still fail to acknowledge them.

These limitations were never better illustrated than in World War II, when the Germans were able to maintain some twenty-six divisions south of the Alps in Italy, using a few mountain passes to keep them supplied for two years, regardless of uncontested Allied air supremacy. In Korea, where we had air mastery over practically the whole peninsula, MacArthur himself acknowledged our inability to isolate the battle area by air bombardment or to choke off the flow of reinforcements and supply. In Vietnam, results to date have repeated this lesson: rails and bridges are repaired and functioning within a few days of a bomb attack, and infiltration routes have not been cut off. Yet we still hear calls for saturation bombing that will, its proponents insist, cut off North Vietnam from the south.

I am doubtful too if we have learned from Korea the further lesson that agreements with the Communists are of no account unless ironclad sanctions which can and will be enforced are included. Two years of trying negotiations in Korea taught us that Communists will fulfill agreements only when it is to their clear advantage to do so or when the threat of retaliation is too clear to be ignored. Whatever settlement is finally reached with the Communists in Southeast Asia, the inclusion of enforceable sanctions is bound to present extreme difficulties. We must be prepared, however, to face up to the necessity of postponing final agreement until such sanctions have been settled on.

One mistake we avoided in Korea was an insistence on "total victory" or "unconditional surrender" or even a "halt to aggression" before talking peace. But in the light of many of the slogans that fill the air and the public prints nowadays, I am moved to wonder if all our citizens have come to understand the concept of limited war. A limited war is not merely a small war that has not yet grown to full size. It is a war in which the objectives are specifically limited in the light of our national interest and our current capabilities. A war that is "open-ended"—that has no clearly delineated geographical, political, and military goals beyond "victory"—is a war that may escalate itself indefinitely, as wars will, with one success requiring still another to insure the first one. An insistence on going all-out to win a war may have a fine masculine ring, and a call to "defend freedom" may have a messianic sound that stirs our blood. But the ending of an all-out war in these times is beyond imagining. It may mean the turning back of civilization by several thousand years, with no one left capable of signaling the victory.

In setting our military goals we need first of all to recognize that most of the world's most basic woes do not lend themselves to purely military solutions. In our clashes with ideologies that deride the dignity of man and deny him his individual freedom, solutions must be sought through combined political, economic, and military efforts. The world is not likely to settle into equilibrium while less than one-third of its population lives on a plateau of comparative luxury and the other two-thirds knows only poverty, squalor, and want.

The objectives of our foreign policy, therefore, must take these basic realities into account and must be stated clearly enough so they cannot become mere war cries behind which we conceal selfish and materialistic aims. I have considerable doubt, for instance, that the objectives of our Vietnam war effort, as articulated by certain government officials, mean exactly what they say, even granting the plain fact that diplomacy can seldom deal in truth, or seldom in truth complete and unadorned. President Johnson's stated objectives, as of this writing (January 1967), seem to me clear of ambiguity and hidden meaning, and about as far as our government can go with honor and. without appeasement. But the pleadings of others in official or influential position that our war aims in Vietnam are wholly altruistic and bent merely on guaranteeing to the people there the "freedom to choose their own government" strike me as open to question. It was not too long ago that President Eisenhower* equated the loss of Vietnam with the "loss of valuable deposits of tin and prodigious supplies of rubber and rice." Perhaps one may be allowed to suspect that these commodities, rather than "freedom," are the real prize that certain eyes are fastened on. And those who state our aim as being "to cause Hanoi to cease aggression" ignore the fact that Hanoi's effort could not long continue without support and supply from Peking.

If we were to place credence in that latter statement of our objective, we would in effect be saying that our aim is to force both Hanoi *and* Peking to cease their support of armed aggression and subversion, not only against Vietnam but against Laos, Cambodia, Thailand, and Burma, to all of which the United States has commitments under the Southeast Asia Treaty. And logic then would dictate that the United States should, either openly or through secret diplomatic channels, convey an ultimatum to Communist China to cease and desist. For myself, I have grave doubts of the wisdom of any course that would involve an ulti-

* *Mandate for Change,* p. 333.

matum to the Red Chinese. The present Chinese leaders would, I believe, spurn any ultimatum, by whatever means it might be conveyed to them. If we should be obliged to extend our military operations to thwart aggression aimed at the overthrow of the other states in Southeast Asia, under the aegis of the Southeast Asia Treaty, I believe we would find it necessary greatly to increase our troop commitment there. And, in my opinion, whatever over-all strength we might feel justified in committing there would still prove insufficient without the tactical use of nuclear weapons, the consequences of which can only be surmised. Finally, I believe the use of nuclear weapons against industrial and population centers—unless an enemy uses them first against our territory or forces—would so revolt free world opinion as to leave us, quite possibly, friendless and isolated in a hostile world.

It behooves us therefore to decide among ourselves what the objectives of our world policy should be—to define them with care and to make sure they lie within the range of our vital national interests and that their accomplishment is within our capabilities. Our resources are not endless, and to expend them all in the pursuit of vague and unreachable objectives might render us unable to meet the ultimate test that, I feel, is surely on its way.

As for our immediate aims in Vietnam, those outlined by Ambassador Arthur J. Goldberg to the United Nations General Assembly in September 1966 are authoritative and presumably mean what they say: We do not seek to establish permanent military bases in Vietnam, or a "sphere of influence" in Asia; do not seek the unconditional surrender or overthrow of the government of North Vietnam; do not exclude "any segment of the South Vietnamese people" from peaceful participation in their country's future; and are ready to negotiate a settlement based on strict observance of the 1954 and 1962 Geneva agreements. The United States is willing, he stated, to leave the unification of Vietnam to the "free choice" of the people of both areas and to accept the result, and finally, would be prepared to cease all bombing of North Vietnam on being assured privately or otherwise that this step would be "answered promptly by a corresponding and appropriate de-escalation on the other side"; and, if North Vietnam would agree to a time schedule for a phased withdrawal from South Vietnam of all external forces—American and North Vietnamese—the United States would allow such a withdrawal to be supervised by the United Nations or other machinery. Unlikely of immediate attainment as these aims seems to be, they are nevertheless far removed from the insuring of our control over the region's tin, rubber, and rice, and so are far more consistent with the moral position before the world that our people have long sustained, and more in consonance with our long-range vital interests.

Our general world objectives—those that clearly lie within the zone of our vital national interests—are more open to debate. But some, I believe, are clearly definable. These include, but are not limited to, the following:

1. To prevent Western Europe, outside the Iron Curtain, from coming under Kremlin control.

2. To prevent the establishment of a Kremlin-dominated government in the Western Hemisphere (an objective temporarily lost sight of with respect to Cuba, but still an objective).

3. To maintain our forward defense line in the Far East, i.e., the line of the Japanese Islands—South Korea—the Ryukyus—Formosa—the Philippines. (Whether all or part of Southeast Asia is to be included is, in my judgment, a debatable point.)

4. To continue support of the United Nations under the principles of its charter, particularly with regard to the promise of the charter preamble: "To save succeeding generations from the scourge of war. . . ."

(Many Americans may disagree with the inclusion of that point as an objective within the zone of our vital interests. But so be it.)

By my way of thinking, to save our children, and their children, from the scourge of war lies within the sphere of vital interests, not only of the American people, but of the people of the whole world. And starting a war—deliberately provoking a nuclear war, for example—is not the way to save them. Indeed that phrase from the preamble seems to me to set forth the most vital aim of the United Nations.

From the time of Rome's greatness until now—a period of two millennia—the peoples of Europe have been periodically deluged in blood by wars which, within the last two centuries, have grown increasingly murderous and have laid wider areas to waste. Now, with the existing potential for destruction, a new world war would charge a price in blood and in annihilation of human values that would be past all reckoning.

In the very ghastliness of this possible catastrophe should lie the hope that the sanity and wisdom of statesmen will devise ways to prevent it. No present obstacle, no foreseeable difficulty—certainly not human greed and lust for power—should be permitted to defeat or weaken collective efforts to stave off the unthinkable. No group of nations has greater stakes at issue, or stronger reasons—apart from the inherent moral imperative—for attaining this objective than do the peoples of Western Europe and America—Europe, because of its long history of death and devastation by war; America, because of the identity of its cultural and economic interests with those of Europe, and both together because of the extreme vulnerability of their highly developed social, economic, and cultural structures.

The problem of Vietnam lies at the very heart of this challenge to the wisdom and moral courage of our statesmen. There will be decisions to face, as with the problems of Germany and Korea, that will try their souls and test the character of our people. I feel that the American people own, in abundant measure, the energy and the moral principles that give any nation its spiritual strength, and I am confident of their ability to stand up to the test.

I believe firmly that our Western civilization evolved on this planet in accordance with some high, though inscrutable, purpose. This purpose, I believe, does not cast the American nation in the role of Messiah among the less fortunate peoples of the earth, but rather in the role of strong, courageous, and broad-minded associates, fully aware of our own limitations, conscious of our own capabilities, and devoid of any desire to force our institutions

249

and our way of life on others. Our material as well as our spiritual strength is sufficient to fulfill this high purpose, provided only that we develop the wisdom to accept our role.

For the present I believe there is no higher duty than the preservation of our freedom. That requires us to husband our strength, not squander it, for use when we face the supreme test. But the mere statement of a purpose is valueless. It must be translated into concrete and pragmatic political objectives that, as I have noted before, should conform to our vital national interests and be subordinated to them.

I am frankly doubtful that we are, in Southeast Asia, setting our objectives within this frame. A citizen outside the flow of high-level governmental intelligence, as I am, cannot of course resolve that doubt with any certainty. Yet, under our form of government, it is every citizen's duty to attempt, on the basis of what he is permitted to know, to evaluate the foreign-policy problems that face us, to utter his honest views, and to be mindful of the many erroneous assessments of the Southeast Asia problem that have been pronounced from Washington in the recent past.

While I am, as I said, not at all convinced that our political objectives in Southeast Asia—manifold, tenuous, and imprecise as have been those set forth by our government officials—really harmonize with our national interests, I do not believe that these misstatements should be our primary concern. Rather we should ask ourselves now if we are not, in this open-ended conflict, so impairing our strength through overdrawing on our resources— political, economic, and military—as to find ourselves unduly weakened when we need to meet new challenges in other more vital areas of the world. For there surely will be threats that bear more closely on our true national interests.

If we find the wisdom to husband our strength against the day when those threats appear, then I am utterly confident in America's future, in the capacity of our leadership to meet those threats, and in the ability of our armed forces to contribute in full measure to that leadership.

KOREAN WAR CALENDAR

GEORGE F. HOFMANN, Ph.D.
Adjunct Assistant Professor of History
University of Cincinnati
College of Evening and Continuing
Education
(ML 19)
Cincinnati, OH 45221-0019

Home Address:
5912 Bridgeview Ct. • Cincinnati, OH 45248-4009
Tel.: 513-451-9798 • Fax: 513-451-9798

1950

June 25	North Korean Peoples Army (NKPA) invades South Korea in force.
June 28	NKPA seizes Seoul, capital of Republic of Korea.
July 5	Task Force Smith makes first contact wih Communist forces near Osan.
July 20	Taejon abandoned by UN forces.
July 31	Chinju falls to NKPA. General Walton Walker announces: "There will be no more retreating!"
August 1	UN forces in Pusan perimeter.
August 6–8	General MacArthur confers in Tokyo with Averell Harriman and Generals Norstad, Almond, and Ridgway concerning Inchon landing.
September 15	Inchon landing. Harbor and harbor islands seized by UN forces.
September 18	Kimpo Airfield seized by UN forces.
September 22	Walker's forces break out of Pusan perimeter.
September 27	UN forces moving north link-up with UN forces moving south, near Suwon.
September 28	Seoul retaken by UN forces.
September 30	Republic of Korea (ROK) 3rd Division crosses 38th parallel.
October 7–9	U.S. 1st Cavalry Division crosses 38th parallel.
October 11	ROK 3rd Division takes Wonsan.
October 19	The Eighth Army takes Pyongyang, capital of North Korea.

October 24 MacArthur directs his commanders to move forward with all possible speed, using all their forces. He removes all restrictions on forward movement of non-Korean forces.

October 26 6th Division of the ROK III Corps reaches Yalu River. 26th Regiment of the ROK I Corps takes Chinese prisoners at Sudong.

October 27–31 Chinese first-phase offensive is launched.

October 27 7th Regiment of the ROK 6th Division badly mauled by strong Chinese forces near Yalu.

October 30 Advance elements of U.S. 24th Division reach to within 40 miles of the Yalu.

October 31–
November 2 Strong Chinese forces attack Eighth Army at Unsan and force withdrawal across Chongchon River.

November 6 MacArthur warns Joint Chiefs of Staff (JCS) that movement of Chinese forces across Yalu "threatens the ultimate destruction of my command."

November 23 Thanksgiving Day.

November 24 MacArthur flies from Tokyo to Korea to give signal for opening of drive to Yalu. He announces: "The Chinese are not coming in." 17th Regiment of U.S. 7th Division reaches Yalu at Hyesanjin. The Eighth Army initiates its advance toward Yalu.

November 25–
December 9 Chinese second-phase offensive is launched.

November 25 The ROK II Corps in central Korea near Tokchon is smashed by Chinese attack.

November 26 200,000 Chinese attack the Eighth Army north of Chongchon River and inflict heavy casualties.

November 27 U.S. 24th, 25th, and 2nd Divisions retreat across Chongchon and the Eighth Army begins withdrawal. CCF attack 1st Marine Division on west side of Changjin Reservoir and elements of U.S. 7th Division on east side.

December 5 Pyongyang abandoned by the Eighth Army.

December 9 1st Marine Division completes fighting breakout, begun on November 27.

December 11 1st Marine Division and U.S. 7th Division withdraw into perimeter at Hungnam.

December 15   The Eighth and ROK Armies withdraw below 38th parallel.

December 23   General Walker killed in jeep accident. General Ridgway appointed to succeed him.

December 24   The X Corps completes evacuation of Hungnam beachhead and North Korea.

December 26   General Ridgway takes command of the Eighth Army.

December 31– January 5   Chinese third-phase offensive is launched, the New Year's offensive.

1951

January 3–4   Seoul evacuated by UN forces, which withdraw to general line Pyongtaek-Wonju-Samchok and regroup.

January 7   The Eighth Army initiates strong reconnaissance probes to north to regain contact with Chinese Communist Forces.

January 15   Operation Wolfhound, reconnaissance by a reinforced regimental combat team (RCT), re-establishes contact with enemy near Osan.

January 25   The Eighth and ROK Armies take the offensive. Operation Thunderbolt begins, with advance north toward Han River by the I and the IX Corps.

January 31– February 17   U.S. 2nd Division heavily engaged. Its 23rd RCT, with Monclar's French Battalion attached, smashes attacks of five CCF Divisions at Chipyong-ni and CCF break off their offensive.

February 5   Operation Roundup, advance by the U.S. X Corps begins on eastern flank.

February 11–17   Chinese fourth-phase offensive is launched, with main effort in U.S. 2nd Division sector.

February 21   Operation Killer, a general advance by the U.S. IX and X Corps, begins.

February 28   Last enemy resistance south of Han collapses.

March 7   Operation Ripper begins in central and eastern zones with advance across the Han by the IX and X Corps.

March 14–15   Seoul retaken by the Eighth Army.

March 31   UN forces on the Idaho Line. All geographical objectives taken.

April 5   Operation Rugged, a general advance to the Kansas Line, begins.

April 11   General MacArthur relieved as Supreme Commander. General Ridgway appointed in his place.

April 14   General Van Fleet assumes command of the Eighth Army. All UN forces on the Kansas Line.

April 19   The U.S. I and IX Corps on the Utah Line.

April 22–28   First effort of Chinese fifth-phase offensive is launched.

April 30   UN forces, after withdrawing to new defense line, halt Chinese offensive north of Seoul and north of Han River.

May 16–23   Second and final effort of Chinese fifth-phase offensive is launched.

May 20   Chinese offensive halted. UN forces resume advance.

May 30   The Eighth Army back on Kansas Line once more.

June 1   Operation Piledriver begins, with elements of the I and the IX Corps advancing toward the Wyoming Line.

June 15   Terrain objectives of Operation Piledriver attained.

June 23   Jacob Malik, Deputy Foreign Commissar of Soviet Union, proposes cease-fire.

June 30   General Ridgway, on orders from Washington, broadcasts to Chinese the UN's readiness to discuss an armistice.

July 10   Negotiations between UN forces and Communists open at Kaesong.

August 17   Communists demand apology for alleged ambush near Kaesong. Request refused.

August 22   Communists ask for confession and apology for "bombing raid." Talks suspended when request denied.

August 31   1st Marine Division opens assault in Punchbowl.

September 2   U.S. 2nd Division opens attack against Heartbreak and Bloody Ridges.

September 3   Marines and 2nd Division reach initial objectives.

September 18   Marines advance to Soyang River, north of Punchbowl.

256

October 12   The IX Corps advances to the Jamestown Line.

October 15   U.S. 2nd Division takes Heartbreak Ridge.

October 25   After two weeks of discussion between liaison officers, truce talks resume.

November 12 Ridgway orders Van Fleet to cease offensive operations and begin active defense. Operation Ratkiller.

1952

January 1   Artillery and air campaign against Communist positions begins, to last all month.

January–April Disorders in prison camps as screening of prisoners begins.

May 7   Prisoners at Koje-do camp seize General Dodd and hold him hostage.

May 11   General Dodd released.

May 12   General Ridgway leaves to take over NATO command from General Eisenhower at SHAEF. General Clark assumes command. (Supreme command ceased to exist with prior signing of treaty.)

June 6   Operation Counter begins, to occupy eleven patrol bases.

June 14   All objectives of Operation Counter occupied by 45th Division.

December   Breakout attempt by prisoners at Pongam-do suppressed.

1953

February   General Van Fleet returns to U.S. for retirement. General Maxwell D. Taylor assumes command of the Eighth Army.

March 25   Chinese seize and hold one outpost, Hill 266.

May 28   Chinese, in regimental strength, attack five outposts of U.S. 25th Division.

May 29   Chinese occupy three outposts.

June 10   Chinese open assault against the ROK II Corps near Kumsong.

June 16   ROK II Corps pushed back to new Main Line of Resistance, about 4000 yards farther south.

June 15–30   Chinese attacks in the U.S. I Corps sector take two outpost positions.

July 13   Final Chinese offensive begins with attack on the IX Corps' right flank by three divisions and on left flank of the ROK II Corps in division strength.

July 19   Negotiators at Panmunjom reach agreement on all points.

July 20   New Main Line of Resistance established by the U.S. IX Corps and the ROK II Corps along south bank of Kumsong River.

July 27   Armistice signed, ending three years of conflict.

APPENDICES

McCLELLAN AND MacARTHUR

The parallels between McClellan and MacArthur are striking, even if only of passing interest. Basically, each was the antithesis of the other, but there were many strong similarities in their careers. Both men were graduates of West Point, McClellan standing No. 2 in his class (1846), MacArthur No. 1 in his (1903). Both were in the Corps of Engineers. Both early attained high rank. One openly harbored political ambitions over a considerable period. The other several times gave evidence of entertaining them, though this he denied. Both enjoyed powerful support from influential political figures who were not above using these officers for their own political purposes. Two years after his relief from command, McClellan ran for the presidency. Two years before his relief, MacArthur stated publicly that, while he did not "actively seek or covet any office" . . . he "would be recreant to all" his "concepts of good citizenship" were he "to shrink, because of the hazards and responsibilities involved, from accepting any public duty to which" he "might be called by the American people." Neither came near the presidency, though McClellan coveted it and MacArthur seemed to be not unwilling to try for it. Like the former, the latter, writes Trumbull Higgins, "was already confusing his popularity as a symbol of patriotism in a Nation at war with his duty as a general on active service."

Text of Eighth Army General Order assuming command, sent from Tokyo, December 26, 1950, marked "PERSONAL FOR ALLEN"*:

I should like the following General Order in the hands of troops this date, immediately following my message to Commanders concerning General Walker, which was sent you last night over the Commander-in-Chief's signature, to the effect that it will be read as soon as practicable by every officer assigned, attached to, or serving with the Eighth Army; and that as circumstances permit, its text be made known to as many of the men as may be practicable, and made available through prompt translations to members of each of our foreign language United Nations contingents.

The order itself read:

I have with little notice, assumed heavy responsibilities before in battle, but never with greater opportunities for service to our loved ones and our Nation in beating back a world menace which free men cannot tolerate.

It is an honored privilege to share this service with you and with our comrades of the Navy and Air Force. You will have my utmost. I shall expect yours.

M. B. Ridgway,

Lieutenant General,
United States Army,
Commanding.

* Major General Leven C. Allen, Chief of Staff, U.S. Eighth Army.

HEADQUARTERS EIGHTH U.S. ARMY

11 Jan 1951

To General Chung Il Kwon
Chief of Staff
Republic of Korea Army

Now that I have had sufficient time to see the situation as it now exists, to view the terrain, and personally to talk to the principal Commanders, I deem it opportune to share my personal basic conclusions with you.

First, there is here but one ultimate objective—freedom for your people. To attain that objective, there is only one force—our combined Allied Army.

Second, there is but one single common destiny for this combined Allied Army. It will fight together and stay together whatever the future holds.

I would like you to feel free to convey to all ranks this simple statement which I send to you with complete sincerity and all the emphasis I can command.

Sincerely,

M. B. RIDGWAY
Lieutenant General,
United States Army,
Commanding.

WHY ARE WE HERE? WHAT ARE WE FIGHTING FOR?

During my first few weeks in Korea it seemed to me two questions were uppermost in the minds of the members of the Eighth Army. These were: "Why are we here?" and "What are we fighting for?"

As Commander of that Army I believed that all its members had a right to know my answers, which on January 21, 1951, I directed to be conveyed to every individual assigned or attached to Eighth Army. The answers follow.

The answer to the first question, "Why are we here?" (I wrote) is simple and conclusive. We are here because of the decisions of the properly constituted authorities of our respective governments. As the Commander in Chief, United Nations Command, General of the Army Douglas MacArthur has said: "This command intends to maintain a military position in Korea just as long as the Statesmen of the United Nations decide we should do so." The answer is simple because further comment is unnecessary. It is conclusive because the loyalty we give, and expect, precludes any slightest questioning of these orders.

The second question is of much greater significance, and every member of this command is entitled to a full and reasoned answer. Mine follows.

To me the issues are clear. It is not a question of this or that Korean town or village. Real estate is, here, incidental. It is not restricted to the issue of freedom for our South Korean Allies, whose fidelity and valor under the severest stresses of battle we recognize; though that freedom is a symbol of the wider issues, and included among them.

The real issues are whether the power of Western civilization, as God has permitted it to flower in our own beloved lands, shall defy and defeat Communism; whether the rule of men who shoot their prisoners, enslave their citizens, and deride the dignity of man, shall displace the rule of those to whom the individual and his individual rights are sacred; whether we are to survive with God's hand to guide and lead us, or to perish in the dead existence of a Godless world.

If these be true, and to me they are, beyond any possibility of challenge, then this has long since ceased to be a fight for freedom for our Korean Allies alone and for their national survival. It has become, and it continues to be, a fight for our own freedom, for our own survival, in an honorable, independent national existence.

The sacrifices we have made, and those we shall yet support, are not offered vicariously for others, but in our own direct defense.

In the final analysis, the issue now joined right here in Korea is whether Communism or individual freedom shall prevail; whether the flight of fear-driven people we have witnessed here shall be checked, or shall at some future time, however distant, engulf our own loved ones in all its misery and despair.

These are the things for which we fight. Never have members of any military command had a greater challenge than we, or a finer opportunity to show ourselves and our people at their best—and thus to do honor to the profession of arms, and to those brave men who bred us.

Notes on my meeting with General MacArthur after his dismissal.*

By noon on the 12th of April I was on my way to Tokyo, for a preliminary conference with General MacArthur. I went directly to his office from Haneda Airport, and he received me at once, with the greatest courtesy. I had a natural human curiosity to see how he had been affected by his peremptory removal from his high post. He was entirely himself—composed, quiet, temperate, friendly, and helpful to the man who was to succeed him. He made some allusions to the fact that he had been summarily relieved, but there was no trace of bitterness or anger in his tone. I thought it was a fine tribute to the resilience of this great man that he could accept so calmly, with no outward sign of shock, what must have been a devastating blow to a professional soldier standing at the peak of his career.

* Quoted from *Soldier,* Harper and Brothers, New York, 1956, by Matthew B. Ridgway as told to Harold H. Martin, page 223.

Extract from Letter of Instructions to the Commanding General, Far East Air Forces, April 30, 1951.

• • •

2. Your primary missions are to:

a. Conduct air operations to:

(1) Maintain air superiority over Korea and waters adjacent thereto.

(2) Provide general air support for the United Nations forces in Korea, to include:

(a) Close air support of surface forces.

(b) Interdiction, including isolation of the battle area.

(c) Air transport, troop carrier and air evacuation.

(3) Assist in maintaining the security of the Far East Command, and of United Nations forces in Korea, including the protection of air communications within the Theater.

(4) Provide air defense for the Far East Command and the forces and facilities assigned thereto.

(5) Provide air support as directed by CINCFE • • •

b. Be prepared to conduct airborne operations as directed by CINCFE

3. • • •

Hydroelectric installations in North Korea in the vicinity of the Yalu River will *not* be destroyed.

In the event of air or sea attack against your forces outside of Korea, you will take immediate and aggressive measures in self-defense, but initial retaliatory action against targets on the Chinese mainland, in Manchuria or in the USSR will be on my order only.

No element of your forces will cross the Manchurian or USSR borders of Korea except on my explicit prior authority.

Extract from Letter of Instructions to the Commander, Naval Forces Far East, April 30, 1951.

• • •

2. Your primary missions are to:

a. Conduct naval operations to:

(1) Maintain control of the sea in the Far East Command.

(2) Provide Naval defense for Japan and other areas under control of Commander-in-Chief, Far East and CINCUNC.

(3) Maintain Naval blockade of Korea.

(4) Provide Naval support for the Eighth Army and Far East Air Forces in the conduct of their operations in Korea.

(5) Protect shipping on the high seas within the Far East Command.

b. Defend Formosa and the Pescadores against invasion or attack by Chinese Communists and insure that Formosa is not used as a base of operations against the Chinese mainland by Chinese Nationalists.

Basic provisions of common application to all services were generally the same as those quoted in the Letter of Instructions to the Commanding General of the Eighth Army.

Extracts from an exchange of letters between Presidents Eisenhower and Rhee, between June 6 and 19, 1953.

". . .

"The moment has now come," wrote President Eisenhower, "when we must decide whether to carry on by warfare a struggle for the unification of Korea or whether to pursue this goal by political and other methods.

". . .

"It is my profound conviction that . . . acceptance of the Armistice is required of the United States and the Republic of Korea. We would not be justified in prolonging the war with all the misery that it involves in the hope of achieving, by force, the unification of Korea.

"The unification of Korea is an end to which the United States is committed, not once but many times, through its World War II declarations and through its acceptance of the principles enunciated in reference to Korea by the United Nations. Korea is unhappily not the only country which remains divided after World War II. We remain determined to play our part in achieving the political union of all countries so divided. But we do not intend to employ war as an instrument to accomplish the world-wide political settlements to which we are dedicated and which we believe to be just . . .

". . .

"The United States will not renounce its efforts by all peaceful means to effect the reunification of Korea . . ."

APPENDIX 9

Telegram received July 1, 1955, from General Marshall on General Ridgway's retirement.

LEESBURGHVIR JUL 1 933AME

GENERAL RIDGWAY
FT MYER VIR
DEAR RIDGWAY, GOD SPEED YOU IN YOUR NEW CAREER. MAY YOU AND PENNY AND THE BOY ALL CONTINUE WELL AND ENJOY LIFE.

MY FORMAL CONGRATULATIONS ON A SPLENDID MILITARY CAREER OF MAGNIFICENT FIGHTING LEADERSHIP AND GREAT EXECUTIVE ABILITY. YOU HAVE VERY MUCH TO BE PROUD OF BUT MOST OF ALL FOR THE DASH OF YOUR CORPS TO THE BALTIC AND MOST OF ALL FOR THE OUTSTANDING BRILLIANCE OF YOUR CAMPAIGN IN KOREA

G C MARSHALL

Extract from my letter to General Van Fleet, sent on April 26, 1951, by hand of then Lieutenant Colonel (now Major General) Paul F. Smith:

". . .

"The second idea, likewise merely for your consideration, would be for me to send a General Officer to see Ambassador Muccio and get him, in the presence of General Coulter* and no others, to tell President Rhee substantially as follows:

'Your primary problem is to secure competent leadership in your Army. You do not have it, from the Minister of Defense on down, as is clearly evidenced by repeated battle failures of your major units.

'This is your first and basic responsibility in the military field. Until you get that leadership, there is little reason to expect any better performance of your troops, or any higher degree of confidence in them than presently exists among their UN comrades.

'Until you get it and demonstrate its worth, there should be no further talk of the U.S. equipping additional forces. Such action would be a criminal waste of badly needed equipment, since the forces you already have in the field continue to abandon major items of equipment without justification.' "

To this suggestion to General Van Fleet, I added this caution:

"This should have your most careful consideration, because as I see it, there is an element of danger, and that lies in the possibility that such action might tend to impair if not destroy such self-confidence as ROK troops now have, and, therefore, increase the possibility of even worse conduct."

---

* Appointed by me as Liaison Officer to President Rhee.

APPENDIX 11

GENERAL RIDGWAY'S NINE POINTS FOR VIETNAM *

1. We should emphatically reject the two extreme courses—"Pullout" or "All-out war"—that have been advocated by certain groups.
2. We should give our full support to the President's determined efforts to fulfill our treaty obligations and to honor our pledges, while at the same time seeking an honorable solution of the basically political problem in Vietnam.
3. With due regard for diplomatic secrecy, our Government should spell out, more specifically and pragmatically, our immediate and long-range political objectives, firmly rejecting any unlimited political objective that might entail unlimited military effort.
4. We should also reject any political involvement that might gradually commit us to military efforts that would jeopardize our basic security and those vital American interests that cannot be compromised.
5. Once having announced our political objectives within the framework stated above, we should then employ whatever force is needed to attain them.
6. We should categorically reject "preventive" war, employing nuclear weapons, the use of which would be, in my opinion, a deliberate move down the road of international immorality past the point of no return.
7. We should enter into formal agreements with the Communist leaders of Southeast Asia only after establishment of enforceable sanctions to guarantee the permanent protection of the South Vietnamese people.
8. We should sign no instrument with these leaders without prior agreement in good faith among a group of nations, including, if possible, the Soviet Union, to join in fairly sharing the task of applying proper sanctions.

* Quoted from *Look* magazine, April 5, 1966, page 84.

9. We should repose complete confidence in the capability of our military leaders in Southeast Asia to accomplish any mission they may be assigned, for these men are among the best that our nation has produced.

BIBLIOGRAPHY

Books

Appleman, Roy E., *South to the Naktong, North to the Yalu,* Department of the Army, Office Chief of Military History, 1956

Battle-Ground, Korea, U.S. 25th Infantry Division History

Beloff, Max, *Soviet Policy in the Far East,* Oxford University Press, 1953

Cagle, Malcolm W., and Frank A. Manson, *The Sea War in Korea,* U. S. Naval Institute, 1957

Canzona. *See* Montross.

Chamberlain. *See* Willoughby.

Childs, Marquis, *Eisenhower, Captive Hero,* Harcourt, Brace & Co., 1959

Clark, Mark W., *From the Danube to the Yalu,* Harper & Brothers, 1954

Coblenz. *See* Reitzel.

Department of State, American Foreign Policy 1950–55, Vols. I and II, Department of State Document 6446, 1957

Eisenhower, Dwight D., *Mandate for Change,* Doubleday & Co., 1963

Fehrenbach, T. R., *This Kind of War,* The Macmillan Co., 1963

Finletter, Thomas K., *Air Power and Policy,* Harcourt, Brace & Co., 1956

Futrell, Robert F., *United States Air Force in Korea, 1950–1953,* Duell, Sloan & Pearce, 1961

Goodrich, Leland M., *Korea: U. S. Policy in the UN,* Council on Foreign Relations, 1956

Gunther, John, *The Riddle of MacArthur,* Harper & Brothers, 1951

Hermes, W. G., *Fighting Front & Truce Tent,* Department of the Army, Office Chief of Military History, 1966

275

Hicks. *See* Kuokka.

Higgins, Trumbull, *Korea and the Fall of MacArthur,* Oxford University Press, 1960

Historical Division, U. S. Air Force, *Korean Conflict, US AF Operations in 1 Nov. 1950 to 30 June 52 and 1 July 52 to 27 July 1953,* Historical Division, Department of the Air Force, 1955 and 1956

Hubard. *See* Kuokka.

Joy, C. Turner, *How Communists Negotiate,* The Macmillan Company, 1953

Kaplan. *See* Reitzel.

Karig, Walter, Malcolm Cagle, and Frank A. Manson, *Battle Report,* Vol. 6, Rinehart & Co., 1952

Kennan, George F., *American Diplomacy, 1900–1950,* University of Chicago Press, 1951

Korea 1950 and *Korea 1951–53,* Department of the Army, Office Chief of Military History

Kuokka, Hubard, and Hicks, *U. S. Marines Operations in Korea,* Vol. IV, Historical Branch, G-3 Division, USMC

Leckie, Robert, *Conflict,* G. P. Putnam's Sons, 1962

————*March to Glory,* World Publishing Co., 1960

MacArthur, Douglas, *Revitalizing a Nation,* Heritage Foundation, 1952

————*Reminiscences,* McGraw-Hill, 1964

Manson. *See* Cagle.

Marshall, S. L. A., *Pork Chop Hill,* William Morrow & Co., 1956

————*The River and the Gauntlet,* William Morrow & Co., 1959

Montross, Lynn, and N. A. Canzona, *U. S. Marines Operations in Korea,* Vols. I, II, and III, Historical Branch, G-3 Division, USMC, 1954, 1955, 1957

Mossman, B. C., *Ebb and Flow,* Department of the Army, Office Chief of Military History, pending

Oliver, Robert T., *Why War Came in Korea,* Fordham University Press, 1950

Rees, David, *Korea, the Limited War,* St. Martin's Press, 1964

Reitzel, Kaplan, and Coblenz, *U. S. Foreign Policy 1945–55,* Brookings Institution, 1956

Rhee, Syngman, *Korea Flaming High,* Vols. I, II, and III, Korean Research and Information Office, 1955–59

Ridgway, Matthew B., *Soldier,* Harper & Brothers, 1956

Rovere, Richard, and Arthur M. Schlesinger, *The General and the President and the Future of American Foreign Policy,* Farrar, Straus & Young, 1951. Includes text of Wake Island Conference, Mac-Arthur's address to Congress, April 19, 1951, Harriman's statement on Yalta, and other important documents.

Sawyer, R. K., *Military Advisors in Korea—KMAG in Peace and War,* Department of the Army, Officer Chief of Military History, 1962

Schlesinger. *See* Rovere.

Schlesinger, Arthur M., Jr., *Bitter Heritage: Vietnam and American Democracy 1941–1966,* Houghton Mifflin Co., 1967

Schnabel, James F., *Policy and Direction the First Year,* Department of the Army, Office Chief of Military History, pending

Spanier, John W., *The Truman-MacArthur Controversy and the Korean War,* The Belknap Press of Harvard University, 1959

Stallings, Laurence, *The Doughboys,* Harper & Row, 1963

Stebbins, Richard P., *United States in World Affairs 1949–1951,* Harper & Brothers, 1952

Streit, Clarence K., *Freedom's Frontier: Atlantic Union Now,* Harper & Brothers, 1940 and 1961

Truman, Harry S., *Years of Trial and Hope,* Doubleday & Co., 1956

U.S. 1st Cavalry Division History

U.S. 2nd Infantry Division History

U.S. 3rd Infantry Division History

U.S. 24th Infantry Division Pictorial History—Korea

U.S. 25th Infantry Division History

VFW, *Pictorial History of the Korean War,* 4 vols., Veterans Historical Book Service, 1951

Whitney, Courtney, *MacArthur: His Rendezvous with History,* Alfred A. Knopf, 1956

Willoughby, Charles A., and John Chamberlain, *MacArthur, 1941–1951,* McGraw-Hill, 1954

Wolff, Leon, *In Flanders Fields,* Viking Press, 1958

Magazines

Boatner, H. L., "POW's for Sale," *American Legion,* August 1962, page 14

Cottrell, A. J., and J. E. Dougherty, "The Lessons of Korea: War and the Power of Man," *Orbis,* April (or May) 1958, for Policy Research Institute

Dougherty. *See* Cottrell

Editors of *U. S. News & World Report,* questions answered by General MacArthur to Joseph Fromm, December 8, 1950

"The JCS Bounce Back," *Army,* October 1963

Lawrence, David, "Lest We Forget," editorial, *U. S. News & World Report,* July 20, 1951

Marshall, S. L. A., "Big Little War," *Army,* June 1960

Montross, Lynn, "The Christmas They'll Never Forget," *Leatherneck,* December 1951

Morton, Louis, "Soviet Intervention in War with Japan," *Foreign Affairs,* July 1962

———"Twin Essentials of Limited War," *Army,* January 1961

Newsweek, April 20, 1964, pages 37–43

Stevenson, C. S., "What About the Katusas?", *Army,* July 1960

Tannenbaum, Frank, "Balance of Power Versus the Coordinate States," *Political Science Quarterly,* Vol. LXVII, No. 2, June 1952

Teller, Edward, "Plan for Survival," *Saturday Evening Post,* February 17, 1962

U. S. News & World Report, Interview with Senator Tom Connally, May 5, 1950

Various writers, "Korea Ten Years After," *Army,* June 1960

Watson, Mark, review of *FDR as Military Chief,* by K. R. Greenfield, *Army,* March 1964

Young, Warren R., "Group Shelters Are a Start," *Saturday Evening Post,* January 12, 1962

Congressional Hearings

"The Military Situation in the Far East," Committee on Foreign Relations, U. S. Senate, 81st Congress, 2nd session

"General of the Army Douglas MacArthur and the American Policy in the Far East," joint statement by the Armed Forces Committee and the Committee on Foreign Relations, U. S. Senate. Senate Document No. 50, June 28, 1951

"Discussion with General M. B. Ridgway re Far Eastern Situation, Koje-do Uprising of POW's, and NATO Policies," 82nd Congress, 2nd session (microfilmed on Reel 45, Carnegie Library)

Government Documents

Numerous documents published by the Department of State have been consulted in the preparation of this book. These, along with other official records, are available from the General Services Administration, National Archives, Alexandria, Virginia.

Personal Files

Ridgway, General Matthew B.
Truman, President Harry S., Truman Library, Independence, Missouri

INDEX

281

L21

Other titles of interest

CONFLICT
The History of the Korean War,
1950–1953
Robert Leckie
480 pp., 60 photos, 1 map
80716-5 $16.95

TEARS BEFORE THE RAIN
An Oral History of the Fall
of South Vietnam
Larry Engelmann
New postscript by the author
417 pp., 30 photos
80789-0 $15.95

REMINISCENCES
General Douglas MacArthur
440 pp., 30 photos
80254-6 $15.95

A SOLDIER REPORTS
William C. Westmoreland
New foreword by the author
488 pp., 32 pp. of illus.
80376-3 $15.95

TET!
The Turning Point
in the Vietnam War
Don Oberdorfer
400 pp., 42 photos
80210-4 $11.95

HELL IN A VERY SMALL PLACE
The Siege of Dien Bien Phu
Bernard B. Fall
535 pp., 48 photos
80231-7 $15.95

PAVN: People's Army of Vietnam
Douglas Pike
384 pp., 5 illus.
80432-8 $14.95

SURVIVORS
Vietnam P.O.W.s
Tell Their Story
Zalin Grant
New introduction by the author
355 pp., 1 map
80561-8 $14.95

THE 25-YEAR WAR
General Bruce Palmer, Jr.
264 pp., 23 photos
80383-6 $13.95

STRONG MEN ARMED
The United States Marines vs.
Japan
Robert Leckie
600 pp., 56 illus., 16 maps
80785-8 $17.95

THE GI's WAR
American Soldiers in Europe
During World War II
Edwin P. Hoyt
638 pp., 29 illus.
80448-4 $17.95

JAPAN'S WAR
The Great Pacific Conflict
Edwin P. Hoyt
560 pp., 57 photos, 6 pp. of maps
80348-8 $16.95

NOW IT CAN BE TOLD
The Story of the Manhattan
Project
Gen. Leslie R. Groves
New introd. by Edward Teller
482 pp.
80189-2 $14.95

THE WAR, 1939–1945
A Documentary History
Edited by Desmond Flowers
and James Reeves
New introduction by
John S. D. Eisenhower
1,142 pp., 20 maps
80763-7 $24.95

THE RISE OF THE
CHINESE REPUBLIC
From the Last Emperor to
Deng Xiaoping
Edwin P. Hoyt
355 pp., 33 illus.
80426-3 $13.95

THE WAR MANAGERS
American Generals Reflect on
Vietnam
Douglas Kinnard
225 pp., 8 photos, 1 map
80449-2 $12.95

Available at your bookstore

OR ORDER DIRECTLY FROM

DA CAPO PRESS

1-800-321-0050